Best Wishes
Bruce S.

Dear Chief

By

Bruce R. Sims

This book is a work of non-fiction. The events and situations are true.

© 1995, 2003 by Bruce R. Sims. All rights reserved.

No part of this book may be reproduced, stored in a retrieval system, or transmitted by any means, electronic, mechanical, photocopying, recording, or otherwise, without written permission from the author.

ISBN: 1-4107-5948-2 (e-book)
ISBN: 1-4107-5947-4 (Paperback)
ISBN: 1-4107-5946-6 (Dust Jacket)

This book is printed on acid free paper.

MISSION:

"To prevent the illegal entry of aliens and to apprehend those that are already here."

This is the story of the author's twenty-year career as he attempted to enforce the Immigration and Naturalization laws.

The author as a U.S. Border Patrolman.

CHAPTER ONE: GETTING THERE

In the middle of April the roadside was covered with wildflowers as I drove south through the King Ranch looking for Harlingen, Texas, a town I had never heard of until I received a telegram to report for duty with the Border Patrol in Harlingen. At first I thought, "Oh, I know just where that is; that's the little town between Dallas and Fort Worth," until I looked on the map and realized that was Arlington, Texas, not Harlingen. I finally found Harlingen on another map and saw that it was on the very southern tip of Texas, very close to the Rio Grande River. That would be my duty station for the next four years.

After ten years' duty in the U.S. Air Force, I was looking forward to this change of careers which had started over six months before when I took the written Civil Service test for the Border Patrol. That was the hardest test I'd ever taken in my life. I took it in Albany, Georgia, with 12 other people whom I never saw or heard of after the test. I did pass the written test and was then told to report to Tallahassee, Florida to the Border Patrol Office where I would be given an oral interview.

There were only three of us for the interview, and the first man inside to meet the board seemed to be inside an awfully long time. Naturally, it seemed longer to the other two of us who were sitting outside waiting our turn. When he finally did leave the office, he just looked at us with a pitying glance and went right on out the door without ever saying a word.

The next man in was a policeman from Pensacola, Florida, as I'd found out when we talked outside. He wasn't in the interview room but a very few minutes. When he came back out, he looked at me and said, "They told me to lose 20 pounds and they would reinterview." Then he told me to go in.

Well, as they say, it was my turn in the barrel. I found myself standing before two Chiefs in their green dress uniforms and one Supervisor-Investigator in civilian clothes who were the sternest-looking people I have ever faced. That was appropriate for the situation, as they would decide my fate for the next 20 years.

Bruce R. Sims

The interview consisted of a review of my personal history statement, which was a part of my application, and answering questions based on hypothetical situations, a couple of which I remember. The first one was: If I were a Border Patrolman patrolling the river and observed three aliens coming up the riverbank out of the water and one fell back in the water, and I could apprehend the two or assist the one who had fallen back in the river and was about to drown, what would I do? My answer must have been the right answer because we went on to the next situation.

If I were inspecting a train and encountered a group of aliens being smuggled into the United States on the train, how would I determine who was the smuggler? I got through the part by saying that I would ask the conductor to assist me and check their tickets. We established that the tickets were in sequence. I was stumped as to how to identify the smuggler, but since the tickets were in sequence, it was logical that the smuggler would be the person with the next numbered ticket, either the lower number or the next higher number.

After that we went on to review the personal history statement, and I had to give an explanation to one of the questions which asked, "Were you ever convicted of a crime?" I had answered, "Yes." I had received a summary court martial while in the Air Force. I gave an explanation of how this incident had occurred and how it began with my First Sergeant's conducting an inspection of my room and finding a sock stuffed into one of my boots. The incident progressed into an argument with the First Sergeant's reporting me to my Commanding Officer, who wanted to take a stripe. Since the First Sergeant had lied to the Commanding Officer about my using profane language against him, I wasn't willing to sign the article of company punishment and be reduced a stripe because I knew I wasn't guilty. That displeased the Major, my Commanding Officer, who didn't like my attitude, so he said. If I was unwilling to sign my company punishment and give up one of my stripes, he would have every stripe on my arm in a summary court martial.

The outcome of the summary court martial was decided before I ever went before the Lieutenant Colonel, and I didn't have a chance to give a good explanation even though a witness had confirmed that I did not use profanity against my First Sergeant. My explanation must have been satisfactory because the investigator, Mr. Wagner, told me that if I successfully passed my physical exam and had a favorable background investigation, which would be conducted by the FBI, that I would be hired.

As I arose and started to leave the room, Mr. Wagner said he had one more question. Where was that other sock?

A physical exam was no problem as I had stayed in good physical condition during my ten years of active duty with the Air Force, but I didn't realize I would be faced with such a lengthy wait while the FBI was conducting the background investigation.

August came and found me an unemployed college graduate taking civil service exams. I had graduated from Florida State University at Tallahassee, Florida in June and did two weeks of military reserve duty and was now seeking employment. One of my neighbors told me that there was work for me in the carpet factory in Albany, Georgia. It was a minimum wage job with no future. He also said that it was better to be working and looking for a job than to have no job at all. I agreed, and the following week I went with him to work at the carpet factory.

Besides the Federal Service Entrance Exams, there was one other application pending. Immediately prior to graduation I had applied for a commission in the U.S. Navy and had gone to Jacksonville, Florida to the Naval Air Station for an oral board interview. I passed the interview, and the Navy Lt. Commander in charge of the board seemed certain that I would be selected for commissioning in the Navy. He told me that I would be hearing from the Navy within 60-90 days.

In the meantime, I had another offer of employment as a security guard at the Army Missile Maintenance Plant at Turner Air Force Base where I was previously stationed. This came about when the Army decided to use civilian guards instead of Army personnel for the plant security. They needed five people to commence work immediately.

Changing jobs from the carpet factory to security guard was no problem, but I told Mr. Jones, the supervisor, that I had other job applications pending and that I expected the security guard job to be only temporary. He said that was all right. He said if we were there for 90 days that all the guards would be upgraded from GS-3, the beginning grade, to GS-4, and at the end of six months one of us would be selected as the Senior Guard at GS-5 grade.

The 90 days came, and I had received job offers from two other Federal agencies as the result of the FSEE test, but I only considered one of them—that of the job of Park Ranger in the Smoky Mountain National Park. That was at a GS-5 grade, and I still had hopes of entering the Border Patrol at a GS-7.

At the end of the 90 days, none of the guards received their upgrade to GS-4, which was bitterly disappointing to all of us. As a result, they were leaving and going to other employment. A former Sergeant in the Air Force found that he could reenlist without losing his grade, so he returned to the Air Force. Another Air Force retiree took an administrative job at a higher grade. A former deputy sheriff obtained employment through the Federal prison system. The other guard and I continued to wait and see what would happen.

Finally, I knew that the decision on the Border Patrol application was nearing, as one day a well-dressed young man in a suit and tie parked in the parking lot and approached the gate where we were on duty and began asking my friend Gus in rapid-fire questions everything about Bruce Sims. Finally, Gus told the person who identified himself as an FBI agent that if he wanted to know anything about Bruce Sims, why didn't he ask me. That was me sitting right inside the gate.

The FBI agent got red in the face and asked if I was still interested in the job. It had been so long since my application that I had to ask him what job he was talking about. He said didn't I make an application for the Border Patrol. I told him yes, that I had, and I was still interested. He then went inside to interview my supervisor. Not long after that, I received a telegram saying I was accepted and to report to Harlingen.

In the meantime, true to the Navy's word, they had informed me that I was not selected for a commission in the U.S. Navy, which was not so surprising or disappointing. The other civilian guard decided that because the Army hadn't kept their word about the upgrade to GS-4, that he would return to his prior job where he had been a GS-4 Civilian Guard and had only come to Albany because it was home. He had hopes of being selected as the Senior Guard.

Dear Chief

  A telegram directed me to report to the Border Patrol at Harlingen, Texas, on April 16, 1962. I gave a letter of resignation to the Army Missile Maintenance Shop on April 15, and with my departure, the Army Missile Maintenance Shop had lost all five of its original civilian guards. I was off to a new, fascinating career.

CHAPTER TWO: HARLINGEN

I found a hotel to spend Sunday night in and asked instructions on how to find the Border Patrol station. On Monday morning I reported for duty at the station on Rangerville Road. There I met the Station Senior, Al Gilman, and six other men who were also reporting for duty.

We found that it would be two weeks before the Border Patrol Academy started classes at the old Naval Air Station at Port Isabel, Texas. We would be sworn in and receive our issue of badges and weapons. We also learned that the old Port Isabel Air Station was the location of one of the Border Patrol's Alien Detention facilities as well as the Sector Headquarters and that the Sector Chief was George W. Harrison, a name that I should remember well.

We also learned that the Border Patrol Academy would be thirteen weeks of instruction. We would be called Border Patrol Inspector Trainees until we completed our probationary year in the patrol.

That morning we were transported from Harlingen out to Sector Headquarters on an old government bus normally used to transport aliens. The driver was a sharp young man with the insignia of a Border Patrol Senior on his shoulder. Since we didn't know the significance of that insignia, some of our more boisterous trainees just called him "bus driver." The "bus driver" was Page Brewer, who gave us a coffee break at San Benito, Texas. The same boisterous young trainee noticed that the restaurant menu showed Wop Salad to be the salad of the day, and he began to tease the waitress about Wop Salad. He told her he was Italian and wanted to know if that was something derogatory. The waitress got red in the face, was highly embarrassed, and refused to wait on our table.

In spite of all this, Officer Brewer ushered us through the day of orientation at Port Isabel, and then we loaded on the bus to go to Brownsville, Texas, where we would be measured for our Smoky Bear hats and where we would be able to buy our uniforms at Sam Purl's Store. Mr. Purl had been furnishing uniforms for the Border Patrol for Lord knows how long. He was highly regarded by the Patrol.

The thing I remember about buying the hat was the fitting. They used a wooden rack that was adjustable to the shape of your head and printed out a shape of your head as well as the size of your hat. The little card with the printout of my head looked like an egg with lumps on the side. So I ordered an oval hat. I also bought a pair of black Wellington boots.

We returned to the Harlingen station that evening loaded down with our bright green rough duty uniforms. Mr. Gilman told us that since it would be two weeks before we went out to Port Isabel to attend the Academy, it might be better that those of us who were living in motels find a boarding house for that two-week period. I took his advice and ended up with Don Devaney and James Garafalo at the same boarding house.

The landlady told us that since we would be away from the boarding house and would miss both breakfast and lunch that she would pack a sandwich for us to take the following day and leave it in the deep freeze where we could pick it up and take it with us when we went to work.

That first day on duty was quite an experience. I was teamed up with an older Patrol Inspector that we just called "PI", and Don was teamed up with another "PI" to patrol a section of the river adjacent to the one I was in. We checked out our jeeps that morning, traveled about six miles down Rangerville Road to the Rio Grande River, and the "PI" showed me the area we would be working in. That area had irrigation canals where water was pumped from the river for irrigating farmland and also a large canal where water was pumped from the river up to the City of San Benito for their city water supply.

This big canal bank was several feet high. We were sitting on the canal bank near Highway 281 when my partner suddenly threw the jeep into gear. We shot down the canal bank onto Highway 281 and started chasing a Volkswagen just as fast as our jeep would go. I wondered what he had seen, if it was a carload of aliens, or just what. I was somewhat surprised when we came to a sliding stop in the gravel in the parking lot of Weaver's Store. It seemed that one of the Weaver girls was a very good friend of this Border Patrolman, and when he saw her pass in her little Volkswagen, he just wanted to talk to her.

After his conversation with Miss Weaver, we went back to patrolling along the river, just getting acquainted, and nothing else exciting happened until lunch. At lunchtime he asked me if I had brought anything to eat. I told him yes, I had brought a sandwich. He said we would meet the other team and eat lunch together, but first we would stop and wash our hands and take a leak and then eat lunch. I hoped he didn't mind if I did that in a different order.

We met the other jeep, and it turned out that Don had a lunch just like mine. That consisted of one bologna sandwich with no dressing—just two pieces of dry bread. I was never so disappointed with a lunch. Since Don hadn't looked inside his lunch bag, I told him, "Oh boy, two sandwiches and an apple!"

Don eagerly opened his lunch bag, and I never saw a more disappointed look on anyone's face in my life. He looked in his bag, which also contained a bologna sandwich just like mine. He looked at me in disbelief and with disappointment in his voice said, "I didn't get an apple."

I learned that most PI's carried a knapsack to hold their lunch, a thermos bottle, and extra boxes of wad cutter ammunition. I learned that the ammunition was to shoot turtles to break the monotony of patrolling up and down the river on what was called "line watch duty."

The afternoon was uneventful, and we returned to the station where I learned to fill out the day's activity report on a form called an I-50, which we were to later call the Lie-50 because we reported as a part of the day's activity the number of foot miles patrolled along the river. If anyone ever put in any foot miles patrolling the river, it must have been whenever they were alone because few of the PI's I worked with ever walked any foot miles.

That night James, Don and I discussed our first day on duty in the U.S. Border Patrol. We found that James had a day much like my day, but Don had not had a good day at all. During his day with George Hendry, they had discussed their background, where each of them was from, and the subject of education arose. Don told Hendry that he had some college and asked had he ever gone to college. When George told Don he had never been to college, Don replied, "Oh, nary a day, huh?" Since this sounded like sarcasm to Hendry, he was offended and took Don to the only hill in the whole Rio Grande

Valley, which was a large pile of dirt dredged up for an inlet from the river for the San Benito pump station and made this sarcastic trainee run up and down the hill a half dozen times. This misunderstanding caused an animosity between Devaney and Hendry, which was evidenced many times during my tour at Harlingen.

The next two weeks were fairly uneventful. Fortunately the lunches got a little better. We became acquainted with the other PI's in the Harlingen station and learned that the insignias on the shoulder epaulets indicated the Supervisory Patrol Inspectors who would be our shift leaders.

By the end of the two weeks, Jim had convinced me that he could help me with my Spanish and that we would be roommates at the Academy. After settling in with my new roommate at the Academy and being briefed by Chief John Eager about the do's and don'ts while we were attending the Academy, we then had a Spanish placement test.

Since the only Spanish I knew was Si, Senor, I was at a loss until I looked down the list of words and saw Journalero. I brightened a bit and said, "Well, at least I know what a journalist is." And to confirm my belief, Jim leaned across the aisle and whispered, "Journalero—newspaper man." So I believed I would get at least one word right. I picked out a couple other words on the list that appeared similar to their English counterpart and ended up with three wrong answers. I was relegated, along with Jim who was going to help me with my Spanish, to the lowest section of the class.

I learned that "Journalero" in Spanish means "laborer." Another one of the things I learned was the mission of the Border Patrol, which was to prevent the illegal entry of aliens and to apprehend those who are already here. It would become clear later on that a lot of officers wanted to de-emphasize the apprehending of those who are already here.

Much of the training at the Academy would be similar to basic military training. Living in the barracks, eating at the mess hall, marksmanship training, and the physical fitness reminded me of basic training. But the emphasis would be on learning the immigration laws, duties and authorities, and Spanish. We also would receive tracking training called "sign cutting" from one of the Senior Patrol

Inspectors stationed at Harlingen. That was Mr. Strobel who I would work with many hours after completing the Academy.

Except for a rattlesnake at our front door, there would be very few interruptions or distractions from our studies. Chief Eager had discouraged the trainees from bringing their wives to the Academy, as there was very little housing available in the area nearby the Academy, and he wanted us to concentrate on our studies.

The facilities were also used by the Alien Detention Facility and the sector headquarters from the Port Isabel Sector. Occasionally an alien on kitchen detail would walk away, and everyone including us trainees would be called upon to search the buildings and the brush around the facility to try to recapture the alien. Since there were so many bushes with stickers and mosquitoes in back, in fact, everything in south Texas seemed to either scratch, bite or sting, the alien would sometimes come back by himself after a few hours of freedom in such surroundings.

There was one mysterious distraction during the next few weeks. There were explosions in the outer areas of the facility, and we wondered who was causing them and why. We never did find out who or why, but it seemed that it was being used as a training area for a group of people to learn demolition techniques. These Latin Americans stayed by themselves, and we were told to have nothing to do with them. They ate by themselves in the mess hall, and the only encounters I had with them were after duty hours in the recreation room. I was a pretty good ping-pong player, and they loved the game of ping-pong, but they never gave their names or explained where they were from or where they would be going. At the end of their training, several civilian-type helicopters came swooping in and took them away to destinations known only by the agency responsible for their training.

My own training was not easy. I had no trouble with the physical fitness or the armed defense because it was a repetition of what I had done in the military. But I was having a little trouble with my marksmanship training shooting the revolver rapid fire. I was able to qualify, but not with a very high score.

Spanish was not easy for me. I had trouble trilling my R's in an alphabet in which two letters like C and H were combined for one letter in the Mexican alphabet. It seemed strange. Fortunately my instructor, Miss Clotilde Guerra, was a good instructor, usually very patient. As I knew French from my school days, when I was stumped for a word in Spanish and I happened to know the word in French, I would throw that in. But Miss Guerra was always alert and would remind me, "Spanish, Mr. Sims, Spanish!"

To add to my problems, I lost my official identification card. ID cards have changed since then and now are thinner, wider, and fit into the shirt pocket where they can be buttoned. But at that time most of us carried our ID card in our hip pocket.

I really dreaded notifying the Chief that I had lost my ID card, and think as I might, I couldn't remember where I might have lost it. Eventually I garnered enough nerve to report the loss and was called into Deputy Chief McDonald's for an interview. Deputy Chief McDonald began telling me a story about someone else who had lost his identification card, and eventually it was recovered by the Mexican police in the red light district called "Boys Town" in Matamoros. He then asked me if I had been to Mexico. I don't know what he expected me to say, but I told him, "Certainly I've been to Mexico, but I'm sure I didn't lose it on the Mexican side of the river."

The explosion I expected from Mr. McDonald never came. He listened to me and then counseled me in a very gently, kind, fatherly voice, but I was about to be introduced to the writing of the service memo. Mr. McDonald told me I would have to notify every law enforcement agency in the area. That included the various Police Departments, Sheriff's Office, Highway Patrol, and the Border Patrol.

Now my problem was, how did I start a memo? How should I address the Texas Department of Public Safety, the Sheriff's Department, the Police Department, and the Border Patrol? Should I just say, "Dear Chief?"

As I struggled with my own problems, my roommate, Jim, was not doing anything to endear himself to the Academy faculty. Jim was the type of person who hated to lose at anything from pinball machines to sports. Some of us had joined the softball team. The Academy staff had joined the church league softball in the little town of Los Fresnos. As there were not really enough members to form the team, some of the Academy trainees were on the team; and Jim and I were both playing softball.

One evening we were in a very close game, and Jim charged into second base in what looked like a sure out, but he hit the second baseman so hard that he jarred the ball loose and really ran over the second baseman. There was an outburst of displeasure from the locals, and Jim was thrown out of the game for unsportsmanlike conduct. A few minutes later he was in the stands in the bleachers cheering on the Border Patrol team and drinking beer. It seems that beer was not allowed. And the person he had just beaten into the dirt at second base was the Town Marshall who then had the pleasure of chasing Jim out of the stands. This was just one of the embarrassments.

Another one of the little things which of itself didn't amount to a whole lot was an expression. Instead of "Ain't that something?" or some such, as most of us would say, Jim's expression was, "Ain't that a tit?" And at everything unusual he quipped out with "Ain't that a tit?" which also sounded embarrassing. Also, he was not living up to the image of the Border Patrol trainee. Jim seemed to be quite happy with the Border Patrol. It was just that the Border Patrol was becoming unhappy with Jim.

At that time we were working at one of the stations either in Brownsville or Harlingen on the weekend. The Border Patrol was authorized overtime pay of 15 percent, but to earn the 15 percent one was required to work at least six hours overtime. In order to claim this overtime, we were detailed to one of the stations and worked with an older PI, usually on line watch. Occasionally someone would get a little different duty. Jim had worked a day of farm and ranch check with none other than George Hendry. They had apprehended several aliens at a farm near Harlingen.

Jim came back at the end of the day very elated because it was unusual for anyone to assist in the apprehension of aliens. He was telling me how the Patrol Inspector had told the aliens to set in front of the jeep and told him to guard the aliens while he was talking to the rancher. Jim told me how he took out his revolver and whirled it around his finger and stuck it back in the holster like Roy Rogers and said, "Bruce, you should have seen their eyes." You should have seen my eyes, too.

Jim was also excusing himself to go to the restroom during class more than any other trainee. I knew he didn't want to wait until

Dear Chief

the breaks between classes for a fast cigarette, and he was also taking some prescription medicine. This must have aroused the suspicion of our instructor, for one day we came back to the barracks at noon and saw that our room had been searched. It wasn't messed up bad, but just enough was out of place for us to know that everything had been moved. We never heard a word about who or why it was searched, but we knew it had been.

The end of Jim's Border Patrol career was fast approaching. By now he had bought a car and was spending all of his day off duty time away from the Academy. He had found a young lady in the little town of La Feria, Texas, who was willing to help him with his Spanish, and she wanted to correspond with Jim. She wrote him a letter at the Academy, and evidently tried to contact him telephonically because the Deputy Chief McDonald found out about the girl in La Feria and went to interview her. In his gentle, fatherly voice, he persuaded her to tell him all about her involvement with the Border Patrol trainee and to even give him the full details in a sworn affidavit. He then returned to the Academy and confronted Jim about his relationship with this young woman.

Jim admitted knowing the young lady but claimed he had never done anything improper and had certainly never had sexual relations with her and was willing to say so in his own sworn affidavit. Mr. McDonald then had two sworn affidavits with conflicting stories. He began to hint that this would be a good time for Jim to resign from the Border Patrol.

At first, Jim was reluctant. But after hints that it would certainly be embarrassing if word got back to his wife in Boston about his activity in Texas, we talked it over in the room. Jim felt sure there was not evidence against him to be dismissed from the Academy, but he said he could still get his old job back. Rather than go through the hassle, he decided to submit his resignation, and I was to finish the Border Patrol Academy without a roommate.

The days drug by, and I was issued another ID card. A very few days after being issued the second ID card, I went to the bathroom, and as I arose from the stool, my new ID card flopped out of my pocket and fell into the commode. I quickly grabbed the ID card before it could become too contaminated and thought, the mystery of my lost ID card is now solved.

Bruce R. Sims

After Jim's departure, I may have concentrated a little more on my studies. Anyway, I continued to barely make a passing grade in Spanish and looked forward to the completion of the Academy. One thing was encouraging. Part of our Spanish training was to practice interviewing an alien sent over from the Detention Facility. We teamed up in pairs to interrogate the alien. My partner was Joe, who already had a working knowledge of Spanish before coming to the Academy. We talked with the alien who had been assigned to us, and after he became at ease he began to talk about where he had been working in north Texas and how the Border Patrol had come to the farm and caught him but had left about seven other aliens that they hadn't seen.

The proper method of communicating such information from one office to another was by use of a form G-330 which Joe and I prepared. Before the end of the Academy, we received an answer from the other office saying they had returned to the farm and apprehended the other aliens.

Despite Chief Eager's advice, a few of the trainees had their wives come down to Port Isabel, and they were living outside the barracks. Don's wife, Myrtle, had joined him, and she was to become my wife's best friend. It appeared that if I could pass the final exam, I was going to successfully complete the Academy, and I was looking forward to my wife's joining me in Harlingen. I would have to go back to Albany, Georgia, where she had continued to work at the Georgia Cigar and Tobacco Company, and help her move. I told her I believe that she would like Harlingen because the land was flat, and it reminded me of her home area of Mississippi, the Delta, which was flat as a floor. When I had traveled down to Harlingen in April, everything was green. The roadside was covered with wildflowers, and I believed she would like it.

By the time I went back to help her move in August, every flower was dead, the grass was brown, and as we traveled south through the King ranch on Highway 77, she began asking me where were all the flowers. By the time we reached Harlingen she said she had seen enough of the valley, and she could already tell me she didn't like it worth a damn.

I had rented a duplex apartment from Mr. George Wallace, who had plenty of vacancies since Harlingen was suffering through an economic depression because of the closing of the Air Force Base. There were blocks of housing that had been occupied by the military which might have just one family left on the block.

We took seven dogs with us down to Harlingen, and some service station operator had asked Jerry in Alabama if she was traveling with the circus because she had so many dogs. The dogs adapted to apartment living, although they had had two acres to wander around on in Albany, Georgia. Two Chihuahuas we kept in the house. Two beagles we kept outside, and noticed that they were disappearing in the hot part of the day. It took awhile to discover that they had learned to go down into the gutter under the street to find a cool place.

We shared the duplex with a family from Ohio who had two little girls. They liked our dogs all right, but the dog they really loved was a beautiful Doberman across the street. The Doberman was owned by one of the coaches at the Harlingen High School. He didn't give too much attention to the dog though he was fond of it.

A few weeks later the little girls' father told me that he was moving to be closer to his work out at Port Isabel, that he was going to take the Coach's dog with him because the Coach didn't care anything about it, and his little girls loved the dog. I said, "Surely you're not going to take the Coach's dog." But a few days later after the man had moved, the Coach came across the street and asked me if I had seen his dog. I told him what my neighbor had told me, that he was going to take the dog with him when he moved, and I supposed that he had.

I also told the Coach I believed our former neighbor had moved to Bayview, which is a tiny village near Port Isabel. That weekend Coach went to Bayview looking for his dog and found it. He brought it home with him.

Another few weeks went by, and the dog disappeared the second time. This time when the Coach went looking for it, our former neighbors had moved, and this time no one knew where they had gone.

As far as duty was concerned, Harlingen turned out to be one of the best stations where I could have been assigned because of the variety of the work. Harlingen did just about everything that the Border Patrol did. We had two-week shifts on line watch, that's patrolling the river, then two weeks on farm and ranch check. We had a midnight shift which fortunately was not assigned very often, and we also worked a team of officers on what was called "city scout." That was civilian clothes work, mostly apprehending maids. Some were live-in maids, and some had just come up from Matamoros to Harlingen on a daily basis. We also had one officer doing transportation check. That was making sure no illegal aliens boarded at Harlingen airport and checking the buses for aliens who might have avoided the Border Patrol line watch operations in Brownsville and walked up the highway a ways before boarding the bus.

We also had traffic check twice a year during the open ports in September on the Mexican Holiday, September 16, and what was known as Charro Days in February. Throughout the year we would then find illegal aliens who claimed they had crossed the bridge during open port and stayed in Brownsville until the traffic check was over and then moved into the Harlingen area to work. We always wondered why these open ports were necessary, but the answer was that it had always been that way.

That's the same answer we got when we asked why we went to work at 5:00 a.m. on line watch duty when it was too dark to see any tracks in the dusty roads and trails leading up from the fiver even if there were any. As a result, we usually reported for duty, received our vehicle assignments, and headed down to San Benito to Clayton's Drive In to have coffee and wait for daylight. It had always been that way.

Another duty which was rotated among us trainees immediately after we came from the Academy was Processing Officer. The Processing Officer stayed in the office and answered the telephone, typed the duty roster for the station Senior, and processed an apprehension report on those aliens brought in by the other units so they could get back out to their specified areas. What I remember about my two weeks on processing was what was called a family unit case.

It was Service policy that if a member of the family was an American citizen, then the alien members of the family would be written up on an I-213, report of an Alien Apprehended or Located, and they would be given a permit to remain in the United States with the U.S. citizen member of the family. One of the older Patrol

Inspectors brought in a woman and a baby and told me that the baby was a citizen of Mexico, but the mother was a United States citizen and that I should write a report giving the baby permission to stay in the United States with the citizen mother. As proof of her citizenship, she had a Xeroxed copy of a birth certificate. I asked her a few questions in my none-too-fluent Spanish, and even though I couldn't really understand her answers, it was obvious, even to me, that she knew nothing about the data on the birth certificate—even the place of birth.

I talked to her as best I could and waited for the PI to return to the office and explained to him that I didn't believe that this woman was a United States citizen, as she didn't know anything about her birth certificate. After awhile of talking to her, she decided that she would tell the truth—that she wasn't really a U.S. citizen and just wanted an opportunity to stay in the States with her baby.

The guys teased me about my first false claim, but I really didn't feel that it was my apprehension or success because she admitted the truth to me. Someone with more experience and better Spanish had to talk with her to get the truth. Later on I would know my own technique in getting the truth from those falsely claiming U.S. citizenship, but I would have to improve my Spanish a good bit.

To help me improve my Spanish, I contacted my instructor at the Academy, Miss Guerra, and asked her if she would continue to tutor me until I passed my two exams during my probationary year. She agreed that she would, and I attribute to her much of the credit for my successful completion of my probationary year. That was the year that James Meredith decided to attend Mississippi University at Oxford, Mississippi.

There was much opposition to the integration of "Ole Miss," and his attendance and his entrance into the school would be by the use of U.S. Marshals. As a result, the Border Patrol was deputized as marshals and was sent to "Old Miss" to escort Meredith into the building and keep the rioters out.

The officers from Harlingen included one Mississippian who was to come face to face with his brother on opposite sides of the barricade. We trainees were not detailed to Mississippi. The six of us were left behind under the supervision of one Senior Patrol Inspector and one other PI who was on leave at the time the order to go to

Mississippi was issued. That was a very skimpy force of officers guarding 23 miles of river during temporary duty. We had been working with a Senior or an older PI, but during that time we were on our own.

I remember checking a field of laborers harvesting onions near the river and finding a girl with a baptismal certificate. She was very nervous when I approached her and looked at her certificate, asked her a few questions, which she couldn't answer, and I made up my mind that she was not a citizen of the United States, but didn't know what to do about it.

I called for some assistance from one of the other trainees, Don Devaney, and we talked to her some more on the edge of the field beside our jeeps. We decided that, yes, she certainly was not the person named on the baptismal certificate and that we should take her to the office to get the older PI to help us get the truth from her. Getting an admission was called "breaking an alien."

Mr. Gilman, our Station Senior, had told us before he left for Mississippi that when we encountered a situation like that we should break the aliens in the field or let them go. On the way to the office, Don and I remembered his instruction and didn't think we had a complete story that the girl had broken well enough, so we stopped a few minutes on the side of the road and talked to her again. This time she saw that she was away from her friends in the field and that her case was lost, and she decided to tell the truth—or as much of it as she wanted to tell. We then proceeded on to the office without worrying we had violated someone's rights and brought an alien to the office without being broken. That was the highlight of the period while the other officers were on detail.

Several weeks had gone by, and I still hadn't caught anyone coming up from the river or entering illegally on foot on line watch duty. Things were slow at that time of the year. There were very few entries, and I was beginning to believe that I would never catch an illegal alien. Catching your first alien on line watch is something that stays with you all of your career.

Finally I was assigned to work the evening shift on line watch with Arnold Cope. Arnold and I checked the roads and trails leading up from the river to make sure there were no tracks when we went on duty. Before dark we threw fresh dirt across one of the most accessible roads that the aliens were apt to take, since at that point they could see the red lights on the radio antenna towers to guide their way up to the highway in La Feria.

The reason we threw dirt onto the road was because it was hard packed, and there was very little soft sand or dust in which to see tracks. By throwing several shovels full of dirt across the road in what we called a bear trap, we could get at least two good footprints where they stepped in the fresh dirt.

That night about 9:30 we had checked our bear traps, and sure enough there were clear footprints in one of them showing where two aliens had walked that road headed towards La Feria. Arnold decided to take me well ahead of where he thought they would be, since they couldn't have had much of a head start, and put me out at a little field crossroad to wait for them to walk up to me. He was going back to the bear trap, drive out the road watching the sides just in case they had turned off the road so he could find their tracks leading away from the road.

I waited and waited for what seemed like an eternity. Finally I saw headlights coming up the road toward me. At first I thought it was Arnold in the jeep, but then I could tell the vehicle wasn't making the distinctive noise that a jeep motor makes. So when the vehicle was almost to me I stepped out in front of it waving my flashlight, and a man, woman and child were quite surprised that I had just appeared in front of their vehicle so suddenly.

When I asked them if they had seen anyone walking the road, they said they had not. So they went on about their business, and I stepped back into the weeds beside the road to wait. In what seemed like another eternity, I saw more headlights coming up the road toward me, and this time I could hear the distinctive whine of the jeep engine. I thought, well, there's no chance of catching the aliens now. They must have stepped off the road and hidden and let the vehicles pass or turned off someplace before they got to me. But then I heard footsteps. They weren't really running, but they were walking as fast as they could walk and evidently were going to wait until the jeep got much closer to them before hiding in the weeds beside the road.

I jumped out in the road in front of them, shined my flashlight in their face, told them to halt, and my heart was racing a mile a minute. Of course, they were just as scared as they could be, too. In a flash I had them handcuffed together. In a couple more minutes, Arnold arrived on the scene. We had apprehended my first two illegal aliens.

Line watch duty is the primary method the Border Patrol uses to fulfill its mission, preventing the illegal entry of aliens and apprehending those who are already here. Line watch duty can be very monotonous duty if there aren't many people crossing the river. This was the case in the Harlingen area. The hours seemed long and monotonous, and our method of operation was to report for duty at 3:00 in the afternoon and work until 11. Then we would usually work an extra hour to qualify for our overtime pay.

In the evening after reporting for duty, having a cup of coffee to get the shift started on the right foot, we would go to our assigned area along the river and see if there were any fresh tracks and prepare our bear traps across the trails and roads leading up from the river. Then we would select a spot for "laying in." "Laying in" is simply parking the jeep in an area where it can't be seen and watching a particular trail you suspect might be used by illegal aliens. "Laying in" was never a productive way of apprehending aliens for me. Maybe it was my impatience. Some PI's I worked with could sit for hours at a time smoking a cigarette or swapping war stories, but after awhile I became impatient and wanted to get back to check the bear traps.

One of the most patient people I ever worked with was Hugo Braesicke. He was a very conscientious Border Patrolman, and I enjoyed the hours I spent working with him. We had an interest in hunting and fishing, so we swapped our stories until we'd told them all two or three times. He was careful to hide the match he lit a cigarette with to keep it from being seen some distance away. He even cupped the cigarette in his hand so anyone coming up the road would not see the red glow. Near quitting time we would leave our place of concealment and check our bear traps one more time before going off duty, and another monotonous shift would be over.

Morning line watch was not much more exciting. As I've said before, we waited for daylight. Then we checked our access roads before the field workers and the vehicles traveled over them and stirred up the dust and blotted out the tracks. Then in the middle of the morning we would go for another cup of coffee, come back down to the farm land near Highway 281 and check truckloads of workers working in the fields near the river. These labor trucks, as we called them, would come out of Brownsville with loads of workers massed at a particular area where they could be picked up for day labor.

These people would go several miles from Brownsville to any part of the valley to harvest whatever crop was in season. Occasionally an illegal alien would be among the workers, one who had waded the river near Brownsville and successfully avoided the Border Patrol to join the group of day laborers. There was always a possibility by checking the whole crew you would find one or two illegal aliens. But you were much more likely to encounter all types of fraudulent documents. A common fraudulent document was a baptismal certificate called a fe de bautisimo. These baptismal certificates were issued by churches, and they showed the child's name, date and place of birth, and the godparents. These certificates could be rented or purchased in Mexico from false document vendors from anywhere from $5.00 to as much as the market would bear.

I never saw so many baptismal certificates coming from Crystal City, Texas in my life. If everyone who claimed birth in Crystal City returned at the same time, it would have made it one of the most thriving metropolises in Texas.

Another type of document was either a Xerox or photocopy of a birth certificate. These birth certificates included more information. It was really easier to find questions that an imposter couldn't answer than it was to break someone with a baptismal certificate. This birth certificate contained information such as number of brothers and sisters, when this child was born, ages of the parents, and things that the real owner of the certificate would know while it would be hard to remember for an imposter who was trying to memorize everything on the certificate. To me getting the truth from someone falsely claiming to be a citizen was much more important than catching a person who had waded across the river without any documents who probably would work a few weeks or months at most and then go back home to Mexico. The successful person with a false document could move anywhere to any city within the United States and eventually bring his family, either legally or illegally, to join him somewhere in the U.S.

Normally, the officers working line watch only checked those field laborers working near the river between Highway 281 and the river and stayed in our assigned areas unless someone found tracks of illegal entrants and requested help. Everyone working line watch might team up with one team following the tracks step by step and other teams leap frogging ahead to the crossroads places where they might find tracks or wait for the aliens to approach them. If that didn't work, the team following the tracks step by step would sometimes find where the aliens had decided to hide in the brush or in the ditch, or even in somebody's barn or equipment shed to stay out of sight during daylight and travel only at night.

If we weren't successful in apprehending those whose tracks we found, we had a book in the office in which we logged the number of tracks and a description of the footprints. There was usually something distinctive about the heel that would identify those particular footprints from any others. Those were called "gotaways."

The Border Patrol's method of performing the second part of its mission, apprehending those who are already here, was through farm and ranch check and city scout. I enjoyed farm and ranch check as we had a large area stretching from the river on the south to the Hidalgo County line on the west. The area we called the brush line, where the farming stopped and the ranching began, north of Raymondville, Texas, and all the way to the Bay on the east. We usually kept at least two teams assigned to farm and ranch, and we let each other know what area we would be working in so we wouldn't be following along one behind the other and checking the same workers twice. This was how we located our own "gotaways" and quite a few who had entered in the McAllen sector, then wandered into the Port Isabel sector to work.

Chief Tommy Ball was the Border Patrol Sector Chief for McAllen. His emphasis was on line watch more than farm and ranch check or city scout. His main concern was that nobody got through his line watch area without being caught. He would go to great lengths to show how efficient his line watch operation was performing. We learned that every time we made an apprehension report and he learned that we showed the alien's place of entry in his sector area instead of the Port Isabel area, the following morning he would be seen flying down Highway 281 to Port Isabel to reinterview the aliens we had placed in the detention camp there. Then he would come back by the Harlingen station and tell the Station Senior that he had reinterviewed the aliens we caught and that our PI's had made a mistake in their location of entry. He claimed they had told him on his interview that they really hadn't entered at the Mercedes pump but entered a couple of miles further down river at the San Benito pump which was in the Port Isabel area. This got to be so funny that a couple of older PI's would deliberately show the alien's place of entry in the McAllen sector just to have a laugh at Chief Ball's expense.

The weeks went by, and each week the six of us trainees and the trainees from the Brownsville station would meet with Robert McKennon, the Sector Training Officer, who would review the work we had done at the Academy and prepare us to pass our five and a half month's exam.

This was a good day to get away from line watch or any other duty. We would stop on the way to Port Isabel for coffee at San Benito, and then the driver would slow down beside a Resaca near the highway. By the way, a Resaca is like a pond of water, which was previously a riverbed, and see if we could spot any nutria. Nutria is a muskrat-type animal that was imported into Louisiana and had made its way around the Gulf coast and was considered pests. If we saw any, we got our target practice by shooting at them. This was in a remote area, and there was no danger that our bullets would do any damage to anything. We then proceeded on to Port Isabel for our day of training and a welcome break from the monotony of line watch.

I would eventually perform every type of duty and work with each one of the Senior Patrol Inspectors at the Harlingen station, but it seemed like during my probationary year I worked more with SPA Oscar Strobel and Hugo Braesicke than with any other PI's. My performance rating was always average with Mr. Strobel. I was never rated excellent at anything. But other PI's who had gone through their probationary year under Mr. Strobel told me that an "average" officer was better than an "excellent" by someone else. My Spanish was improving as I had bought a cheap tape recorder on which to practice. Somehow I squeaked through that first exam and it faded into memory.

As my second and final exam approached, I was more confident that I was not going to be fired from the Border Patrol. I thought I had done a pretty good job during my probationary year, but I do remember sitting in front of that Board of three officers who would give me the oral part of the exam. The test could be as easy or as difficult as the officers chose to make it. We trainees always believed that their minds had been made up before we met the Board, whether we were going to pass or going to fail. I certainly needed that help in order to pass.

One of them would give a story such as an illegal alien would give about his date and place of birth, where he lived, how he had entered and why he came to the United States, and we would have to interpret that back and answer in Spanish. One of the things I could not remember to save my life was an expression the pretending agent uttered when he was apprehended at the airport trying to board a plane. He said in surprise, "So soon?" I could not remember the Spanish for "so soon."

The Board members saw I was stumped and began trying to help me. They said, "What happens when a person goes to the beach?" And another said, "Yes, but what is the purpose of going to the beach?" And then it struck me. They went to get a tan. And "So soon" was "Tan pronto." And I blurted out "Tan pronto." And they all laughed and said, "Of course."

My barely passing grade gave me a real sense of relief and assured that I would become a journeyman Patrol Inspector at the end of my probationary year.

That first year was filled with learning experiences. Like the day I was assigned to work with Lloyd. Mr. Gilman, Station Senior, said, "Lloyd will help you with your Spanish." And sure enough, he was eager to help me, and we conversed in Spanish. He gave me the names of vegetables and other bushes and trees that were growing in the valley, and he was very helpful, even when we spied a person in a blue shirt chopping weeds in the middle of a field.

A tractor driver was plowing the field, and the man was coming along behind the tractor chopping the weeds that the plow had missed. We stopped at the end of the field where the tractor would come to the end of its row and turn around, and the man on the tractor, out of politeness, stopped to talk to the Border Patrolmen in our gaudy green uniforms; and I learned that Mexicans are basically honest. If you ask them something that they don't want to tell you, they will say they don't know. But if they do answer and tell you a person is all right, that they have their Residence Card, then you can

Dear Chief

believe they have a Residence Card. But an "I don't know" answer can mean they do know and that the alien is illegal, and they just don't want to say so.

In this case, I saw a look of amazement come over the face of the tractor driver, and then I realized why he looked so surprised. Lloyd had asked him in his best Spanish, "Who is that man in the blue dress?" The Spanish word, *camisa*, had escaped Lloyd, and he had substituted the word *vestida*, which means dress. I really did learn something that day.

That reminded me of the story the instructors told at the Academy about the Border Patrolman who was going to speak before a civic organization. He arrived a few minutes late and wanted to express his embarrassment for being late. The point of the story was that one should not try to add an "o" to an English word to change it into a Spanish word. Sometimes that will work, but usually it doesn't. In this case the Border Patrolman forgot that to be embarrassed was *tener verguenza* and told his audience in Spanish that he was *muy embarrasado*. Imagine his surprise at the outburst of laughter when he realized he had told them he was *very pregnant*.

Another incident I found humorous occurred one morning when I was on line watch duty with SPI Red Dennis. We patrolled down the levee and observed a man who appeared to be in his fifties and a young man who might have been in his early twenties with a little fire built beside the river fishing for catfish. We spoke to them and asked if they were catching anything. They said, "Not much." They had been there all night. We proceeded on down the levee until we came to a pepper patch owned by a farmer named Mr. Sojak. Mr. Dennis stopped beside the pepper patch and said, "Jump out there and get us a handful of those peppers." Not knowing what kind he liked, I got a few red ones, some dark green ones and some bright green ones, and climbed back in the jeep. We went back up the levee to where the men were fishing. The older man was cooking breakfast. He had some coffee boiling, some bacon frying and was scrambling some eggs. It smelled good. They invited us to join them for breakfast, but we declined. Mr. Dennis told the older man, "I have something here that would really spice up those scrambled eggs," and offered him a handful of the jalapeno peppers. He said he believed that it would add something to the scrambled eggs, so he chopped up several of the peppers, and stirred them into the scrambled eggs. It was obvious that the young man could hardly wait for breakfast. He spooned out a heaping helping of scrambled eggs, took two bites, and then realized that his throat was on fire. The coffee wouldn't quench the fire. He gulped about two gulps of air, stuck his head into the Rio Grande River, and I thought he would drink it dry. I hoped it didn't prove fatal.

I didn't get to work very much with Mr. Dennis, although he was an enjoyable man to work with. I had to learn what was permissible and what was not. I remember working with SPI Strobel and checking a group of laborers picking oranges. As we left the orange grove, I reached over and picked the largest, yellowest orange I could spot. When we got back to the jeep I proceeded to peel the orange with my fingers and tear it into sections. Mr. Strobel just watched me and didn't say anything until I'd finished the orange. Then he reached over, and what I was to learn was one of his fatherly gestures, slapped me on the knee and said, "Well, compadre, did you enjoy the orange?" I told him, yes. It was a juicy orange, and it sure was delicious. He said, "Well, I hope you enjoyed it, but don't do that again." He said we never take anything from a field or orchard; and as long as I worked with him, I never knew him to accept anything that was offered to him by a farmer or rancher, whether it be vegetables, fruit or anything else. He was the most honest man I've ever worked with in my life.

During the fall of 1962, while we trainees were still going out to Port Isabel for our in-sector training, we noticed a group of trainees at the Academy who obviously were not Border Patrol trainees. These people were shorter than the Border Patrol height requirements. Most of them were chubby with potbellies. Many were wearing thick glasses, and it was obvious they could not have qualified for the Border Patrol. We asked our instructor who this new group was, and he told us they were Investigator Trainees from New York. He explained that it was difficult to get anyone to transfer to New York City, and in order to fill the vacancies they decided to hire a group of Investigator Trainees off the street. Off the street didn't necessarily mean they had literally come "off the street." Many of them were already Immigration employees who had held some type of clerical position in the New York district office.

Some of the most athletic appearing ones were retired New York City police officers. We were a bit disturbed because Investigator jobs were our route to promotion within the Service. Our instructor said not to worry about those people. They were being hired specifically to fill the New York vacancies, and they would never interfere with our opportunities to be promoted from the Patrol.

At that time the promotion system was a three-tiered evaluation. An officer was highly recommended or recommended. In order to be recommended a new Border Patrolman had to have about five years in the patrol. Only those with the most time and doing the best job were highly recommended. Those highly recommended were offered promotions where vacancies existed. That was usually Chicago, New York, occasionally Los Angeles, or some other smaller district office.

Occasionally someone who was disgusted with the way things were at Harlingen would accept one of those offers. But the response was usually like that of Hugo Braesicke who would write on his announcement that he would accept Senior in the Border Patrol only. I don't know how many times he responded to his offer of promotion in that manner, but it was every time that he was offered a promotion until he was eventually promoted to Senior in the Border Patrol at Brownsville, Texas. It would be a long time before any of us six trainees would be offered a promotion.

During my probationary year, some of the officers had asked if I was interested in joining the union. That was the American Federation of Government Employees, the AFGE. I told them I believed I'd better wait until I had completed my probationary year before I joined. So I kept my word, and immediately after my probationary year was over I joined the AFGE. Shortly thereafter they wanted me to be the Harlingen representative. That was the Shop Steward. I agreed, and was enthusiastic about getting a few more members so we could have what was known as "exclusive recognition." The union only needed a couple of new members to have the percentage to claim exclusive recognition. So I contacted the other stations in the Port Isabel district, the offices at Kingsville and Corpus Christi, Texas. Two men agreed to join if I would bring the membership application to them and collect their dues. I agreed to do that. On one of my days off, my wife, Jerry, and I traveled up to

Kingsville, collected the dues and application form from the men who had agreed to join at Kingsville and proceeded on over to Corpus Christi.

We enjoyed our day in Corpus Christi. I got the other membership necessary to give us exclusive recognition, and we started to do some shopping that afternoon before heading back to Harlingen. There came a little shower of rain; the roads were slick. I didn't know my way around, and I had a minor accident. The accident wasn't serious. It did a little damage to both of the cars involved. No one was injured, but it was definitely my fault. I put in an insurance claim, and the first thing I knew I got a notice that my insurance was cancelled. That was my first dealing with GEICO Insurance Company. I had to shop around Harlingen and find another company that would give me liability coverage. So my gaining two members for AFGE turned out to be very expensive.

The president of the local chapter of the union was from the Brownsville station. He was Billy Marshall. During the next few months I would get numerous calls from Billy saying, "Meet me out at Port Isabel at the sector headquarters. We have to talk to Chief Harrison." There was no problem getting out to Port Isabel. I was Shop Steward, and they allowed me to represent the members; but we got very little satisfaction from Chief Harrison. It was obvious that he had nothing but contempt for the AFGE union.

One of the problems we discussed with him was holidays. We thought we should be getting more of our holidays off. Chief Harrison said that he didn't give a damn what we thought. If he had to, he could prove statistically that more aliens entered illegally during holidays than any other time, and that was when the most people should be on duty. There were other little problems that we went out to see the Chief about. It was obvious that we were a nuisance to him, especially Billy as he was the spokesman. I just went along as the silent partner.

On one of our trips out to Port Isabel the Chief said to Billy, "Billy, if you could transfer in the Border Patrol anywhere you wanted to go, where would you go?" Billy told the Chief that he hadn't really thought about transferring anywhere; but if he could go anywhere he wanted to go, he guessed he would go to New Orleans. Within three weeks a telegram came for Billy. And you guessed it, he was transferred to New Orleans. I was convinced that Chiefs in the Border Patrol were the most powerful people in the United States government.

My five classmates and I were no longer trainees. Another class had graduated from the Academy. From that class we got four trainees. They were Homer, Floyd, John and Andy. I had a small tape recorder that I had used to practice Spanish, and one of those trainees, John, thought that would be helpful to him, and he bought my tape recorder. The tape recorded wasn't destined to be much help for John, as when they reported back from the Academy for their first day on the job, the older PI's went through the same routine they had used on; me and the others by putting a jeep four wheel drive transmission in neutral and giving the trainee the key and telling him to go ahead and drive. The trainee would crank the engine, race the motor, shift through the various gears, and nothing would happen. If they had not had military experience driving jeeps like I had, then they were the butt of the joke. The older PI said, "Now look what you've done!" But in my case I had simply shifted the transmission back into drive. There was no joke. Poor John was in a more serious predicament. Mr. Gilman, our Station Senior, had parked his sedan at the back door to the office. When the older PI told John to drive, and they got into the jeep, John backed from his parking space into Mr. Gilman's sedan causing some damage.

At that moment destiny had stepped in and decreed that John would never make it through his probationary year. Despite his ability, which I thought was about average in Spanish, his appraisals were so bad that he just couldn't overcome them. After John resigned from the Border Patrol, we would occasionally see him delivering milk on his milk route. That was just a way of life on the Border Patrol.

There had been other personnel changes during that first year. The number of PI's assigned to the Harlingen station had reached 32. Our Station Senior, Mr. Gilman, wanted more people assigned, as the number assigned to the Brownsville station entitled their Station Senior to a grade GS-11, while Mr. Gilman was only a GS-10. He thought if he had as many people as Brownsville, then he would be upgraded to a GS-11 grade. But it never worked out that way. We began to lose some officers through promotion, transfers and resignations; and the station's strength got smaller instead of larger.

One of the people who transferred to the Harlingen station had been working in Florida and was to be one of my best friends. That was Robert McCord. It was customary in the mornings that Mr. Gilman would gather several people along with himself and go to the Seville Coffee Shop for coffee. We would play a numbers game in which everybody contributed a nickel or dime more than their coffee cost, and then we would select a number and the person guessing the number would get everything in the pot which would pay for the coffee and leave enough left over to pay for his coffee and sometimes a few cents extra.

That particular morning I was on another two-week tour of processing; and when Mr. Gilman got ready to take the people with him to play the numbers game at coffee break, he told me to come along and told Bob to stay behind and answer the telephone, even though Bob had about four years or so more in the Service. Mr. Gilman told him to do the processing, as he needed the practice. I could see that Bob resented that remark, and he was never fond of Mr. Gilman as long as he knew him. I always liked Mr. Gilman, who some of the PI's referred to as "Uncle Al," and I hated to see him leave when he was transferred to California.

Completing that first year was important. We would now be GS-8 Journeymen Patrol Inspectors and would be assigned to work alone either in a vehicle by ourselves on line watch or on transportation check. Transportation check consisted of checking the airplane departures from the city airport and checking the northbound buses as they came through either the San Benito station or the Harlingen station. This duty was performed in the Class A uniform and was one of the duties that I enjoyed most. I never apprehended anyone trying to leave Harlingen by aircraft, but I was very productive in apprehending aliens at the bus stations.

One day I returned home at end of the shift, and as I got out of my Class A uniform I noticed that my badge was missing. Oh, how I dreaded the thoughts of notifying the Chief that I had lost my badge. I could just see those memorandums, "Dear Chief, I regret to report the loss of my badge." I put off reporting the loss as long as I could. Thankfully, the next day at the San Benito bus station a little boy approached me with my badge in his hand. I had never been more thankful to see a piece of equipment in my life.

Another item of the uniform we had very little use for in southern Texas was the overcoat, and subsequently only a few people in the station had bothered to purchase an overcoat. I bought a used overcoat from one of the men who was transferred away from Harlingen. So when our annual uniform inspection rolled around, I had all of the necessary equipment in items of uniform.

The inspection was performed by Assistant Chief Bill Jordan. Mr. Jordan came to the station early in the morning and began his inspection. We who had our full complement of uniform items were the first ones to be inspected. Then we went outside and passed our overcoat over to another officer who did not have an overcoat, and he went inside. As a result the overcoat was inspected time after time.

Mr. Jordan, realizing that we truly didn't need overcoats and that it was an asinine requirement to purchase one, never let on that he was inspecting the same overcoat over and over. He just checked "yes" that we did have an overcoat because we'd shown him one.

He did make a comment while I was standing before him in my Class A uniform with my Smoky Bear hat which did not fit my oval head because the hat was a round hat. When we were measured for our hats in Brownsville, the little card that the machine punches out showed that my head was shaped like an egg with some bumps on the sides. So I ordered the proper size hat in an oval. When the hat came it was the right size, but it was not an oval shaped hat—it was a round hat which touched my head on the back and front but left spaces along the sides that you could run your hand up the side. Chief Jordan looked at me in that hat, and in his gruff, Louisiana voice drawled, "Damn, son, why don't you just wear the box and throw the hat away. The box would fit you better." I always hated that Smoky Bear hat and wore it only when absolutely necessary.

There were just a few times when we wore the Class A uniform. One was while performing our duties as transportation check and another was during traffic check operations. We performed traffic check operations for a few days during two holiday seasons in Mexico. That was the 16th of September and during Charro Days in February. During those two Mexican national festivities we would set up a traffic checkpoint on Highway 77 just south of San Benito and another on Highway 281 near the river on the road leading out of Brownsville. We would maintain those traffic checkpoints about five days to prevent the aliens who entered at Brownsville during open port from proceeding northward into the interior of the United States. The traffic checkpoints were not very effective as throughout the rest of the year we would apprehend aliens who claimed they had entered during the open port and remained in Brownsville until they knew our traffic checkpoint had been taken down. Then they had proceeded northward.

Traffic check was also very dangerous, and I don't remember ever getting through a five-day period of traffic check without an accident at our checkpoint. There were so many people that had gotten soused in Matamoros and headed back home that weren't used to a traffic checkpoint being there and would come flying up Highway 77 disregarding our warning lights and signs and either plow into a vehicle that was already stopped or lose control of their vehicle and have some other type of accident.

The only Cubans I remember were apprehended at the Highway 77 checkpoint while working with Ted Milner and Robert McCord. I was the junior man when a bus from Brownsville stopped at our checkpoint. I jumped on the bus and announced that this was an Immigration check and checked the citizenship of each person on the bus. As I neared the rear of the bus, I saw two people sitting side by side who evidently didn't comprehend what was going on. So I said to them when I came to their seat, in my very best Spanish, where are you from? They answered me in their very best Cuban and said, "Somos de Uva, Senor." Uva is the Spanish word for grape, and I had never heard of Grape, Mexico. So I asked them again, "Where are you from?" They again told me the same thing, that they were from Uva. So I stuck my head back out the bus and asked Bob if he had ever heard of Grape, Mexico. He replied, "They're telling you they are from Cuba, not Uva." So those were the first two Cubans I remember apprehending.

I owe Ted a debt of thanks, for it was also during that traffic checkpoint tour that I had leaned over with my head inside a car to talk to the occupants on the passenger side and I wasn't paying any attention to the cars coming up behind me, as I expected them to slow down and stop. Suddenly someone grabbed my shoulder strap of my

Class A leather, jerking me backwards just as a car crashed into the rear end of the car that I was leaning into. I could just imagine my head going up the highway about 20 feet with that car while the rest of me stood in the middle of the road. One could never be too careful on traffic check.

Now that my five classmates and I had completed our probationary year, I could relax and really enjoy being in the Border Patrol. I continued to work mostly with Oscar, but I rotated through all the different duties we had to perform. I worked city scout with Carl Shults. I worked some farm and ranch with Page Brewer and worked alone on transportation check. I gained confidence in my use of the Spanish language and wasn't afraid to tackle anyone with any documents that I thought were fraudulent. We PI's considered breaking one documented false claim worth catching ten pure wets.

Each officer had to develop his own special little technique for getting a documented false claim to tell the truth. One of the first methods I used was to have the older ones swear to tell the truth, and since they were usually Catholics and really didn't want to tell a lie after they had sworn to tell the truth, you could appeal to their religious training. Occasionally they would say, "Well, what will happen to me if I tell you the truth?" Once you explained that it wouldn't be so hard on them, in fact that it would be easier if they did tell you the truth, then they would go ahead and tell you they'd purchased the documents from a vendor whom they had met in the park or in the plaza in Mexico. Many times one wouldn't want to tell you that he had purchased the document, so he would claim that he had found it in the plaza. If the plazas had as many documents as they claim to have found, then the whole thing would have been littered with birth certificates, baptismal certificates, and Social Security cards.

The more documents one had, the easier it was to find something on the documents that the person hadn't memorized. Once you caught them in a lie, it was just a matter of keeping the pressure on until they would continue to tell more lies and more lies until eventually they would see that it was impossible to claim that they were their documents and they were the person named on the documents. However, if you encountered a really tough false claim who had presented the documents at the bridge and had been admitted, then it was really tough to ever get them to tell the truth afterwards. They would tell you, "They accepted me at the bridge." And they wondered why you were questioning them once they had been admitted to the United States. If you persisted trying to get the truth from them, it would eventually get to the point where they would say, "That is my paper. This is me. You do whatever you want to with me. You can even kill me if you want to. But this is me, and this is my paper." When you came to that point, you might as well let them walk away, because they were never going to tell you anything.

The Service, in an attempt to assist us in detecting altered documents, had sent us an ultraviolet light. One of the officers built a shadowbox to protect the ultraviolet light from the other sources of light. Once you slid a document into the little crevice in the box underneath the ultraviolet light, one could hopefully detect any alterations in the ink on the document. We'd had the light for quite awhile without its being any use to us, until I worked the midnight shift with Jerry Apfel. Jerry worked the midnight shift the way I liked to work it. We would look for any sign of illegal entry along the river until daylight when the morning line watch crew came to work and relay any information about crossings to them. Then we would get a bite of breakfast and take a sedan and finish up our shift any way we desired.

One morning Jerry decided we would go by some rented cabins where a bartender/prostitute worked and lived in La Feria. Sure enough, we found an undocumented alien just getting out of bed after having spent the night with this woman named Irma. We apprehended him and checked her documents, which consisted of nothing more than a baptismal certificate. We processed the one we apprehended and sent him back to Mexico.

A couple of days later, Jerry suggested we go back by the cabin and talk to Irma some more because he suspected that she was really an illegal alien who had somehow obtained a baptismal certificate. We convinced her that we would have to talk to her at our office and took her into the Harlingen office to again question her about the information on the baptismal certificate. She had answers for every question—her birth date was her correct birth date. She remembered who the godparents were and had everything on the baptismal certificate well memorized. We had almost reached the point where it was, "You do anything you want to; kill me if you want to, but this is my paper. Now let me go." As a last resort I slid the baptismal certificate underneath the ultraviolet light. I let out a yell that startled her and Jerry, for everything on the baptismal certificate except the church pastor's signature had been eradicated. The reason she knew all the details so well was because they had been rewritten over the eradicated spaces with her actual name, her actual parents' names, and her godparents' names. She knew all of that because it actually related to her. The only thing was that we could clearly read under the blue light all the information that had been originally entered on that baptismal certificate including the actual person's name.

Irma finally conceded that, yes, she had the baptismal certificate altered and her own information entered on it. But she had to see for herself the writing underneath the blue light before she would admit the truth. We sent the baptismal certificate to the Southern Regional Intelligence Officer as an example of what blue light could be used for.

My classmates and I were now occasionally assigned to work with each other, but I continued to work mostly with SPI Oscar Strobel on farm and ranch check and on line watch, and we got to share some of each other's stories. One night after we had spotted a car parked near the river and approached in our usual careful way, parking close to the car, approaching it on foot one on either side of the car, then shining our flashlight into the car, it was a young man and woman. The man saw that we were some sort of law enforcement officers and was really shaken up. He tried to put on his clothes, tried to put two feet in one leg, and was just all thumbs and couldn't get dressed. The young woman who he was with was cool as a cucumber. She just lowered her dress and was not flustered at all. She looked up into our faces and said, "It's all right, officers. We're married. We were just married today, and we don't have a place of our own. We're going to have to live with his parents at their house, and we just wanted some privacy."

We walked back to our jeep, and Oscar told me one of the funniest sights he had seen was a similar situation with an elderly man and a young lady who had parked near the river. He had discovered them making love in the back seat. The elderly man looked up into the face of the officer peering into the window of the car with the gold name tag on one side of his chest and the gold badge on the other side shining in the moonlight, and the old gentleman said, "Just a minute, officer. Just a minute."

Oscar and I got to be fishing buddies. We caught quite a few catfish out of the Rio Grande River in the area of the San Benito pump. Oscar used a commercially produced brand of stink bait, and I usually used stale beef liver for bait. I usually caught the most fish, but Oscar had bragging rights because he usually caught the biggest fish. I also invited some of the other PI's to go with me once in awhile. One night I had invited George to go with me. His wife, Jean, would visit with my wife for awhile, while we fished at night in the San Benito Reservoir.

It was dark when we left the house. George had parked his car behind my car in the driveway and said maybe we should go in his car. But I said I already had the rods and the bait in my car, and the driveway was wide enough for me to get around him. He could just leave his car parked where it was and we could go in my car. We got in, and I pulled up a few feet in order to back around his car in the driveway. When I pulled up, I saw that the water sprinkler had been in one place so long in the backyard that it was beginning to puddle and should be moved. I stopped and jumped out of the car, pulled the hose and sprinkler several feet to a new spot, jumped back into the car, and in that few seconds I forgot that George's car was parked directly behind mine. As I started backing up, George yelled, but too late. I struck his car and broke out three of his headlights. We went on fishing and caught three catfish that would weigh about two pounds apiece. We brought them back, and neither of us wanted to clean the fish that night. So he said to just keep them. I said they would be okay until the next day.

The next day at the office I told some of the guys there that George didn't want the fish, and I already had some in the freezer. They could have them if they wanted them. I had just rolled them up in a newspaper and stuck them in the bottom of the Frigidaire after we caught them the night before, but I was sure that if we put them in a tub of water to revive they would be just as fresh as when they were caught. I had read about how catfish can go into some sort of hibernation, even burrow in the mud if a pond goes dry and survive for some time until it rains and the pond refills. I had verified this by putting them in the Frigidaire previously and then putting them in a tub of water when I got ready to clean them. In a few minutes their gills would start opening and closing, and in a few more minutes they would be completely revived.

One of the guys said he liked catfish and he would come home as I came home at the end of the shift and take the catfish. He didn't believe what I told him about their reviving, so I started filling the washtub in the backyard, unrolled the catfish in the newspaper, threw them in the tub, and continued spraying some more water on them. Sure enough, his eyes opened in amazement as he saw their gills begin to open and close. In a few minutes they were swimming around just as frisky as they ever were. He said to me, "When did you catch those fish?" I told him George and I had caught them the night before and they had been rolled up in a newspaper all day. He looked at the fish a long time as if they were possessed by some evil spirit, looked at me again and said, "Bruce, I don't believe I want them fish."

Of course, he couldn't wait to tell the guys at the office the following day how he had witnessed those fish coming back to life after being in the Frigidaire all night. People around the office who hadn't actually seen it naturally were skeptical and didn't believe it. They asked me about it, and I told them, yes, it was true. Oscar heard him telling about how those fish had come back to life. He drew me aside and said, "Bruce, several years ago I was fishing down in the river just where you and I had been fishing at night. I dropped my lantern in the river. A week later I went back to the same spot, hooked my lantern, and pulled it out of the river, and it was still lit. Now, if you'll kill them catfish, I'll blow out my lantern."

Some days are so momentous in history that one never forgets them. One day that I vaguely remember was December 7, 1941, when listening to the radio and learning about the attack on Pearl Harbor. Another day that I remember more clearly is the day Kennedy was assassinated. On that particular day I was working alone in my jeep on the day shift line watch. As I neared the end of my shift at one-o'clock in the afternoon, I came up from the river back towards the station using field roads and stopped at a hay storage shed where a farmer and two Mexicans were unloading hay. I checked the identification of the two Mexicans who showed me their alien registration cards and talked a few minutes with the farmer. In the course of our conversation, I mentioned that our president was visiting Dallas and what a big day it was for Texas. Evidently he didn't agree because he said to me, "Someone should shoot that son of a bitch." I was a bit shocked that anyone would use that kind of language in front of a Federal officer and especially that anyone could harbor such hatred for such a popular president.

I came on into town to the Texaco service station where we usually got gas to leave our jeep full for the next shift coming on duty. The radio was saying, "Kennedy has been shot!" Over and over, "Kennedy has been shot!" I immediately went into the station and used their telephone to call Jerry and asked her if she had the television on. She said, no she didn't. So I told her to turn it on immediately. The radio was saying that Kennedy had been shot, and I rushed down to the office, turned in my jeep, and went home to watch every second of television coverage of his assassination.

We watched as the tape of the parade was run and rerun on television. When the announcement finally came that Kennedy was dead, I was in shock. The nation was in shock. The United States had lost a dynamic, young president, and history was altered forever. Lyndon Baines Johnson took the oath of office as our next president on the plane, Air Force 1, on his way back to Washington, DC, and the Rio Grande Valley settled down to its normal routine.

Our Station Senior, Uncle Al, left us. He transferred to Chula Vista, California, and we got a new Station Senior from Falfurias, Texas. His name was Roland Lomblot, and he had been the Station Senior for the small station with about ten Patrol inspectors whose primary duty was maintaining the traffic checkpoint on Highway 281 as it left the Rio Grande Valley. We didn't know what to think of our new Station Senior. He was overweight and had leaned on his pistol so much that it looked like it might discharge and he would shoot himself in the crotch.

We were used to having a schedule posted in advance so we would know when we went home Friday or Saturday, whether we were to come back to work Sunday or Monday, and what days we would have off the following week. Obviously, Roland was not used to posting a schedule for his small group of men. In fact, when I talked to one of them later, he told me that they often all came to work in the morning and Roland would tell them, "You and you and you are on traffic check; you two can go back home and change into civilian clothes and do city patrol; and you two can change into rough duty uniform and do farm and ranch check." Well, that was no way to treat a large station of approximately 30 men, and we didn't get along from the very beginning.

Roland also came to our station with the preconceived notion of how things should be done, even though our station was running along like a well-oiled machine. It wasn't broken and didn't need fixing. But Roland decided he didn't like the way we wrote our Apprehension Reports and told us what changes he wanted made. He stated that if we didn't know how to write an Apprehension Report, he would get one of his men to come down from Falfurias and show us how it was done. It was obvious from the start that he was not going to be a well-liked Station Senior.

As the men grew restless there were some transfers, and my classmates began to talk about leaving the Patrol. George, who had been a policeman, was interested in going back to a civilian police department and went to Los Angeles to be examined for a police job. Ron, who had been an Air Force pilot, wanted to become a Border Patrol pilot, but there were no vacancies in the Border Patrol at that time. He became restless and looked into going to another agency. Ed decided that he could afford to take some time off and went to Mexico to study Spanish for six months. He came back with one of the stories that I remembered. When I repeated it later, it never failed to get a laugh.

It seems that once during the Mexican Revolution, a Captain and his soldiers camped for the night. The Captain put his guards around the camp and told his Sergeant that if anyone approached during the night to tell him immediately. Sure enough, during the night the Sergeant came running to the Captain's tent and told him, "Captain, Captain, get up! Two men are coming!" The Captain said, "Well, Sergeant, are they enemies or friends?" After thinking a moment, the Sergeant said, "Well, Captain, I believe they are friends because they are coming together."

In a very short time, morale at the Harlingen station was lower than a snake's belly. The matter of the schedule was soon to come to a head, and I was to play a part in that. One day about 9 o'clock, after I had had a long day and didn't get home until 6 o'clock, Roland called me to inform me that he was changing the schedule. Instead of coming to work the following day, I would come back to work that night at midnight. There could have been several reasons for this, but I always suspected that he had chosen me to double back because of my Union activities. I told him that there were other alternatives, and I didn't think that was right, but I learned one of his favorite expressions that night. It was that everything he did was for the exigencies of the Service. And by God, if he said I would come back to work at midnight, I would come back to work at midnight. I told him since he was ordering me back to work I would come back, but I didn't believe it was right, and I offered some other alternatives. He wasn't interested in any alternatives, and I told him that I was going to see the Chief. He said, yes, I might see the Chief all right, because he would probably take me to see the Chief.

As soon as he hung up the phone I started dialing our sector office trying to contact the Chief and was successful in getting Mr. Blackwell, the Deputy Chief. I explained to Mr. Blackwell what had been going on for some time with the schedule—how we never knew what days to work. When we left work Friday or Saturday we didn't know if we would have the following Sunday and Monday or what days we would be off, or what uniform to wear. He listened and then told me to go ahead and pull my shift and that he would be at the Harlingen Station at 8 o'clock the following morning to try and straighten things out.

The next morning shortly after 8 a.m. when we went in to turn in our car keys and go off duty, Mr. Blackwell was already there and was in Roland's office with the door closed. The door being closed didn't prevent us from hearing what was going on. Roland was getting a chewing—a real chewing! In fact, in my ten years in the military I had seldom heard a better chewing out than Roland was getting.

No one in the station said anything about what had happened. We just sat back and waited, and we saw the results immediately as the schedule was posted well in advance and continued that way into

Dear Chief

the future. There was a benefit in knowing when we would work, but it brought up another situation that involved me as the Union representative.

One morning on my day off I was called by the Processing Officer and told to get down to the office immediately. There was a situation that required my being there as the Union representative.

I rushed to the station not knowing what to expect, and when I got there I found Joe and Roland glowering at each other like two torn cats, and Joe was refusing to go into Roland's office to talk with him until he had a Union representative as a witness. It turned out that the problem was his schedule over the holidays. We had just had a holiday, and Joe had been scheduled to work. Joe explained as soon as he saw that he was scheduled to work that he needed that holiday off duty and asked Roland to change the schedule. He told him that he would be glad to work the next holiday, but he needed this one off. Roland, in his usual manner, refused to consider Joe's request and had told him, "No, you're scheduled to work. It is for the exigency of the service. You will work as scheduled." The problem was, Joe didn't work like he was scheduled. He had not come to work on his shift, and I believe he had claimed he was sick. Since he had already asked Roland to be off, Roland knew he was not sick and had just defied his orders. This was an intolerable situation to Roland. The discussion ceased to be a discussion very quickly and deteriorated into a profanity match, which was not solving anything. Roland had said by God, he would just have Joe fired. I had to remind Roland that he had not hired Joe, and that he couldn't fire Joe. The most he could do as a Station Senior was to write a memorandum recommending that some disciplinary action be taken against Joe.

After tempers cooled a bit, things settled down, and I never heard of any disciplinary action being taken against Joe. But he was in the doghouse. Later on, Joe took some more sick leave, and it became a joke around the station what had occurred while he was at home.

There was an orange grove around Joe's house, and what should he see out in the orange grove but the Border Patrol sedan. Someone was parked near his house where they cold see and observe what Joe was doing on the day he was claiming to be home sick. Joe just laughed about those damn fools sitting out there trying to catch him.

Ed would be one of the first of my classmates to leave the Patrol. He would be going to the FBI. Before he left, he and I enjoyed a good two weeks' schedule together on farm and ranch check, and we had another experience. He and I and Ron and Homer May were told that we were on one day detail to the District Director's Office in San Antonio, Texas for an interview with a regional representative. We were curious as to why we four were selected to go to San Antonio for the interview with Mr. Martindale. We knew that Mr. Martindale was nicknamed "Slick" without knowing why. But once we met him, it was obvious that he was nicknamed "Slick" because of his bald head. It turned out that we were meeting with Mr. Martindale with others from the Brownsville Station who had college degrees.

The Service was looking for college graduates who would volunteer to be Administrative Officers for the various district offices in the Immigration and Naturalization Service. Mr. Martindale explained the procedure for becoming an Administrative Officer, how we would train first at the Central Office in Washington, then at a Regional office and finally be assigned to a permanent assignment at a district office. We would be promoted from GS-8 Border Patrolmen to GS-9 Administrative Officers with the possibility of promotion to GS-11.

Leaving the Patrol didn't appeal to me at all because Administrative positions no longer authorized 20-year retirement and overtime. Administrative Officer didn't appeal to Ed or Ron either, but Homer saw that as a short cut to a promotion and said yes, it was just what he wanted to do. A couple from the Brownsville office also decided that they would give it a try because Mr. Martindale had explained that at any phase along the way, if they were dissatisfied, they could go back to the Border Patrol.

That is just what happened to one of my buddies from Brownsville at the central office. He decided it was not what he wanted to do, and he came back to Brownsville. But Homer would stick with it until he finally became an Administrative Officer.

George and Ed were best friends, and after Ed left, George became more and more dissatisfied with the Border Patrol. By then

Dear Chief

he and I were working on the evening line watch shift for B. L. Melton, A Senior who had transferred to Harlingen replacing T. C. Milner, who had finally achieved his ambition of becoming a Station Senior at Stockton, California. For some reason we were very short handed at that particular time, and George and I had the whole 23 mile section of river border to patrol by ourselves. B. L. would come in at the beginning of our shift, assign us vehicles, and tell us which end of the area we were to work, and then we would seldom see him unless some situation arose where he was needed. If we called him on the radio he never refused to answer. He was always in radio contact, but we knew when he said, "If you need me, you will know where to find me," we knew he was going home for supper. But evidently he could park his vehicle so close that he could hear the radio. If we called him, he always answered. But the solitude of being alone was just too much for George. Occasionally he took a day off, and I occasionally found myself the only person preventing the illegal entry of aliens on that 23-mile stretch of river.

Everyone was always looking for a chance to do something different and break the monotony of patrolling the river on line watch. I found that one of the things I could do was volunteer to be a guard on the airlift. The airlift was flown from the detention center in Port Isabel to El Paso to El Centro with occasional stops in between to pick up aliens who should be transferred from one detention center to another. This duty was on a voluntary basis with Brownsville furnishing a guard two weeks to Harlingen's one week because Harlingen had fewer men than the Brownsville station. I learned that I could sit up there in an airplane for eight hours and work on my correspondence courses which the Service offered.

There were ten of these courses. Nine of these correspondence courses dealt with the primary functions and authorities of the Immigration and Naturalization Service, and the tenth was a supervisory course. It was rumored that if a PI wanted to be recommended for a promotion he should complete the correspondence courses. They were designed for home study, but by volunteering often for the airlift, I managed to do most of my work while guarding the aliens on the airplane.

The duties on the airlift were very simple. The Border Patrolman stood fire watch as the pilots started the engines. He made sure the aliens were seated and fastened in by their seat belts and explained to them if they were sick at their stomach how to use the paper bag on the back of the seat in front of them.

The first leg of the trip was usually from Port Isabel to El Paso where we unloaded and loaded aliens. We then flew to Stafford, Arizona, where we would pick up those who were being released after serving their federal sentences and were to be deported and transported them to El Centro. Occasionally there was a stop in Arizona before our final destination of El Centro. That was one day's flying time. We spent the night in El Centro and then took a trip the next day, either to San Diego or up to Stockton, California. Then we came back to Port Isabel.

It was very routine except for one trip when we stopped in Tucson, Arizona, and ended up staying two nights in Tucson because one of the airplane's engines was malfunctioning. It was a convenient place for the engine to malfunction, as the pilot's mother lived on a ranch just outside Tucson.

Wherever we stopped for the night the Border Patrol was very considerate of the pilots and furnished them a car to get back and forth to the airport. When we stopped at Tucson, we went to the Chief's office to get the keys to the car and say hello, and I was surprised to see Chief Bruce Long behind his desk. He was a man of few words, and I would not realize how few until sometime later. I was glad to see the Chief who had been on one of my Boards while I was on probation, and I told him I was glad to see him and reminded him that he had been on my Board. All he said was, "I know."

I enjoyed my two-night layover in Tucson, and we then completed our trip otherwise uneventfully.

Ron would be the third of my classmates to leave the Border Patrol. Before he left I enjoyed the two-week tour with him on farm and ranch check. We really worked good together and located illegal aliens ranging from a 12 year old boy to a 70 year old woman who was living as the wife of an American citizen and had been posing as his deceased wife for several years. When we first talked to her, she was so nervous when she presented the birth certificate of the woman she was impersonating that the paper literally fluttered in her hand. There was no reason for her to be so nervous around a Border Patrolman unless there was something wrong, so we talked to her.

Dear Chief

We talked with her very patiently for a long time before she realized that we really weren't going to arrest her on the spot and send her back to Mexico. We explained to her the law on suspension of deportation of people who had resided in the United States for over seven years. She saw this as an avenue for legalizing her status in the United States and ended up being thankful that she had decided to tell us the truth.

Ron and I also joined forces for the best day as far as apprehensions that I had on line watch while I was stationed at Harlingen. He was working in one jeep assigned to the middle area of the Harlingen station while I was in another jeep assigned to the westernmost area that adjoins the Hidalgo County line, Hidalgo being in the Mercedes station area and Cameron County in the Harlingen area. There had been one of the infrequent rains in the valley, and sign cutting was really easy as the people were leaving clumps of mud. I saw the tracks of so many aliens I couldn't tell exactly how many there were in the group. I called Ron to come and give me a hand tracking them, and we started following their tracks away from the river. It looked like they were headed to La Feria.

We used the leapfrog method of going ahead and finding their tracks and following step by step while the other person went ahead and found them again. We used this method for several miles until we came to a stream that is called the Arroyo. Just before crossing the Arroyo we saw where part of the aliens had turned off and gone into the brush alongside of the stream. There were signs that two of them had continued to cross the bridge. Ron said he would follow the two sets of tracks that crossed the bridge, and I went after the largest group.

Several yards from the bridge I saw a bag hanging on a mesquite bush. These bags are multi-colored mesh bags that the aliens carry their clothing and personal effects in. There was a levee running along the stream, and I stopped my jeep on the levee and looked with my binoculars into the brush where I could see the bag but couldn't determine how many aliens were there. I thought if I went into the brush after them, they would run like a covey of quail, and maybe we could track them all down or maybe we could only catch a couple of them. Then I noticed one standing up to get a better view of me. Since they knew I was there, there was no element of surprise, so I climbed onto the hood of my jeep where I could see the brush and they could see me and yelled for them to come out. Others started standing up, and I could see them talking to each other trying to decide what to do. To hasten their decision I fired two shots into the air and again told them, "Everybody come out."

It turned out there were six aliens in the group, and they all walked up to the jeep. I had them sit down in front of the jeep while I called Ron on the radio and told him that I had apprehended six and also called the station to have the panel truck sent out to meet me. As soon as the panel truck guy arrived, I started on up the road to overtake Ron and help him locate the other two. That gave us eight aliens for a morning's work, and we were really proud of that. We stopped in the coffee shop in La Feria to congratulate ourselves before going back to the river. Eight aliens was a good day's work, but the day wasn't over yet.

After our coffee break, we headed down the highway back to the river with Ron a few yards in front. As we neared the river, Ron turned left on a field road and told me he was going back to his own area and would see me later. I was watching his jeep as it turned left, and immediately after he turned onto the dirt road, an alien jumped out of the weeds beside the road and crossed the road behind him. I knew he hadn't seen him in the rear view mirror, or he would have slowed down and stopped; so I called Ron on the radio and told him to come back, that one had run across the road behind him and had lain down in a field beside the little dirt road. He came back, and we went into the field following the tracks of the one I had seen. We were surprised when we overtook him that instead of laying in the field, he had lain down beside another one that we hadn't seen. That gave us ten apprehensions for the day. That was the most I ever apprehended at one time on line watch. Eventually I would assist in apprehending a larger group and would even apprehend ten by myself. But it wasn't on line watch.

The ten I apprehended by myself were working for a farmer named Mr. Dudley. Mr. Dudley had large cotton fields and a small field that was enclosed by mesquite brush. It would have been unhandy to harvest the cotton by machine in the small field because he would have been turning around so often. He needed so much room for the machine to turn around, so he had decided to harvest the small field by hand. I had been on coffee break at Clayton's Drive-In at San Benito and was on my way back to my assigned area along the river when I noticed there were tracks into the field. I backed up, pulled over a little bank into the edge of the field where I could see. Boy, was I surprised to see so many illegal aliens picking cotton by hand. I quickly counted ten aliens. It's obvious to a Border Patrolman who is a wetback. There's just a look about them.

I called the first one over to the jeep and asked him if he had papers. He said, "No, sir." I asked him about the others, and he said he didn't know. The "I don't know" answer is common among the illegal aliens because they don't want to lie to you. If they know something favorable, they will tell you. But if they know something unfavorable, they will just say they don't know.

I figured the other nine were also illegal, but I didn't want to disturb them and have them running all over the field. So I just waited at the jeep, and as they picked their row of cotton back to my end of the field, I motioned for them and told them to come over to where I was. The ones on the far end of the field looked at me suspiciously, not knowing what to do, but since there was no big disturbance and no one was running, they continued to pick cotton. In a little while, everyone had picked their way from the far end back to my end of the field. I had them all sitting on their bags of cotton in front of my jeep, and once again I called the office to have the panel truck come down and meet me for transportation.

Roland was curious as to how I had discovered the aliens and wanted me to say that I had apprehended them online watch. I would not agree to that as they were employed and should be reported as "aliens located working in agriculture."

Aliens working in the fields near the river were a constant and perplexing problem. The larger operators usually contracted with a labor contractor in Brownsville to bring a load of legal workers in to harvest the fields near the river, but some of the smaller farms enticed aliens to wade the river and harvest the fields near the river. Of course, there was always some harvesting going on against the owner's wishes as the local people would sneak across the river to steal an armful of vegetables. I remember Ray Young calling for assistance. He had spotted a small group working in the field near the river, and they had spotted his jeep as he approached. They all ran back to the river, splashed across to the other side, and waited for him to leave so they could come back and resume their work. Usually a group like that would leave their clothing on the far side of the river and come over to do their work wearing only a pair of shorts. Ray had told the Station Senior where the field was located and they decided they would wait until the evening crew came to work for the 3:00 to 11:00 shift before trying to apprehend the aliens again.

Ray briefed us as to where they were and how close we cold get before having to hide our vehicles and sneak up on the people in the field. We concealed our jeeps, went across the levee to try to approach in the brush along the river's edge. We got pretty close before the alarm went out. We had been spotted, and the aliens started running out of the field back towards the river. I was giving it my best to get between them and the river and had to jump across a fence. Then I jumped across a log, and one of the young men had made the mistake of not leaving his clothing on the far side of the river. He had tied up his pants and shirt in a bundle and left them near the water's edge on this side of the river. By running just as hard as I could, I managed to arrive at the bundle of clothing just as he did. I grabbed on to him with my left hand while he was trying to pick up his clothes. He wrenched free from my grasp, and I grabbed his bundle of clothes. So we were both hanging on to the bundle. Since he didn't want to surrender and wasn't as meek as most of the illegal aliens had proven to be, I reached for my pistol which usually will intimidate an alien just by letting him know that you are wearing a gun. I got a sinking feeling as I felt an empty holster. I could just see myself writing those "Dear Chief" memos. "I hate to report the loss of my pistol." But to subdue the alien, I reached down and picked up a piece of driftwood to threaten him with. He decided resistance was useless, and I marched him back to our vehicles. He was a downcast alien, as he was the only one of the group that we caught.

Another time, Jerry Apfel had called the station asking for his relief to hurry down to the river. I reported for duty about 2:00 o'clock in anticipation of working my 3:00 to 11:00 p.m. shift. The processing officer told me to grab some keys and take a jeep down to the river—and hurry! Jerry had been calling for someone to hurry down and meet him. He told me the river point that Jerry had reported. As I approached that bend in the river, I heard gunfire. A little further ahead of me I spotted Jerry, leaning across the hood of his jeep with his pistol pointed towards the river. Very cautiously I pulled in behind his jeep because I could remember the windshield with the bullet hole in it that had been leaning against the fence the day I reported on duty with the Border Patrol. Someone with a rifle had fired from across the river and put a hole through the windshield of one of our vehicles. They left the windshield there as a souvenir and reminder for young PI's. I walked up to where Jerry was pointing, asked him what was the trouble, and he said, "See those bundles of clothes across the river?"

I looked across the river, which at that point was about 50 yards wide, and laying there on the sand bank were four or five bundles of clothes. I looked a little closer, and every once in awhile we'd see a head rise up from an irrigation ditch on the other side of the river. Each time someone acted like they wanted to get out of the irrigation ditch and come and retrieve the clothes, Jerry would send another wad cutter sailing across the river into the bank. Sometimes dirt would fly up very close to a bundle of clothes. Sometimes there would be no spray of dirt at all, so I believe he was occasionally hitting one of the bags or bundles of clothes. Jerry was really teed off, as he had tried to catch the aliens out in the field. They had run around him on both sides and escaped to the safety of the other side, and he didn't want them to retrieve their clothing. He told me to keep an eye on them, and if anybody moved to do as he had been doing. I told Jerry O.K., I had everything under control, and he was relieved. As soon as he was out of sight, I had no further desire to worsen international relations by shooting across the river, so I left as soon as Jerry was gone.

I had a little better success one day working the day shift on line watch. I was driving down the levee, stopping occasionally to look at the river through my binoculars when I spotted a mule and a wagon backed up to the edge of the river on the Mexican side. The mule had been taken from the harness of the wagon and had been tied out where it could graze. There was no person in sight, but I knew it was a common practice for people living near the river on the far side to come to the United States side and cut willow trees. The bigger trees were used for firewood, and the smaller bushes were trimmed and used as bean stakes.

I parked my jeep behind the levee out of sight of anyone near the river, sneaked across the levee into the patch of willows in that particular bend of the river. While sneaking along very quietly and listening often, I soon heard the chop, chop, chop of a machete. I knew that someone was in the brush cutting the willow bushes. I continued to sneak along as quietly as I could and soon saw ahead of me a middle aged Mexican man wearing only his shorts, chopping the willow poles. By moving only when he was chopping, he couldn't hear me as I approached within a few feet of his back. Then I let out a blood-curdling scream, yelled, "Gotcha!"

The man was so startled he stood motionless while I reached out and took the machete from his hand and told him to come with me. A person like that really benefited from being apprehended. We would usually give him an old pair of pants and a shirt that the Salvation Army had given to the Immigration Service just for such purposes and would send him down to the bridge that same day that we caught him and put him back across the bridge. He was only out the few hours he had spent in our custody.

Of course, everyone was curious about where I had caught the old man, and I explained to Fred Munt that he had been chopping willow poles and that I had sneaked up on him, surprised him, and caught him before he could run back to the river. Fred was going to be working that same area. And a few days later, I rotated to the evening shift. I was in the office when Fred came in with a torn uniform, scratches on his forehead and nose, and I wondered what had happened. "Fred, what happened?" I asked.

He told me that the old man had been back to the willow trees. He had spotted the wagon on the other side of the river just like before and had tried to sneak up between him and the water just as I had done. The old man was more alert the second time and had sprinted back towards the river with Fred in hot pursuit. What I hadn't told Fred was that there was a small, barbed wire fence running through the willows. In Fred's haste to catch the woodchopper, he had hung his toe in the top strand of the barbed wire fence and fell flat on his face. Needless to say, the woodchopper escaped.

The largest group that I assisted in apprehending was a group of 20 that George Hendry had spotted working in an okra field right alongside the river. George had tried repeatedly getting close to the workers, but they had a lookout in a willow tree, and the lookout gave the alarm every time he saw anything suspicious. After several attempts, George decided we needed a different approach. He was determined to catch this group one way or another and put the dreaded and hated lookout out of commission. He asked for assistance from the three of us. He told us he would drive his old station wagon that he usually hauled his bird dogs around in, that he would come down to the very edge of the river bank and possibly cut the aliens off while they were still out in the field. It all depended on whether or not the lookout would be suspicious of the station wagon. He thought it might work since it was a beat-up old wagon, no resemblance at all to any type of government vehicle. He put three of us laying down in the back of the station wagon where we couldn't be seen. He took off his green shirt, and all that the lookout could see as it approached was one person in a white T-shirt in an old beat-up station wagon. We approached closer and closer, and the alarm wasn't sounded. We parked within a few feet of where the lookout was perched in the willow tree.

As soon as the door started opening and we started crawling out of the station wagon, the lookout dropped to the ground and with one leap was in the water on his way to the other side without giving any kind of alarm to the workers in the field. We then spread out along the riverbank and started going through the field, rounding up the workers and having them go in front of us towards the levee. When we got to the far end of the field, no alarms had been sounded; no one ran away, and we had a group of 20 aliens. We marched them up the levee a short distance away from the field and had them sit down at the field road where our panel truck could come and pick them up.

Once they were transported to the office, we walked back down the riverbank to retrieve George's station wagon, and the lookout was on the other side of the river yelling, "Mis zapatos, my shoes, my shoes." In his haste to get back to the other side, he hadn't picked up his shoes, which were still at the base of the willow tree. One of the guys, said, "I've got your f— zapatos," picked one up and threw it in the river, and the man on the other side was yelling, "No, no," as he threw the other one in the river. That was just a small bit of revenge for the number of times that he had warned the aliens, and they had run back to the river and got away. I don't know if he ever was able to retrieve his shoes. And as a final gesture, in case anyone was within listening distance, George yelled, "Thank you for the information." We only hoped someone would get the idea that he had cooperated with us in not giving the alarm and would take care of him when they got back home.

By now, due to the decrease in manpower at the Harlingen station, I only occasionally worked with a partner. On one of these occasions, I was working with Floyd Monroe when we received a call on the radio from the office saying Monroe's wife needed him home as soon as possible. We rushed the six miles from the river back to town to his apartment and saw his wife standing in his front door afraid to come down the steps. I wouldn't have been surprised to see some kind of a snake at the foot of the steps, but it wasn't a snake. It was only an earthworm that crawled onto the sidewalk that was constructed by the steps. I don't know who was upset the most—Monroe or his wife—but he found the broom and beat the unlucky earthworm into a pulp.

We returned to our duties on the river, but I suspected that Monroe had some kind of phobia. That was to be borne out a little later when I came to work one morning and spotted a huge tarantula crawling across our parking lot near the rear door to the office. Tarantulas are usually very mild-mannered, docile creatures, and I have no quarrel with tarantulas. But this particular one had been rousted out of his usual nesting place and was on the move and looking for trouble. As I approached within a couple of steps, the tarantula jumped several inches into the air. I was surprised at how high it could jump and that it would be so antagonistic. I decided, well, enough of that from this creature, and I stepped on him and mashed him so badly that he was done for. But I wanted to get a closer look, so I picked him up on a sheet of paper, looked him over, and then put the sheet of paper down on an almost-full trash can in a corner of the office. Monroe came to work shortly after I did. He spotted a movement in the trash can, got his favorite weapon, a broom, and had waste paper and tarantula legs flying all over the office. I was sure this time that his phobia was some fear of bugs or insects. Then I understood Monroe's dislike for the Rio Grande Valley and his desire to transfer back to the northern border, which he was eventually successful in doing. Before I left I had one more practical joke for Monroe that cost a horny toad its life.

Horny toads were interesting little creatures who would lie motionless in the palm of your hand while you stroked their stomachs. I had picked one up while I was on farm and ranch duty when it crawled across the dirt road in front of me, and I brought it back to the office. Without telling anyone, I left it in Monroe's mail drawer. I wasn't there when Monroe came to work and checked to see if he had anything in his mail drawer, but the ones who were there described how he panicked, beat the hell out of the horny toad, and then washed out his mail drawer with alcohol.

There was one more episode at our station that involved Monroe. We had been hearing before from people living along the river of some kind of strange creature's roaming up and down the river. In all of my days and nights working on the river, I had never seen anything unusual. But the rumors persisted that maybe this was a spaceman or some other strange creature with a large head. The mystery was eventually solved. As it turned out, to keep the nasty mosquitoes away from his face, Monroe had purchased a beekeeper's veil and was wearing that when he walked along the river.

Our Chief, Chief Harrison, the man whom I have always believed had more clout than any person in the Border Patrol, was about to retire. But he had a couple more scenes to play before he left us. SPI Page Brewer, with whom I had shared several tours on farm and ranch duty, was from Boston and decided it would be nice to go back to his hometown to be an investigator. He requested a transfer, since Investigators were Grade 9, the same as Senior Border Patrolmen; he saw no problem in being transferred back to Boston. Several people in the Border Patrol had the idea that one should always be loyal to the Border Patrol for their entire career with the Immigration Service. Anyone who would leave the Patrol was looked on as somewhat of a traitor.

In a few weeks, Page received his telegram notifying him that his request for transfer to Boston had been approved. In the meantime, he had reconsidered for several reasons, I'm sure one being financial, that transferring to Boston was not in his best interest. So he notified the Chief that he had changed his mind and would not accept the transfer which he had requested. We didn't know how irksome this must have been to the Chief because a couple of weeks later, he made a special trip to our Station, which was unusual. He had a Station meeting and told everyone that he had no use for Border Patrolmen who requested transfers and then refused to go when the transfer was approved. In another few weeks, Page Brewer received his notification that he was transferred to Immigrant Inspector at Progresso, Texas. This wasn't as bad as it seems because Page could continue to live in his house in La Feria and go to work at Progresso.

I continued to work more with SPI Strobel than anyone else at the station. Each time he and I pulled a two-week tour on farm and ranch check together one of the places we stopped was the El Sauz ranch between Raymondville, Texas and Port Mansfield. This was a large ranch supervised by Mr. Beto Duram. He always came out to meet us when we pulled into the parking area behind the ranch house where the cook shack was located. He always said he was glad to see us and we were welcome to come in and have a cup of coffee. They always had a pot on in the cook shack. Mr. Strobel and I would go in, converse a little bit with Mr. Duram, have our coffee, and then leave without ever finding any illegal aliens. We had even been there during a roundup time and checked several of the cowboys who all had alien registration cards showing they were legally in the United States. I was a bit suspicious that a ranch that big would not have any illegal laborers.

One day when we arrived and went through the usual procedure, I declined the offer of a cup of coffee. While Oscar and Mr. Duram were in the cook shack having their coffee, I crawled across the gate leading into the brush behind the ranch house about 200 yards in a spot concealed by the brush. I spotted two large tents. One of the tents was a second cook tent, and the other was a large sleeping tent with a half dozen cots in it. I had discovered where the illegal aliens were living. The ones who had their alien registration cards and always worked near the ranch house and were inspected each time we came by were just the decoys. The real fence menders and brush cutters were living in the tent.

There were only two present at the time I located the tent. One was the cook, and the other had not felt like working that day and had stayed in the living tent. I rounded up the two of them with their possessions, marched them back down to the gate and crawled across.

Dear Chief

I put the two in the panel truck and went inside just as they were finishing their coffee, and Oscar was ready to leave. They said their goodbyes. Then I told Mr. Duram that before we left I thought he ought to pay the two illegal aliens that I had just apprehended, as they claimed they had about a week's wages coming. Both men were surprised, and both at the same time asked, "Where did they come from?" I told Oscar what I had found out in the back. Dr. Duram paid the two what they said he owed them.

I went back to the office and told the whole Station where the tents were located and how we had been going there repeatedly without ever checking any of the illegal aliens. Needless to say, that was all they wanted to hear. So every time they went on farm and ranch, another team would go by and try to apprehend some of those aliens that I knew were still working there. This was verified by the Sector pilot who started flying over the ranch very frequently and was telling us how far back in the brush the crew was working.

Evidently Mr. Duram was slightly offended by this, because it had not been happening to him before, and the Chief sent us word that we would not go on the ranch again unless we had a warrant because he had just remeasured the distance from the border to the ranch, and it was just outside the 25 mile limit that Border Patrolmen were authorized to enter on private property without a warrant. I was somewhat surprised by the Chief's action and asked around, "Why would he do a thing like that?" They said, "Don't you know? That's where the Chief does his deer hunting, and you've just upset everything."

The Chief retired, and I suffered no consequences from my aggressive attempts to apprehend those aliens who were already there.

The 1964-65 year was good for me. It seemed that no matter who I worked with, we were successful in apprehending illegal aliens. The rating period for that 12-month period for purposes of awards came. I went to work on the evening shift one evening and found Arnold Cope with the apprehension book counting up the past year's apprehensions. When he had them all counted, the Station Senior told me, "Bruce, you have had one hell of a year! Do you know that you had more apprehensions than anybody in the station?"

I told Roland I didn't know I had the most. I knew I had a good year, but I hadn't kept up with the numbers.

"Yes," he said, "you were number one, and Andy was number two right behind you. I guess I will have to give you and Andy an award this year." An award could be either a Sustained Superior Performance Award or an Outstanding Award, and I would have been pleased to receive either one. It surprised me that Roland would even consider me for an award considering our little differences. I told him I appreciated it and forgot about it for several weeks until a call came from the Sector requesting that Andy come out to the Sector for an awards ceremony. There was no mention of me. I didn't say anything, and would have died and gone to Hell before I would have asked Roland about an award.

Several weeks went by, and I never mentioned an award to anyone. But evidently Roland had been thinking about it and waiting for me to bring up the subject, which I was not going to do. He finally met me one day when I came to work and told me, "Bruce, you know that award that I recommended you for?"

I said, "Yes, Roland, I remember you telling me that you were putting me in for an award, and I wondered what happened—especially since Andy was called out to receive his award, but I never heard anything."

"That's what I wanted to tell you," he said. "Your award was turned down at the Regional Office." And that's all I ever heard about the matter.

One of the reasons I had such a good year was because of an informant I will call Juan. Juan was an American citizen of Mexican descent who owned a small farm just south of La Feria, Texas. I went by his farm occasionally on my way to or from the river. I preferred to go by in the early morning hours on my way to the river because I had learned that he usually had two illegal aliens who slept in a shed on the side of his barn. The second time I had apprehended two aliens at his farm, he came out and talked to me and paid them a few dollars as they gathered up their meager belongings and put them in a little cardboard box to take back to Mexico with them. He was asking me why I was picking on him. I told him that I was not picking on him. My job was to apprehend illegal aliens, and I would apprehend every one that I knew about. If he knew about some others and would tell me about them, I would guarantee that I would go by and apprehend them. He thought about that for a while. He didn't want to tell on any of his neighbors who were using illegal alien help. But then he thought, well, if I can't have any, they shouldn't have any either. And he began to tell me which farmers were using illegal laborers. This resulted in several apprehensions that I would not have otherwise made.

In fact, Juan got pretty brazen about telling me about the illegals he knew about. One of the ones he told me about was living in town. I had trouble finding the little shack that he was living in. So I went by again to get new directions from Juan. He said, "Well, get in my pickup, and I will take you by there and show you where he lives." I was in my green Border Patrol uniform and didn't want somebody to recognize me riding in Juan's pickup. He suggested, "Take off your shirt, and nobody will know."

We got in his truck and went into the edge of Harlingen, down the street, past the building that the illegal alien was living in. Sure enough, he was sitting on the front porch with a friend. Juan said, "That's him right there on the front porch. Do you want to take him now? If you do, we'll just stop, and you can catch him."

Since I wasn't wearing my shirt, I said no. I could now return to the place early in the morning and find him before he got up to go somewhere to work. We went to the driveway next door and started to turn around. As Juan backed up he dropped the wheel of the pickup into the ditch, and we were stuck. The two men on the porch became curious. I left my gun and hat on the front seat, and there I was in my green pants and white T-shirt trying to lift a pickup out of the ditch as Juan raced the motor. But the wheels couldn't get traction, and there we sat spinning.

Juan was undaunted. Since the two men were already curious, he asked them to come over and give us a lift, which they did. There we were, the three of us lifting the pickup. Sure enough, we succeeded in getting it out of the ditch. But true to my word, the next morning, early, I went back and apprehended the alien who had been so helpful the evening before.

New Year's Eve came, and only a skeleton crew was working over the holidays. I was scheduled to work transportation check. One of the men said if I was going to be in San Benito, would I go by a bar where a barmaid was known to come back to work every time we caught her and sent her back to Mexico. I told the PI that I would try to get by there that afternoon and see if she was there. I drove down the street very slowly and could see through the door that there was a woman behind the bar. I stopped, went in, and asked her for her Immigration papers. She readily admitted that she didn't have any, and I told her she would have to go back to Mexico. I remember that her first name was Elena.

When a person working alone apprehended a female, he would call Port Isabel Sector radio operator reporting that he had a female in custody and was transporting her to the bridge in Brownsville. He then would report his arrival at the bridge. The radio operator would keep a log to account for the time the alien was in custody, and therefore prevent any claim that the PI had taken any improper action with the female. On the way to the bridge, Elena wanted to know if we were going to stop anywhere. I don't know who apprehended her previously, or how long it took them to get to the bridge with her, but I was not about to stop and must have set some kind of record getting from San Benito to Brownsville. I wanted to get rid of her just as quickly as I could.

The next day, New Year's Day of 1966, I was still one of the few working the holiday. I repeated my actions of the day before. I proceeded to check buses in Harlingen, then went down to San Benito, slowly drove down the street in front of the bar, and who should I see behind the bar but Elena Briones. She was a little more alert this time when she spotted my car. She ducked behind the bar but not quickly enough to prevent being apprehended the second time. I wrote another apprehension report. I noticed when I entered her name in our Apprehension Book, the other officers working line watch had not apprehended anybody on the last day of December. So Elena Briones was the last entry in our Apprehension Book for 1965. She also had the distinction of being the first apprehension of 1966. She seemed to be proof of the standing joke, which was too common to be funny, that if you stopped in Brownsville for a cup of coffee before returning to Harlingen, the illegal alien would get back before you did.

Smuggling was not much of a problem in the Harlingen area. I never caught a smuggler. The closest I came was on evening line watch as I drove down the levee in the evening just before sunset. I noticed a couple of people sitting in the edge of a cornfield on the

Dear Chief

other side of the river. It was not unusual to see several people on the other side of the river, lying on the riverbank waiting for darkness and a chance to slip across the river. But there was something suspicious about these two. Rather than being in the open, they seemed to be trying to conceal themselves as I drove down the levee in plain sight on my side of the river. I drove down the river a ways until I was out of sight, and then I drove back fairly close to the point where I had seen the two people. I parked my jeep behind the levee where it couldn't be seen from the other side of the river. I took my binoculars and crept through the brush to a point almost directly opposite where I had seen the two people. I looked through my binoculars and could see a couple more hidden back among the cornstalks. There was a small irrigation ditch. Every once in awhile one of them would raise up high enough to see over the irrigation ditch and look in my direction. I was concealed in the brush, so I just waited.

The sun sank lower, but I would still see fairly well through my binoculars. As the sun sank out of sight, a man on horseback came from the village on the other side of the river, rode down the riverbank to where the people were waiting in the cornfield. As they rose to meet him, I counted nine people. I thought, well it will just be a few minutes before the man on horseback leads them across the river, and I will be waiting for them. I heard him say in a loud voice, "Estoy Listo." That's "I'm ready," and nine people started walking behind his horse toward the river. On my side of the river someone else had also hidden in the brush whom I had not seen yelled in Spanish, "Don't cross. The Immigration's here." When the man on horseback heard that, he stopped and looked around, changed his mind about crossing, and he and the nine Mexicans walked back towards the village. Whoever had shouted the warning also got away quickly, and I was very disgusted.

I went back to the office at the end of my shift and left a note for the midnight crew saying where I had seen the aliens and that I felt sure they would try again later in the night. The midnight crew assured me they would keep an eye on the place where I expected them to cross.

The next day I went to work and checked the Apprehension Book to see if they had caught anyone, and they hadn't. I asked the Station Senior, and he said the midnight team had reported nothing happening during the night. I went back to the place I had seen them and walked along the edge of the river. Within 40 yards of where they had originally been, there were horse tracks and footprints climbing the bank on our side. So at least I knew there was one successful smuggling operation that we missed.

Drugs were not a problem, either. In fact, SPI Carl Shults apprehended an alien with several pounds of marijuana in a cardboard box, and everyone gathered around to feel of the weed and smell it because it was the first most of us had seen. I had seen a small amount while I was in the Air Force, but I didn't know much about it. It would be a few more years before drug smuggling became a problem.

I enjoyed working with Carl Shults. He and I were working city scout duties the first time I looked down the barrel of a gun. I had seen a woman hanging out clothes at a Rancher's house while I was on farm and ranch check, but I waited until I was on city patrol with Carl to tell him about her. We went to the rancher's house to see if she was legal or illegal. We went to the back door of the rancher's house and knocked on the door. He was an elderly man and evidently a very cautious man, because when he opened the door he had his pistol in his hand, and it was pointed right at Carl. I was just a step behind Carl and to his right. After a few minutes of explaining who we were and showing identification, Carl said, "Would you mind pointing that pistol somewhere else?" So he pointed it at me.

We finally convinced him that it wasn't necessary, that we meant him no harm. We just wanted to talk to the maid. He eventually brought her to the door. Sure enough, just as I had expected, she claimed to have no immigration documents, and we had no further trouble apprehending her and sending her back to Mexico.

Carl and I had also worked several tours of farm and ranch duty together. I remember one day we approached two men who had been irrigating and were sitting near the field road by the irrigation pump when we approached. One of them had seen us coming and lain down and pulled his hat over his face. We drove up and spoke to the other one who was very talkative and spoke fairly good English and told us he was a citizen of the United States. He was from the Harlingen area. We chatted on a few minutes and were ready to

Dear Chief

proceed when I asked him, "What about your buddy? Where is he from?"

As I mentioned before, some people are reluctant to tell you a lie, so they just say, "I don't know." When he said, "I don't know," I decided we'd better check a little more thoroughly, so I stepped over to where the man was laying on his back, hands folded across his stomach as if he were asleep, lifted his hat off his face, and he was starting up at me with a great big smile. He didn't speak a word of English and was as wet as a sock.

Carl also was involved in the longest tracking apprehension while I was at Harlingen. He and I were assigned farm and ranch that day. The Station Senior told us when he came to work that the evening shift had spotted the tracks of two illegal entrants near the river and had tracked them until they went off duty at midnight. The midnight crew had lost the tracks when they got on a paved road near the airport. Roland asked Carl and me to go out to the airport where they had last seen the tracks and see if we could pick them up again and follow them that morning.

By making larger and larger circles around the airport, we finally discovered a set of tracks where they had turned towards town, went as far as the railroad tracks heading north to Raymondville, and had taken a path parallel to the railroad tracks. If they had walked on the tracks themselves, we wouldn't have been able to follow them. But by walking on the dirt path beside the tracks we were able to follow their progress as they headed north. Carl would let me follow the tracks step by step in case they turned off in another direction. He would go into the next little dirt crossing where field roads crossed the railroad tracks. If they had gotten that far, he would wait for me to walk up, and we would leapfrog up to the next crossing.

We repeated this for almost 26 miles to the outskirts of Raymondville. I was following the tracks, track by track, and Carl had gone ahead to Raymondville. This was our last opportunity to over take the aliens. Sure enough, just before we reached Raymondville the tracks left the little dirt path, went around the edge of a plowed field into the thickest patch of brush I have ever seen. It was so thick there was no way to stand up in it. The only way to get through it was on hands and knees. And that's what the two aliens had done. They had crawled several yards into the thick part of the thicket, and I could see them by getting on my knees and looking underneath the overhanging vines and brush. One of them was asleep on his back. The other was on his stomach looking directly at me, eye to eye.

I told them in Spanish, "Come out!" They never moved, and I told them again, "Come here!" The one who was awake reached over and nudged his sleeping companion with his elbow. He rolled over, and both of them just lay there looking at me, not wanting to move. I told them one more time, "This is Immigration. Come out!" They didn't respond the third time I told them. I was afraid they would begin crawling away from me through the thicket. Not wanting to tear my shirt going through the thorns, I fired a warning shot, and they decided they would come out. In just a couple of minutes Carl found me. I had them out of the bush waiting by the trail by then. I never saw two more disappointed aliens. One of them just shook his head and said, "Why are you here?" I told him it was my job. Wherever the illegal aliens were, that's where I would be.

The spring of 1966 came, and my two remaining classmates, Warren and Donald, began to wonder about promotion possibility. One of them asked Roland what it took to be promoted or recommended for promotion, and he said, "Why, you guys aren't dry behind the ears yet."

With my military experience and time as a civilian guard, I was approaching 15 years' service and received a notice from the Regional Office that I would begin receiving eight hours per pay period annual leave credit. Roland saw the notice before he gave it to me and told me the date I would begin receiving the annual leave credit, and I said, "Sure, Roland, I know that when I have 15 years' service, I earn eight hours annual leave."

He said, "Well, you old rascal, you."

I noticed a change in his attitude towards me now that I was an "old rascal," and he started inviting me over to his house saying, "The wife and I are having a little barbecue this weekend. Why don't you bring the missus and come on over?" I didn't take advantage of this newfound hospitality. In just a few weeks I would be leaving the Rio Grande Valley and the land of the wetback behind me.

I had mentioned Ted Milner before and that I enjoyed working with Ted and respected his ability. He had left Harlingen to become the Station Senior at a little station in Stockton, California. He occasionally called back to Harlingen and would talk to one of his friends about some rental houses he had bought in Harlingen and other things in general. In one of those calls he mentioned that his station would be increasing by two men.

Ted left word that if Andy Leach and I were interested in transferring to Stockton, he could see that we would be transferred. Andy was glad to hear this and right away contacted Ted to let him know that he wanted to transfer to Stockton, and it took no time at all until Andy was on the way. I wanted to take a little more time to talk it over with my wife before saying that I wanted to transfer. We had been living in a large ranch style house with a swimming pool and very low rent, and Jerry had taken a job as the secretary to the principal of an elementary school near where we lived. I didn't know how she would feel about leaving at the particular time, even though all along she had expressed her dislike for the valley.

She had an interesting job at the school. The principal was named Sealy, like the mattress company, and naturally the children had nicknamed him "Old Posturpedic." Jerry came home one day telling me about a little problem with a girl at school. Some of the girls in the seventh grade were teenagers, and the first person they saw when sent to the principal's office was Jerry. She talked to this particular girl about her problem, asked why she had been sent down to the principal's office. She confided that it was because she had refused to do her physical exercise. Jerry asked her why she had refused to do her exercise with the rest of the class. She whispered that it was because her panties had holes in them. When she would bend over doing the exercises, the people behind her would see the holes in her panties. I told Jerry that shouldn't be much of a problem, that she could just be placed on the back row where nobody behind her would see her when she bent over. Jerry relayed this information to "Old Posturpedic," and she said he was elated the rest of the day telling his teachers, "I sure solved that problem. I just put her on the back row."

Jerry had also been taking some night classes at Pan American University and had made better grades in Spanish than I ever made, even though she was too timid to say very much. When we discussed moving, Jerry was ready to go. I was ready to go. I believe I had

Bruce R. Sims

gained about as much experience in every phase of Border Patrol work at Harlingen that I was going to gain, and a transfer would be welcomed.

CHAPTER THREE: STOCKTON

On a sunny day in May I headed for the golden state. Coincidentally, it was the same day that Robert McCord left Harlingen on his way to his new assignment and promotion to Investigator at San Francisco, California. My transfer to Stockton was a lateral transfer with no promotion and would entail working under very different circumstances than those along the border. Stockton was a medium-sized town in the San Joaquin Valley, three hundred miles away from the border. Our work would be farm and ranch check in uniform. The very little city scout work that we did would also be in uniform. I was glad to get the opportunity to work with Ted and Andy and was introduced to the rest of the crew, which consisted of Loy Taylor, Robert Nelson, and Noel Doran. Andy and I made six men, and the station would eventually be rounded out to an eight-man station by Bob Mucher and a young PI we just called "Tex." The Chief in charge of the sector was Chief Williams, nicknamed "Speedy" Williams, and he was well pleased with the job that Ted was doing with the Stockton station. Ted had wanted to be a Station Senior ever since he went to California on one of our annual details.

My first day on the job was with Andy. I had spent the night with him, and he took me to the office to show me where it was and to let me get entered on duty. On the way to the office, we passed a field on the outskirts of Stockton. Four people working in the field looked up, saw the green Border Patrol panel truck, and started running for the far end of the field. In the Rio Grande Valley it was a rare thing for an alien to try to run away from you. Usually whatever you told them they would say, "Si, Senor" and obeyed. But the aliens in Stockton were a different breed. They had traveled 300 miles to get to the San Joaquin Valley to work in the agriculture. Some of them had paid as much as $500 to be transported, and they weren't about to give up without trying to escape or fight. Even though I fell flat on my face in the middle of the field, Andy and I were still able to get fairly close with the panel truck and overtake and apprehend two of the four runners. We took them to the office, and I processed my first apprehension in California. I mentioned to Andy, "Well, that was my first California wetback," and the alien I was processing told me, "Senor, I am not a wetback, I am an *Alambrista*." So my days of apprehending the river waders with their wet backs and the nickname of wetback, or worse, was behind me. I prefer the term illegal aliens, personally, although some of the men I had worked with called them either wetbacks or gut eaters and had no sympathy or respect for their plight. Those that called them gut eaters would then go down to Maggie Montalvo's restaurant and order menudo, which is made from the cow's stomach and is the derivation of the gut eater term. The term *alambrista* meant fence jumper. Those aliens who entered illegally in the western part of the United States wanted to be called *Alambristas*, and that was fine with me. There were plenty of *Alambristas* in the Stockton area to be apprehended.

Although my flight back on the airlift had not worked out, I did manage to get as far as Edinburg, Texas, where Jerry met me, and I assisted her in the move back to Stockton. We loaded our dogs in the back of the car and made an uneventful trip across New Mexico and Arizona to the triplex apartment that I had rented in the same complex where Andy lived. This was a financial hardship, as the rent in California was much higher than we had been paying in Harlingen.

I quickly settled into the routine at Stockton, which was a task force of all the manpower working as a team with Ted in a sedan in the lead with two panel trucks following along behind. Loy Taylor was the second in charge, and he and Ted usually rode together in the sedan while Andy and I teamed up in one panel truck with Bob and Noel in the other. We often had the sector airplane overhead guiding us to the larger groups of field laborers where we would attempt to surround the field and apprehend all of the illegals, although it was unlikely that we would catch all of them if it was a large group with all of them running.

I managed to get along well with all of the men at the Stockton station, but I was to find out that things were not running as smoothly as they could be. It seemed that Ted in his exuberance to catch every possible illegal alien that he could was not considering the long hours that he wanted us to work and the consequences on our families. We would leave the Stockton office at daylight, and at sundown we would have deposited two panel loads of aliens at the county jail, have two more panel loads to drop off at the jail, and write out apprehension reports before going home. A few weeks of this daylight to dark work began to take its toll, and Ted was getting disgruntled with Noel and Bob, saying that they were not willing to work as long as he wanted them to work, and things were deteriorating. Finally, Ted decided that Noel and Bob should be split up, so Andy worked with one of them while I worked with the other.

Every person has their own particular way of working, and I didn't mind going across a field to check an irrigator or walking into an orchard to check fruit or nut pickers or whatever was required. So when I worked with Bob or Noel, one of them usually drove, and I was the passenger. We would always have some aliens in custody by the middle of the day. The procedure was to stop at some little drive-in at Modesto, or Tracy, or Lodi, or wherever we happened to be working and buy a lunch for each of the aliens in custody. We would get a receipt and be reimbursed for the money we spent on alien lunches. We also bought something for ourselves, and since we were still on duty guarding the aliens we had in custody, we put on our time and attendance report, "No lunch period taken." Ted decided that this was not the correct thing to do and told Andy and me to show at least a thirty-minute lunch period taken. Then he checked our time and attendance reports to see if we were complying with his instructions. Noel and Bob continued to show no lunch period taken, and he decided this should be reported to the Chief. Ted could do no wrong as the Station Senior as long as Chief Williams was his boss, but things were to change, and not for the better.

I learned from the men at the station that a detail from Tucson, Arizona had come to the San Joaquin area to the Sacramento and Stockton stations, and at the end of their detail had expressed their intent to stop in Las Vegas on their way back to Tucson. Ted had overhead this and told the men on detail that they must take a direct route and proceed in the fastest means possible back to their station at Tucson. They were forbidden to go through Las Vegas, and that was his order. He learned that the men from Tucson had disregarded what he told them and had stopped in Las Vegas on their way back to Tucson. So he wrote a memorandum to the Chief at Tucson, who was Bruce Long, stating that he had instructed the Tucson PI's to go directly back to Tucson and not go through Las Vegas and that they had disobeyed his order and should be disciplined.

Chief Long did not look favorably upon receiving such a memorandum from the Station Senior at Stockton. In fact, it was customary for the Station Senior to write a memo to the station where the men came from complementing them on their work on the detail and thanking them, instead of writing a memorandum implying that disciplinary actions should be taken against them. Chief Long let word get back to Stockton that some day he wanted to meet this young Station Senior.

I had always considered Ted to be one of the hardest working Border Patrolmen I had ever known, and this was no exception when I first arrived in Stockton. On my day off, Jerry and I had gone to the movies in Stockton and seen Ted standing in the doorway of some skid row hotel trying to apprehend just a couple more illegal aliens as they went to their rooms. Stockton had the largest skid row for any city its size in the nation. Labor contractors would load up busloads of winos, other citizen laborers, and wetbacks and go to the fields within a fifty-mile radius of Stockton every day. It was no trouble apprehending all the aliens we could process, even though we cut processing to a minimum, and it seemed like we never made a dent in the alien population. There were always new ones to replace the ones we sent back to the border.

Apprehensions were sometimes very difficult and sometimes very easy. I remember working with Andy one day when we spotted twenty people chopping weeds in a tomato field. We approached the field, and I got out on the side next to the highway while Andy drove around the side of the field to the far end. So we had the group between us, and when we had finished we had all twenty of the workers gathered around the panel truck. All of them were illegal aliens, and none of them had run or tried to escape.

On the other hand, we had worked with the airplane, and the pilot spotted a group and guided us along the proper road to get close to them. He told us that he had spotted a field of twelve people and we better hurry, they were all running but one. By the time we got there, no one was in sight but one person. The foreman of the crew was an immigrated alien. The other eleven were hiding. This was in the area we called the Islands, which are a group of fields actually below sea level, and the flood waters from the Sacramento River had been levied and pumped out to leave rich peat soil. It turned out there is some kind of chemical in this peat soil, and Mucher's leg broke out like he had the measles because he was allergic to the chemical in the peat. In this instance, we had to get into drainage ditches waist deep and literally kick the aliens out of the ditches where they were hiding. We eventually succeeded in getting all of the eleven the pilot had spotted but one. Some of them were hiding underneath asparagus. They would lie down between two rows of asparagus that had gone to seed and rake dirt over their bodies and pull a stalk of the leafy asparagus over their face, and you had to be right on top of them before you could see them.

In other cases, with the plane circling overhead, aliens would run in all directions, requiring larger and larger circles by the aircraft while the pilot tried to keep the runners in sight and spot where they were hiding while we rounded them up. We then took them to the county jail where we would prepare our apprehension reports. The aliens would be detained in the drunk tank until a bus came over from Livermore to transport them back to the Livermore Detention center where they would await the bus lift back to El Centro and ultimate delivery to the Mexican border. Very few of the aliens would be detained for formal deportation or prosecution.

A typical day started about seven in the morning, checking the buses and stopping them as they loaded with the laborers to go into the fields. That was followed by eight hours of farm and ranch check, sometimes with the assistance of the Border Patrol plane—often not, as the plane had to be shared with the other stations in the Livermore sector. Our return to Stockton to the county jail and two hours of processing made a twelve-hour day. This went on for the first few weeks I was at Stockton. Bob would leave our detail early. I could see that this really upset Ted. It amounted to almost insubordination. Ted began to express his belief that Bob Nelson and Noel Doran were not fit officers and should not be wearing the Border Patrol green uniform, and they should be fired.

I gradually became more familiar with the problem as I worked with each one of the officers. Noel and I had worked together quite a bit, and I learned that one of the things that he attempted to learn from every alien we apprehended was the location of the camp that he was living in. If we learned the location, we would go there to let the alien in custody retrieve his personal things, what we called "cleaning up the alien." Occasionally we would apprehend a couple more at the camp, but more than likely, they would see our vehicle coming and would all run. It really didn't make any difference to me if the alien told me where his camp was or not. In fact, I preferred that he didn't tell me. I would ask him, "Do you have any personal effects?" If he said no, that suited me just fine, as we could then take him to the office or the county jail, and it made it easier.

Noel insisted and tried every means of getting the alien to tell him where he lived. One day we had gone to the camp after he intimidated the alien into telling him where the camp was located, and as we let the alien gather up his clothing, Noel found a pistol in the alien's possession. It was a little Saturday night special, owl-head brand pistol, worth hardly anything. Nevertheless, we could not let the alien possess a weapon, so we took it from him and proceeded back to Stockton. Noel said, "I'll take care of the pistol," and the last I saw of it, it was on the dashboard of the panel truck when we arrived at the office. I thought no more about it, since Noel had said he would take care of it.

The next morning Ted was waiting for me when I came in the front door, and his first words were, "Well, Bruce, where's the pistol?" I wondered how he had heard about us taking a pistol from the illegal alien so quickly, but I had nothing to hide. I told him that I really didn't know where the pistol was. The last time I saw it was when we arrived back at the office, and it was on the dashboard of the panel truck, and Noel had said he would take care of it, and that was the last I had seen of the pistol. He said, "Okay, that was all I wanted to know."

I walked from Ted's office into the lobby where Noel, Bob and Andy were waiting. They wanted to know what Ted had wanted to see me about, and I told them he had asked about the location of the pistol. Noel also said, "That's all I wanted to know," and didn't mention it again. Unknown to me, that wasn't the pistol that Ted was inquiring about.

There were other little things that displeased Ted. Noel had some GI footlockers in his garage, and Ted expressed his curiosity as to what was in those footlockers. If Noel was keeping things that he confiscated from the illegal aliens, he must have footlockers full of alien property stored in his carport. Ted's attempt to get Noel and

Dear Chief

Bob disciplined or indeed fired from the Border Patrol might have had a chance of success if we hadn't had a change of Chiefs. The Chief who had wanted to meet the young Senior who had written a memo requesting the Tucson men be disciplined was transferred to the Livermore Sector and was our new boss.

An indication of a change in attitude came when Ted, who had been telling us when things slowed down we could take a detail over to Lake Tahoe, requested that orders be cut detailing the men of his station for an overnight detail to Lake Tahoe. He had told me that there were a couple of sawmills in the mountains, and a laundry in Lake Tahoe that always employed some illegal aliens and that was justification for an annual trip over to that area. I looked forward to going to Lake Tahoe, but it was not to be. Chief Long, after receiving the request for orders for the detail, called the Stockton Station to notify Ted that if he wanted to take a vacation and go to Lake Tahoe, to take annual leave. There would be no work detail to Lake Tahoe that year.

It had been several days since the pistol was mentioned. When Noel was finally called to account for the pistol, he had a receipt ready showing that he had turned it in to the Stockton Police Department. Ted continued to send memorandums to Chief Long reporting what Noel and Robert were doing, and I tried to tell Ted that the Chief really wasn't interested in getting those memorandums. If he wanted a report from Ted, he would call our station and let Ted know how to submit a report. Ted was determined. When I talked to him, he said, 'No, those two men didn't deserve to be in the patrol," and he enlisted the assistance of Andy and Loy in reporting to him their activities.

The next incident involved Noel again. He was working with Andy, and they had apprehended some aliens. Noel, as usual, wanted to know where their camp was located. He took one of the aliens behind the truck, and slapped him around a little, until the alien told him where the camp was located. Some time went by, and one morning I thought I would be working with Andy, but he reported to the office, took the sedan, and headed for the Sector Headquarters at Livermore. Naturally, nothing is secret in the Border Patrol. It didn't take us long to find out that he had gone to see Chief Long to report that his conscience had been bothering him ever since he had worked with Doran, that Doran had slapped an alien, and he didn't think that was right and thought the Chief ought to know about it. Once again, that just fomented turmoil at the station. Andy could no longer be trusted. Noel and Bob both refused to work with Andy, so that meant that I would be working with one or the other of them more than usual. I made the best of the situation, and really didn't mind working with either one of them. Bob was saying when we left the station that he was going to drive and that he wasn't turning his hand. He wasn't going to get his boots dirty, and would refer to Ted's birth in England by calling him "a limey bastard." Bob even got carried away occasionally and would let a cuss word slip out over the radio. If this happened, Chief Long, who would have been monitoring the radio, would be heard on the sector radio cautioning, "Now Bob, Bob, watch that language."

I had a knack of agreeing with Bob when he said he wasn't going to get his boots dirty, until we saw some aliens working in an orchard or a field. Then I would tell Bob, "Well, Bob, I really don't mind walking out into that field to check those aliens, you just wait for me there in the truck." He would sit in the truck, and I would start waking across the field to approach the aliens. As soon as they started running, Bob's adrenaline would also start running, and he would drive the truck around the field trying to cut off the running aliens and would chase them just like I did. That way we continued to be successful in apprehending quite a number of illegal aliens.

Ted wasn't satisfied, however, with the number we were apprehending. He always wanted more. So he decided that it would be more efficient if Bob wasn't sent out in the field at all. Instead of coming to the county jail at the end of our shift and processing aliens, we would dump the aliens in the drunk tank overnight. Bob could go directly to the jail the next morning and spend as much time as necessary writing apprehension reports on the previous day's apprehensions. This worked well for about two weeks. Bob really got proficient at writing apprehension reports. He could have forty aliens processed and be back to the office before we returned from the day's activity. This didn't please Ted either, so he started taking Bob to the jail himself, leaving him there for the day. He would be stranded without a vehicle until we returned with the day's apprehensions. After a week of this, Bob got word to the Chief that he was tired of the preferential treatment. He got tired of being stranded at the jail as processing officer. The Chief sent word that this would cease immediately, that everyone apprehended aliens, and everyone would process the aliens they apprehended.

We went back to hours of processing after long days in the field. Despite the long days, there still were days off, and Jerry and I found time to enjoy living in Stockton. We visited San Francisco, Lake Tahoe, and Reno. We also moved from the triplex apartment in town to a duplex apartment on the outskirts of town. We shared the duplex with Dave and Marie Lopez and their son, Ronnie, and daughter, Rene. They were lovely children, whom I enjoyed having as neighbors. Ronnie was pitching baseball and looked like he would have a good future in baseball. Rene was just a live wire whom I nicknamed "Grenade." She would come over to our apartment with some sausage, which her father had brought home from his job as a meat deliveryman, and say, "Here, Brucie boy, here is some linguiza for your freeza."

It was in Stockton that I had my first experience with an earthquake. It happened one afternoon when Jerry had gone to town shopping, and I was on the couch watching a ball game on TV. The house shook, glasses rattled, and pictures on the wall shook, but I was unaware that was an earthquake until I heard it on the news. There was some glass breakage downtown, and some boulders had rolled onto the highway on the mountains east of Sacramento. Fortunately, this was just a minor quake, and I had no desire to see what a stronger one would feel like.

As a general rule, the *Alambristas* continued to run. There wasn't an opportunity for them to run all the time. A second visit to the tomato field with Mucher was one instance. Jim and I counted twenty workers in the field. In a repeat performance almost like I had done with Andy, Jim let me off at one end of the field, and he drove around the side to the far end so we had the group between us. I approached the first ones nearest me and asked them for their papers. Each one said he had no papers, so I told them to go to the truck. Very slowly, they began walking towards the truck at the far end of the field, and as there were acres and acres of open space with no place to hide, they all obeyed my instructions and waited beside the truck until we had checked everyone in the field and sorted out about eighteen of the workers and left two who were there legally.

On another occasion we approached a barracks out in the Islands. The barracks was a two-story army surplus dormitory that had been moved out there to house farm laborers. Visibility was good from the dormitory, and one could see a vehicle approaching a half mile away, at least. By the time we parked beside the dormitory, it seemed to be deserted. There was no one on the ground floor. The walls were lined each side with bunks. We went upstairs; it looked to be deserted also, until someone fell through the ceiling. Then we discovered that, sure enough, they had seen the vehicle approaching at a long distance and had time to scramble up into the attic. There were so many aliens that the rafters were about to break, and one of them had slipped and fallen through the ceiling.

In other instances, everyone in the field would start running in all directions. If we were working with the airplane, the pilot would make larger and larger circles trying to keep up with them, but still some of them would manage to hide or run out from under the airplane. It was really perplexing to drive into a field or orchard and have everyone start running and be able to apprehend only one or two. I learned right away that once they had been caught, you'd take precautions to keep them apprehended. Andy and I took a whole panel truck load back to the barracks for them to get their personal effects. One of them was just waiting for the vehicle to stop and was crouched at the back door of the truck. As soon as I opened the door, before I could even grab him, he jumped out of the panel truck, ran into the cornfield with corn higher than a person's head, and was lost. I told myself I wouldn't make that mistake again, they were too hard to catch to let them escape later on.

I started carrying more than one set of handcuffs, and from then on, I opened the panel door very carefully so that no one could push their way by me. I would handcuff two of them together and never let more than four at a time out of the truck go into the barracks to reclaim their personal things. I never had any more escape. I wasn't the only one at Stockton who was perplexed over the large number of aliens who were running and managed to avoid apprehension. Some of us, me included, were carrying a wad cutter round as the first round to be fired from my pistol, and we would hasten them on their way with a round fired in the air. This very seldom worked. I only remember one time that an alien came to a sudden stop and threw his hands in the air and surrendered. Usually the gunfire just hastened them on the way that much faster.

Naturally, in time, Chief Long heard about the amount of warning shots being fired by the Stockton Border Patrol and sent word that it would cease immediately. For me, personally, the advice was unnecessary at that point. I had already come to the conclusion that it was a dangerous thing and that I shouldn't be doing it. I had taken my wad cutters out of the pistol and reloaded service rounds and decided that I wouldn't be shooting at the fleeing aliens anymore.

The thing that made me decide that was an incident where my partner and I went to a small house in a peach orchard. The house was used as a dormitory for illegal aliens, and there were three or four in the house at the time we arrived. We pulled up beside an old beat up car in the yard. I rushed to the back door while my partner went to the front door, and as soon as the people inside realized that it was the Border Patrol, they looked out the door, both doors, saw there was someone at each door. As it was warm weather and the windows were up, it was an easy matter for them to knock off the screens and start jumping out the windows. As those coming out the windows had a head start, it looked like I would not catch more than one of them if I chased after them. It was better to stay at the back door and see how many we could get who stayed in the house. I could see one running down the lane between the peach trees, so I sent a bullet in his general direction. The instant the gun fired, a child screamed somewhere in the peach orchard that I hadn't seen, and it just scared the crap out of me. I decided then and there a warning shot was not worthwhile, so I had already decided on my own. The Chief's warning had some effect, but did not bring the practice to a complete halt.

Working in Stockton continued to be the hardest work that I could imagine doing, and things had slowed down a little bit. We no longer worked as many days with the airplane, and Ted had decided that maybe teaming Nelson and Doran together would be more efficient if he just wrote them off as a loss and continued to let the other teams who he though would work together team up as partners. James Mucher was easy to get along with and was the newest guy at the station. He could work with Taylor or Andy or me or Nelson or

Doran. Seems like everyone trusted the easygoing Mucher, but I found myself working more and more with Andy since we had worked together at Harlingen and he was my best friend. We worked pretty good together, it seemed like. Andy had an appearance that made him ideal to play the bad guy when he and I would team up to interrogate a person about their documents that we suspected to be false documents.

There's a knack to getting someone to admit that they are carrying someone else's papers, and the same thing doesn't always work. One case in point was a middle-aged man in a car that we checked on a Stockton street. It was occupied by four or five men who showed their identification when we asked them, and everyone seemed to be legally in the United Stated with an alien registration card except one who presented a birth certificate which we immediately suspected. He was hesitant about the information on the birth certificate, and we wanted to talk to him at length.

The driver of the car sat patiently for several minutes while we talked to the middle-aged man whom we had invited to our panel truck. Then the driver explained that they were on their way to Oregon to work in the apple orchards, and that they were in hurry; and if we were going to continue to talk to the man, then they would have to leave him. Our instructions on false claims were either to break them or let them go. We already had the man sitting in the vehicle, and my heart sank when the driver put his personal effects on the side of the road and drove off and left him.

We were in the position that if he turned out to be a citizen, and we had arrested a citizen, we were in deep trouble. We both were convinced that this couldn't possibly be the person named on the birth certificate, but we had no choice now but to take him to our office and get the truth out of him, if we could. It was to our advantage, even though it was making us both uneasy, that his companions had decided to leave him because now he was stranded, and we acted confident that we knew he was carrying someone else's documents. It would be useless to insist further that he was a citizen of the United States. The old man must have had some experience because he was hanging tough, and after we had been at the office and gone over his information as to place of birth, parents, how old the parents were, when he was born, and any brothers and sisters he had that were older than him, and he wasn't certain about any of this. He still insisted that those were his papers, and we were almost to that point where it's do what you want to do with me, but these are my papers, and either put me in jail or let me go.

We had tried the good guy/bad guy routine. Andy would get mad, threaten him with jail time. I would tell him to think of his family, that if that happened, he wouldn't be earning any money, and the family would be starving. I could understand his need to come to the United States, even using someone else's birth certificate, but the old man would just smile at us, shake his head negatively, and refuse to admit the truth.

In a desperate attempt to find some incriminating items, we had checked the contents of his billfold, which gave us nothing. He had emptied everything out, and then we began looking through his personal effects. Among the things in his bag was a writing tablet. I looked at the writing tablet and could see that something had been written and the page torn out. As Andy continued to talk to the old man, I took the pencils from the desk and began to blacken over the writing with the long side of the pencil lead, like I had done when I was a kid, and would put a coin underneath a piece of paper, then lightly blacken over the coin, and the details of the coin underneath the paper would come through. The old man watched me intently. I had finally got his attention, and as the writing underneath began to faintly appear, I would show the tablet to Andy and tell him to look at this. He would look at it, and even though we couldn't read the words, I continued until I got to the bottom of the page. Then I turned to the man we were questioning, looked him in the eye, gave him a big smile and said, "Ah ha, when you write your wife, you don't sign the same name that you are telling us." He grinned back at me with an ear to ear grin, put his hands in a gesture of resignation and said, "Yes, sir, that is the truth." That was a real relief because I had envisioned having to buy him a bus ticket to Oregon and sending him on his way with his assumed identity.

After he told us that it was the truth, he was using another name, he then wanted our sympathy, especially mine since I had told him I understood his problem, and he wanted to know what would happen to him now that he was willing to tell the truth. We knew that the truth would only be a partial truth, with long explanations of how his family was in such need that he had to come to the United States to find work and that he had met a man in the plaza and he had given the man all the money that he had to buy the birth certificate so he could come to the United States. Naturally, he would not know the name of the man, and his description would fit 99 percent of all the Mexicans in Mexico, but we were still glad to take that particular birth certificate out of circulation.

It was the height of the peach harvest when Andy and I again found ourselves working together checking peach pickers in the area around Modesto, California. We had some success and had already apprehended five aliens whom we had seated in the panel truck. Then we spotted another group of pickers off to our left as we drove down a paved road very slowly, looking down the lanes between the peach trees. Evidently someone in the group was alert and looking back towards the road and spotted our green and white Border Patrol panel truck as we pulled over to the left shoulder of the road. We stopped and could see people jumping off of ladders and running towards the back of the peach orchard. By the time we got to their location it looked like eight or ten people had jumped off of their ladders and left only one person standing there. That person was the foreman who kept up with the number of buckets of peaches each person picked.

The group scattered like a covy of quail, and we could still see them running through the trees. So Andy veered off to the right after someone he could see, and I spotted one going away from me slightly to the left of where we were. There were two or three of them that I could see in that direction, so I picked out one who was the shortest and slightly heavy set that I thought I could catch and started chasing him. He had a pretty good head start, and it wouldn't be easy to catch anyone, but I was persistent. In fact, I had earned a nickname because of my tenacity in pursuing someone who was running. I would stay after them until we each were so exhausted we were down to a walk, but eventually I would catch the one that I was running after, and the guys in the station had started calling me the "Big Bear." They said, "If the 'Big Bear' got after you, you were caught." It took awhile, but after the first burst of speed, the person I was chasing slowed down, and I was gradually overtaking him. When I caught him, I put handcuffs on him and ordered him back towards the direction of the truck.

Dear Chief

As we neared the truck, I could hear loud voices and figured that Andy had caught the person he was chasing quicker than I had and was already back at the truck with him. I couldn't understand the words that were being said, but could understand that something was going on. I prodded the boy I had caught a little bit to move faster and hurry back to the truck. The voices stopped before I got to the truck, and when I finally arrived on the scene, Andy was standing in the middle of the road. Someone who wasn't there when we had parked had arrived on the scene in a pickup truck and had backed the truck crossways to the back of our panel truck about ten feet from the back doors of the panel truck. I could see that the pickup truck was occupied by a woman in the passenger's side and a man in the driver's side.

I took the boy I had caught between the vehicles, opened the back door to take off the handcuffs and put him inside when the person seated in the pickup truck began cursing me. I paid little attention to him at first, went ahead and took the handcuffs off the alien I had caught, closed the back door of the panel truck and turned to face the man who was still cursing me. He had called the Border Patrol every dirty name he could think of, brought my ancestry into the situation, and after calling me every dirty name he could think of, he slowed down for a minute. He then started all over again, about what rights he had and what authority the Border Patrol had. At that point I made my only comment to the man, and that was to say, "It's too bad you have such a misunderstanding." At that point, he slung his pickup door open, jumped to the ground, and said, "I don't have no damn misunderstanding. I'll show you a thing or two," and he turned and began dragging something from under the seat of his pickup truck. The woman was still seated on the passenger's side. I have heard people say that when action starts, things seem to slow down and move in slow motion, and that's the way it was in this situation.

Even though it took only a second, it seemed from then on that everything moved in slow motion. I had time to glance at Andy. He was still standing in the middle of the highway, and I thought here comes trouble. This guy is reaching under his seat for a tire tool or something. As he pulled the object from under the seat, it wasn't a tire tool. I could see a shotgun being pulled out from under the seat.

As we were only a few feet apart, by the time he pulled the shotgun from under the seat and turned t o his left, holding the shotgun by the grip with one hand on the grip under the barrel, I held out my left hand. As the barrel came in line with my body it was pointed right at my stomach. I remember reaching for the barrel with my left hand and grasping it near the end of the barrel and pushing it arms length out beside me. With my right hand I instinctively reached for my pistol, brought it up pointing at the man, and fired one shot. The shot struck the man in the upper arm, and the shock of the bullet made him release the grip on his shotgun and stagger backwards one step against his pickup.

There I stood, pistol in my right hand, holding the shotgun by the barrel with my left hand. Since the man was grasping his left arm with his right hand and blood was streaming between his fingers and dripping off of his elbow, he was no longer a threat. But his wife jumped from the passenger's side of the pickup truck, screamed when she saw her husband, and yelled at me, "You crazy bastard, you have shot my husband." She then said, "Give me that," and she tried to grab the shotgun. I turned to keep the shotgun away from her, then moved to the passenger's side of the panel truck and put the shotgun inside the truck. When I went back to the rear of the panel truck she was seeing about her husband's wound, and I told her, "Maybe you had better get a doctor for him." He said, "Yes, you had better get me to a hospital." They jumped in the truck, and she drove away without my even knowing who he was.

I could see the memorandum in my mind that I would have to write, "Dear Chief, I have just shot a farmer." I got on the radio, called the sector headquarters and asked for Chief Long to come to the radio. I also called our station office and asked for SPI Milner if he was hearing the radio transmission. Then I explained to Chief Long that I had had to shoot a farmer. I explained to him that he had threatened me with a shotgun, and I had had to shoot him. Chief Long's only question was, "Was it a service load?" When I answered him, "Yes, Chief, it was with a service load," he said, "Okay," and that was all I heard from Chief Long. SPI Milner came on the radio and said, "Stay right there, I'll be there as quickly as I can get there."

While we were waiting for Ted to show up, the first person representing a law enforcement agency to arrive was a Deputy Sheriff from Stanislass County. He came screeching to a halt in the highway beside us, asked what happened, and I told him I had had to shoot a farmer. He asked who it was, and I told him that I didn't know, that he had not been there when we stopped to check the peach picking crew, and he hadn't introduced himself when I got back to the truck with the alien I had apprehended; but from the description I gave of the man and the vehicle from the location where we were, the deputy said, "Oh, I know who that was," he says, "Down here, we all know him; he is about half nuts anyway, and we just call him 'Crazy Miller.' You have just met 'Crazy Miller.'" Crazy Miller turned out to be George Miller, the owner of the peach orchard, and George Miller had his own story to tell to the press.

Needless to say, his story did not approach anything like the truth. The next day, in the Modesto paper headline, "Border Patrolman Shoots Local Rancher," and Miller gave his version of the events and announced that he would be filing a million dollar lawsuit against the Border Patrol and against Andy and me personally.

The farmers in the area who belonged to the farmers' grange were really up in arms about one of their members being shot by a Border Patrolman. No one knew the facts, other than the way Miller reported them, and his story was that he and his wife were innocently sitting in their pickup where their crew was picking their peaches. Then these men in green uniforms came running through his peach orchard, scared off all of this workers, and one of them had run up beside the pickup where he was seated and put a gun through the window of the pickup and shot him.

No one from the Immigration Service disputed his story for several days. In fact, Andy and I were advised that this incident would be investigated by the FBI, who had authority over federal offenses; and as I was going to charge Miller with assault on a federal officer, that the investigation would be conducted by the FBI, and any prosecution would be handled through the U.S. Attorney whose office was in Sacramento.

I didn't see George Miller again for over a week, and then when I did see him again, it was just by chance. On that particular day, I was working with Loy Taylor. We were in the same general area where the shooting had occurred; and on that day Loy and I were working in a sedan, and I was driving. I didn't know where George

Miller's residence was, but I did know we were in the general vicinity. We stopped on the paved road beside a couple of Latins who were sorting peaches in a large plywood box. We stopped near them and asked them about their citizenship and what kind of documents they had. They both replied that they were immigrated aliens, but their resident alien identification cards were in the cabin about a hundred yards from where they were working. On the other side of the street was a large barn, and a house was near by it. Loy said there was no need of both of us going to the cabin to check the alien resident cards, that he would just take the aliens down to the cabin and see their cards and left me sitting in the car waiting for them to return. Out of the barn walked a familiar figure whom I could tell as he got closer, had a bandage around his upper arm, and he walked up to the car. I recognized the person as being George Miller. He looked at me a long stare, bent over so he could see in the car a little better, and says, "Are you the one that shot me?" I answered, "Yes, I am." He said, "You ought to be fired." He turned and walked back into the barn.

Not knowing what he was intending to do or would do, the hair on the back of my neck stood up a little bit, and I decided I'd better back the car down the street a little further away from the barn and wait for Loy to come out of the house. As I backed down even with the cabin, Loy came out with one of the people he had taken to check his card, and he had a different one with the two of them cuffed together. He got in the car and said, "One of the men had a card and one didn't, and I found this other fellow hiding in the house." By then Miller came out of the barn and was standing in the street beside his box of peaches.

The two people we had in custody said he owed them money and would we collect their wages? Since I could see that Miller had nothing in his hands, I drove the several yards back to where he was standing. Taylor told him the workers claimed they had some wages coming and would he pay them. He reluctantly took several bills out of his pocket, gave each of them some money, and we drove away. I would only see Crazy Miller one more time at the lawyer's office.

The newspaper was still carrying articles about the shooting incident, and I was displeased with the progress the U.S. Attorney was making. He hadn't arrested Miller. When I inquired, he told me that the FBI was still doing their investigation and that he would let me know if the case merited prosecution.

In the meantime, the District Director from San Francisco, who had authority over the whole northern part of California, had scheduled a meeting with the farmer's grange in Modesto. He told me and Ted Milner that no one from the Border Patrol would attend that meeting, that we were specifically told to stay away from that meeting. This only whetted my curiosity as what could he be telling them that he didn't want me to hear, and I was determined to find out.

My wife decided that there was nothing to prevent her from attending the meeting of the farmer's grange, since it was open to everyone in the community, so we proceeded to Modesto, and I sat in the car while she went inside and listened to what Mr. Fullilove, our District Director, had to say to the farmers. We were mildly surprised when we recognized someone getting out of his civilian car, in his civilian clothes, and easing into the meeting unnoticed. It was none other than my Station Senior. Ted had discreetly entered the hall so he, too, could hear what the District Director had to say.

When my wife came outside to tell me what had gone on in the meeting, she was very much pleased with Mr. Fullilove's conduct and what he had to say. She told me that he laid it on the line to the farmers, that he was tired of hearing the complaints about harassment and abuse of aliens by the Border Patrol. Miller had claimed that he didn't recognize who the men were who had shot him, but they had claimed to be Border Patrolmen. He told Miller and all those assembled that the Border Patrol worked in marked vehicles with U.S. Border Patrol decals on the sides of the vehicle, that the men wore uniforms, that they had U.S. Border Patrol on the shoulder of the uniform, they had a badge on the left hand pocket of the uniform, a name tag over the right hand pocket of the uniform, and that if there was any doubt whatsoever, that the person was a border patrolman, to give a call at his office in San Francisco, and he could very quickly verify whether or not the person was a Border Patrolman. I was very pleased with Mr. Fullilove's support.

I wished I had been getting as much support from the U.S. Attorney. It seemed to me that he was really dragging his feet. Every time I inquired I got the same answer, that the FBI would submit their report, he would then take the information before a federal grand jury, and they would decide whether or not there was sufficient cause to prosecute George Miller. It seemed to me like prosecuting a citizen for assault on a federal officer was not very popular with the U.S. Attorney. We had held the two aliens that we apprehended on Miller's property as witnesses, as they were the two nearest he window in the back of the panel truck, and both said they had seen what had happened. It turned out that the two Mexicans were father and son. Andy had caught the old man, and we verified his claim that he was an immigrated alien and that he had left his alien registration card in the building he was living in and was afraid when all these people he was working with had jumped off of their ladders yelling, "Immigration and had started running through the peach orchard. He was excited and ran along with them, but he hadn't run very far or very fast, and Andy had caught him rather quickly and got back to the truck before I did to find Miller had arrived on the scene and had cursed him out just like he cursed me. When I arrived with the second alien in custody, Miller was already raving and ranting like a maniac.

  Since Andy had not moved a muscle to come to my assistance when Miller threatened me with the shotgun, I wondered about that, and Andy explained that he didn't know what had happened on that particular day. He said it surprised him so much when Miller pulled the shotgun out from under the seat of the pickup truck that he was just frozen in this tracks, and it seemed like he couldn't move. He had finally moved and came over to help control Miller's wife after she got out of the truck and while I was putting the shotgun away in the cab of the panel truck.

  Time dragged on, and as I could see no progress being made in the case, I began to tell the U.S. Attorney that if he was not going to pursue the federal case, then I would bring my own civil case against Miller. He assured me that progress was being made, but the two people we had in custody as material witnesses were becoming uneasy and wanting to get out of detention and go back to Mexico. We knew if they were released we would never see or hear from them again. A way to their statements as witnesses on the record was in the form of a deposition, and a meeting was arranged where they would appear before Miller at his attorney's office in Modesto. They could make statements and be questioned by Miller's attorney. The U.S.

Attorney would be there with me, and I would make my statement before Miller and his attorney. This seemed a little bit unusual to me, but I had nothing to hide, and my side of the story would be finally a matter of official record, not just the memorandum explaining the incident that I had prepared. So reluctantly, I agreed to meet the U.S. Attorney at the office of Miller's attorney. They even let his attorney choose an interpreter of their choice.

Evidently, George Miller had told his attorney the same story that he had told to the press, about how he was innocently sitting in his pickup truck when I had approached and shot him through the window of his truck while he was seated in the truck with his wife. As I told his attorney just how things had transpired, he looked questionably at Miller because it was obvious that he had not heard the true facts. The facts were substantiated, as the boy I had apprehended and the man Andy had apprehended told the same story. The old man was particularly impressive as he told of how he had been seated in the back of the panel truck when I brought his son to the back of the truck and opened the door to put him inside. He also repeated how I had been cursed by George Miller and how Miller had gotten out of his pickup truck, and the old man pantomimed bending over, reaching back into the pickup, pulling out the shotgun, how he had held the shotgun, turned around with it in his hands and pointed it directly at my stomach.

When Miller's attorney heard that version of what had happened, you could see all the color leave his face. As soon as Miller's attorney saw his million dollar case flying out the window, he had turned as white as a sheet and immediately asked to confer with the U.S. Attorney and offered to withdraw his million dollar suit against me and the government in exchange for dropping the charges against Miller. But, to the U.S. Attorney's credit, he said there would be no deals, and Miller would be prosecuted for accosting a federal officer.

Weeks flew by, and I heard nothing further from the U.S. Attorney. What I did hear were comments from the other Border Patrolmen who had heard of the shooting incident. They asked me why had I shot him in the arm and suggesting that I might need more training at the firing range.

I continued to work with every officer in the station, even though the station was still torn apart. The shooting incident did not solidify the friendship among the men at the station, but I could see that it didn't have any adverse affect either. I continued to work with Nelson; in fact, I enjoyed working with Bob. I remember one incident when he and I were together. The leaves were falling off the peach trees, and visibility was a little better in the peach orchards when we spotted a fellow who spotted us about the same time. He took off running. Once again, I jumped out of the panel truck to pursue the runner on foot while Bob drove along the peach orchard trying to get in front of the runner. The man was thin and could run like a rabbit, but I continued my pursuit, gaining a little each time he would change directions until I saw him disappear into a ditch. I watched for him to come out of the other side, but he didn't reappear. When I looked over the bank of the irrigation ditch, the bottom of the ditch was muddy, and he had left large footprints, showing that he had turned toward a concrete pipe in which the irrigation was pumped. There was a large puddle at the mouth of the pipe and just enough space to hide a person. Since the tracks didn't come out of the puddle, I assumed that he was hiding inside the concrete pipe.

Sure enough, when I got down into the bottom of the muddy ditch and could look up into the pipe, just a foot or so inside the pipe was nothing but the man's head sticking out of the water. I began to tell him to come out, and he shook his head negatively. I got on top of the pipe and tried to bend over and reach inside, but he moved back a few inches deeper into the pipe, just out of my reach. And again he refused my order that he come out. I got back down into the ditch in the lower end of the puddle, and by squatting down, we could look each other in the eye. I assured him that he wouldn't be harmed if he would come out. He kept shaking his head and saying, "No, Senor." But I could see his arms moving as he squatted. It reminded me of someone squatting to take a crap. I asked him what was he doing, had he shit in his pants, and he said, "Yes, Senor," he had shit in his pants. His motions were his attempts to clean himself up, and as the water was very cold, he finally decided to surrender. When he came out, I placed one handcuff on his right wrist, as a precaution, since he had run so far, I thought he might attempt to run again before we got to the truck, which I could see was some distance across the peach orchard. I kept the other handcuff in my left hand, and as we walked toward the panel truck, the guy was shaking like he had the palsy, either from the wet clothing or from nervousness.

It was a good thing that I did have one wrist handcuffed and was holding the other end because, sure enough, before we got to the truck, he attempted to jerk out of my grasp and run again. But I managed to hold on. Nelson told the story back at the office how the big bear had chased a wetback until he shit in his pants.

More weeks went by before I heard from the U.S. Attorney again. This time he reported that progress was being made in the Miller case, that he had presented the case to a federal grand jury who had returned an indictment, but we had no date for his trial.

I could see that our Station Senior was losing some of his zest for apprehending illegal aliens. He no longer led us on a caravan of vehicles with every man in the office working with the plane. And I occasionally found myself working a weekend with one other person. One of those occasions was with James Mucher, whom I enjoyed working with because he was such an easygoing and likeable person. We had gone into the office, and only he and I were working when we received a call from one of the pilots who was up scouting around even though no one was working beneath him. He wanted to know if we had anybody working near Modesto. I told him, no we didn't. He said he had watched a busload of field workers load onto a bus, and he was convinced from their appearance that they must be illegal aliens; and if someone could catch up with that bus before it unloaded its passengers, he would stay overhead and keep an eye on it and direct us to intercept the bus. Jim and I jumped into a sedan, started toward Modesto as quickly as we could go, and with the pilot's instruction, we overtook the bus in downtown Modesto.

All the passengers were still aboard when we pulled it over to the curb. I got out and boarded the bus, asked the first couple of passengers about their citizenship and if they had any documents. They told me, "No, Senor." I took them off the bus, gave them to Jim, who was waiting outside at the door of the bus keeping an eye on the windows to see that no one jumped out. I checked a couple more at random. They also told me, "No, Senor," they had no documents. I saw that we would quickly overload our car, so I asked them if anyone on the bus had documents. If so, show me. They were all illegals except the driver who was an immigrated alien. We could not transport a whole busload. The easiest thing to do was to ask the driver to take the bus around the block and a couple more blocks down the street to the Modesto Police Station, where we unloaded the whole busload. That was probably the largest group that I ever apprehended at one time, up until that time.

There was another weekend where we were again working together. There was a phone call from a little town called River Bank, California. The Sheriff of River Bank was asking if we could send someone over to this jail to pick up a couple of illegal aliens that he was holding. He said he had received a report from a woman telling him two Mexicans were in her backyard stealing clothes off of her clothesline, and he had apprehended them.

As there was some work to do in the office, and two illegal aliens were nothing to get excited about, I asked Jim if he could go over to River Bank alone while I took care of the things we had to do in the office and bring them back. He said, "No problem." So he jumped in the sedan and headed for River Bank, and in a little while he was back at the office with the two men who were claiming to be illegal aliens from Mexico.

As soon as Jim walked into the office, he said, "Bruce, I can't put my finger on it, but there's something wrong with these two guys." They did appear a little larger and a little huskier than the usual illegal aliens we were encountering. We talked to them, and they didn't seem to know much about Mexico. Their main interest was in how soon they would be on a bus going back to the border. We told them that they would be going either that evening or, at most, the next evening. They were happy to have been apprehended and to be told they would be sent back to Mexico.

They had also aroused my suspicion along with Jim's, and although we didn't usually fingerprint every illegal alien we apprehended, I thought we had better find out more about who these two birds were because the one I was writing the apprehension report on didn't know such simple things as how many pesos there were in a dollar. He told me it had been seven years since he was in Mexico and he no longer knew how many pesos were in a dollar. I had him sign his name, which he claimed was Perez, and he left out the "e" and signed his name "P-r-e-z," instead of "P-e-r-e-z." So we decided to take their fingerprints. Every time I started taking this fella's prints, he moved his fingers and smudged his prints so they would be illegible. This went on for about three attempts. I started over and each time he smudged the prints. So I decided we would take them down to the county jail. There was a big deputy at the jail who took the fella by the wrists, in his firm grip, looked him the eye and told him, "If you smudge my fingerprints, I'll break your fucking arm." Evidently the suspect was convinced, and the deputy took a legible set of prints and put them on the machine to send to the California Criminal Information Center at Sacramento.

In a few minutes we had the results back, and it turned out our two wetbacks weren't really wetbacks. They were escapees from a work camp in the Sierra Mountains who had somehow managed to make their way down to River Bank and were trying to conceal their identity and get a free trip out of the United States. It didn't work. The warden at the work camp was glad to get his prisoners back, and Mucher and I received an "Atta Boy" for their apprehension.

As the pruning season got into full swing, I found myself working with Nelson again. We stopped at a field with two people on ladders trimming peach trees, and I being the walker, walked out to the middle of the field. As I approached the two people on the ladders, the younger one jumped off his ladder and started running across the peach orchard. I hesitated long enough to ask the other man on the ladder what was his citizenship. I got his answer and then proceeded running after the one who had jumped off of the ladder. As he had a pretty good start, I wasn't going to catch him right away.

Nelson, seeing the man running, drove around the field to get in front of him. When he saw the truck in front of him, he changed directions, and I cut across to gain on him. Nelson, once again, drove around to the other side of the orchard where he would come out if he continued in that direction. He changed directions again, and I overtook him. Just as I was in arm's reach, he suddenly stopped and swung the pruning shears, which he was still carrying. I stepped back, just out of reach of the pruning shears, and instinctively reached for my pistol, and then second thoughts overtook me. As I hesitated, the young man turned and ran again, and it took me another few minutes to overtake him again, and the same thing occurred. Just before I reached him, he stopped and swung the pruning shears.

The third time this happened, he finally was exhausted from running so much. As I overtook him this time, he said in good English, "Man, what the fuck are you chasing me for? Do I look like a wetback?" I had to tell him that, yes, he did and was acting like one. He said, well he wasn't, that he was a citizen and that was his father on the ladder. I was convinced that he truly was a citizen, nobody else would be crazy enough to swing at a Border Patrolman in uniform with a pistol at his side. The boy would have been in serious trouble if I had not had that encounter with Miller just a few months ago and was reluctant—in fact, hesitant, to use a weapon until this day. Despite the teasing I got from other Border Patrolmen, I am glad that I didn't injure Miller more seriously or kill him. I would hate to have the death of a citizen on my conscience.

During the winter, things slowed in Stockton. Many of the labor camps were closed for the winter, and it was hard to find anything other than small groups of people pruning grape vines or peach trees. We no longer worked as a station team with everyone driving along in a convoy. We now teamed up to work as individual units with two people to the vehicle. Even Ted's enthusiasm for catching illegal aliens had diminished. We blamed dissention between Ted and the Sector Chief. I wondered what the outcome of the strained relationships would be.

One day I was in the back seat of the sedan with Andy and Ted in the front, and we were on our way to eat lunch at Johnny Homm's Restaurant, which was one of our favorites when we were in town at noon. Ted and Andy were in a conversation of their own and seemed to have forgotten that I was in the back seat. Ted mentioned that it was time for the recommendations for the annual awards and told Andy that he would be recommending him, and since Taylor was his second in command, would have to recommend him also. He then asked Andy what he wanted from the Border Patrol. Andy told him he would like to be a Senior in the Border Patrol and would like to return to the northern border since that was where he lived. Ted said, Well, Andy, I will see that you get that." I sat quietly in the back seat and wondered what was in my future.

I wouldn't have long to wait, however, as things were reaching a climax at the Stockton station. In the meantime, to keep things interesting, I found myself working with Andy. We decided that since things had slowed down in the field, we would check a few bars in Lodi and Tracy. Sure enough, just as we expected, we found a few illegal barmaids. That was interesting, as it would require either a female attendant or a second guard on the bus ride from Livermore to the border. We also decided that it might be productive to work a night shift, so we got another team to help us and check the few of the labor barracks around Modesto that were still in operation. On the way back to Stockton, we stopped at the little cantinas in the towns between Modesto and Stockton.

There was a pretty good crowd at one of them, and as we walked in the door, I saw a figure leave the darkness of the back of the room and go out the kitchen door. I went across the room and out the kitchen door as quickly as I could, and by then the suspect was getting into a Pontiac car. He ground the starter a couple of times, and the car wouldn't start. By that time, I was at the driver's door, and he slid across the seat and went out the passenger's side and ran down the street with me in hot pursuit. I wasn't gaining any on him, and he wasn't able to outrun me as he kept looking back over his should, and I was still there behind him. The street had streetlights, so he decided to cut through a backyard into the darkness. A couple of seconds after he rounded the corner of a house I heard wires squeak. I looked around the corner of the house and saw my suspect lying on the ground with a gash across his forehead. I approached my suspect and confirmed that he was indeed an illegal alien. Then I reached down with a handcuff and attached it to his right arm. I didn't bother to handcuff both hands, as I figured I could hold onto the handcuff with my left hand and guide him back to our vehicles at the bar.

I don't know if I would have caught him so easily if he had not run into that clothesline which nearly took the top of his head off. But he was far from incapacitated.

As we walked back out to the street and started up the sidewalk, he began yelling at the top of his voice, "Ayude me, ayude me." That's "Help me." He was screaming so loudly that porch lights came on, and people came running out of their houses to see what was going on. Several people began following me up the street. As the alien and I went back toward the bar, he would grab onto the fender of a car or a board in a picket fence with his loose hand, and I would have to pry him loose and drag him up he street a little further. All the while he was asking in Spanish for people to help him. He had touched the blood oozing from his cut on his forehead and would hold out his bloody hand and say, "Look at my blood. Help me. Help me. Look at my blood." I could see that he had the people's sympathy, but they were not about to interfere with a uniformed Border Patrolman. So they just followed us up the street. All the time, I was hoping that my partners had finished checking those who remained inside the bar and would come looking for me. But they didn't, and I eventually managed to drag the little fellow back to the Border Patrol vehicle in front of the bar where my buddies sat waiting for me.

The year of 1967 came, and with the new year came the big shake up we had been expecting at Stockton. Chief Long had sent word that there would be some transfers, and anyone desiring a transfer should put in a written request and it would be approved. Ted had the opportunity to transfer to San Francisco as an Investigator, and we asked him if he would accept. He told us no, that he had not lost anything in San Francisco and had no intention of transferring to San Francisco as an Investigator. He stated that he had attempted to get Nelson and Doran fired and that he had started that and he was going to see it through. A little while later, a telegram came, and this didn't give him a choice. It simply stated that he was transferred to El Paso, Texas.

While I was anticipating or contemplating whether or not to request a transfer, I received an offer of promotion. It was like all the other first offers, one of the most undesirable places. But the writing was on the wall, and even though it was to New York, I said yes, that I would accept the promotion and transfer. I gave a February date to enter on duty, and just kind of coasted along awaiting my orders and a transfer.

Andy decided he wanted to go to the northern border, and his transfer was approved. As things would work out, Doran would go to the southern border. Nelson would leave the Border Patrol for a better job with the Law Enforcement Assistance Association. Loy Taylor would eventually leave the Border Patrol for another agency. Mucher and Tex had been the least controversial people in the station, and they were the two remaining Border Patrolmen.

Dear Chief

My orders came, and I had my furniture picked up. My wife packed a U-Haul trailer with a few things we wanted to store in Mississippi and our dogs. I would come along later in my separate automobile. Jerry wouldn't be alone on her trip from California to Mississippi as her mother and a friend showed up the day before she was to leave and said they had come to California so they could travel back with her. At the last minute, I received word from the regional office that my transfer was delayed because I would have to be a witness in the trial of Miller. I was disappointed that my departure was delayed, but I moved into a motel room, thinking that it would only be for a few days. When Ted left on his transfer to El Paso, Joe Turner came over for a little while to be our Acting Station Senior until the person selected could arrange his transfer. We found out our new Station Senior would be named Ware.

My transfer was further delayed due to postponement of the Miller trial, so I ended up staying the motel until the middle of March. By then Howard Ware had entered on duty, and I worked two days for Howard as the Station Senior. My wife was getting more and more agitated because my transfer had been delayed. She called me a couple of times and finally called the sector and complained to Chief Long about my delay. He referred her to the Regional Office, and once again, she got no assistance. So she told him that the next phone call they received would not be from her, but from her Congressman. That must have stirred a little bit of interest because the Regional Officer decided that I could go ahead and transfer to New York, and I would fly back to attend the trial of Miller when it was rescheduled.

I remember my last day in the Patrol very well as I was working with Howard, and we found a small group of workers chopping weeds in one of the fields that grew a winter crop. As we proceeded through the fields, checking each person, an elderly man kept right on working as I came up beside him. I noticed him glance at me, then duck his head and keep right on going as if I didn't exist. Finally, I tapped him on the shoulder and asked him for his papers. With a trembling hand, he showed me an alien resident identification card. It was one of the old type, which were originally green. The name has continued even though the color of the cards has changed twice to blue and white; they still call them "green cards." There were many counterfeit alien registration cards of the old type, and some of the printing didn't exactly match the original colors. This was one of those type cards, the lettering was too yellow, and it could be detected as a counterfeit card immediately. That accounted for the old fellow's nervousness. I knew that he was carrying a counterfeit card, so I just told him without further question, "Go to the truck and wait for me." He obeyed my instructions, and as I went on through the field, I found another card just like the first one and told the bearer to go to the truck and wait for me. We continued to check the other workers in the field. By the time we got over to the truck, the two I had sent to the truck to wait had plenty of time to think over their situation. With very little prompting, they decided it was best to tell the truth and be sent back to Mexico.

I thought my last day in the Patrol was a good day as I had detected two counterfeit alien registration cards. The following day, four years and eleven months after I had entered the Border Patrol, I gave up the green uniform and headed for a new chapter in my Immigration career as an Investigator in New York City.

CHAPTER FOUR: NEW YORK

As I made my way across the United States, I had plenty of time for second thoughts about my decision to transfer to New York. I would take a couple of days en route in Greenville, where Jerry was waiting for me. She would drive one car, and I would drive the other car and pull the trailer. We checked the maps and decided which way we would go and made it very well to Knoxville, Tennessee. In the city of Knoxville, we were stopped by one of the longest trains I ever saw. Other cars were turning around and getting out of the long line waiting at the railroad crossing. Jerry signaled that she was turning around, and by the time I got turned around she was out of sight. In fact, that was the last time I would see her until the following Monday in New York City.

I had no idea that we would become separated. We had made no plans for such an event. In fact, some of her personal things were in the car I was driving. She had most of the cash in her car, and I was left with just a few dollars pocket change and an advance check for travel expenses in the amount of $1,200. I wasn't very worried at first. I felt sure that she would stop by the side of the road and wait for me to overtake her. Then I came to an intersection where I had to make a decision whether to take Highway 11-W or 11-E. As Jerry was not at the intersection waiting for me, I chose 11-E without too much concern, as I saw on the map that the highways rejoined at Bristol, near the Tennessee/Virginia state line. I reached the intersection, and there was still no Jerry waiting for me. Then I began to wonder what had happened to her. She was surely traveling faster than I was, pulling the trailer as I was, so she should have reached that intersection before I did. I wondered had she stopped on the way for something to eat or a break and I had passed her without realizing it, or had she taken 11-W and not reached the intersection yet. Surely she had. What should I do? I decided to keep going as I was moving fairly slowly. If she were behind me, she would soon overtake me. If she were ahead, she would surely stop and wait for me.

As I took inventory of the situation, I realized that I had all of Jerry's clothes in my car, and she had most of the money with her. So, I began to look for a bank that would cash my travel check. The two banks that I stopped at might as well have been on Mars the way they looked at me. No matter how good my identification was, neither of them would cash the $1,200 government check. I traveled along through Virginia, and I remember stopping for lunch and having some of the best lemon meringue pie that I ever tasted. The meringue must have been three inches thick, and the lemon filling was just right. The next day was Sunday. I remember going through Washington, DC pulling my U-Haul trailer down Pennsylvania Avenue, then proceeding into New Jersey and getting on the New Jersey Turnpike, which was a toll road. I didn't realize how often the tollbooths would be appearing, and as I put money in the first one, I realized I had better get off of that toll road because I might not have enough cash to buy gasoline and pay tolls and reach New York City. At the first opportunity, I exited and got back on a non-toll highway and proceeded through New Jersey and the Holland Tunnel into a different world.

The island of Manhattan, New York City, USA—there's no other place in the world like it. After the silence of the Holland Tunnel, coming above ground into Manhattan, I thought that was the noisiest place I had ever been. The taxis were bumper to bumper, horns were honking, and I really didn't know where I was going. I saw an arrow pointing "Up Town," and I thought, well, I should be Up Town, so I followed the arrow and ended up near 42nd Street. I found a parking lot where I could park the car and trailer because it would take up two spaces. I took inventory of my money and found that I had no more dollars and only 50 cents in change in my pocket. What would I do in Manhattan with 50 cents?

I looked around for a place that would hold my check as a security against my hotel expenses and was lucky enough to find a fellow southerner at the Holiday Inn in Manhattan. He told me to go ahead and check in and I could take care of the bill when I was ready to check out. As my shaving kit was in the car Jerry was driving, he also permitted me to put some shaving cream, razor and so forth on my bill at the hotel. So I spent Sunday night at the Holiday Inn and inquired how to get to the Immigration Office. They told me that it was in the opposite direction, that it was at the lower end of Manhattan near the Battery, and I could get there on the subway. I had enough money for the subway token and a thirty-cent hamburger.

At that time, the subway tokens only cost a dime. I arrived a few minutes late to work on Monday morning because I wasn't very familiar with the subway system and how many blocks I would have to walk, so by the time I got to the Immigration Office, Jerry had already called the office inquiring if I had arrived yet. So they were expecting me. I still had ten cents in my pocket. That was really cutting it close. I had left my car in the overnight parking lot, occupying two spaces, and that's where it would stay for several days.

Going to New York City had been a real experience. Now I was ready for a new type of duty, something completely different from the Border Patrol.

New York City is a large office, if not the largest; it is one of the largest in the Immigration Service, and I didn't expect to know anyone there. But the minute I got off the elevator and entered the Immigration Office, someone yelled at me, saying, "Hello, Sims." I turned to look at a total stranger, but the guy was smiling a big smile like he and I were long-lost buddies. He saw my quizzical look and said, "You don't remember, do you?" I said, "No, I'm afraid not." "Oh, you should remember. We were on a ship together in the Navy." I said, "No, we couldn't be onboard ship together; I was never in the Navy. I was in the Air Force." "Well, your name is Sims, isn't it?" I said, "Yes, I am Bruce Sims." He still didn't understand why I wouldn't acknowledge knowing him, and I don't think I ever convinced him that I was not the Sims he knew in the Navy. I learned that his name was George Tarrant, and as I thought about it more, he must have known a cousin of mine who was in the Navy and whom I resemble a great deal.

A receptionist found out that I was a new investigator just reporting for duty and escorted me into the office of the Assistant District Director for Investigations. The ADDI's secretary said, "Oh, Mr. Sims, your wife just called. We have been expecting you." She then told me which hotel Jerry had checked into, which turned out to be only four blocks from the Holiday Inn where I had spent the night. I also met another new Investigator who was just entering on duty that day whose name was York. We both were introduced to Mr. Wroblewski and were briefed about the duties of Investigators at New York. We were informed that the acceptable attire for an Investigator was a suit with preferably a white shirt and tie. We were questioned about our backgrounds, and both of us were coming from the Border Patrol. Mr. Wroblewski, whom we learned later would affectionately be called "The Robe," asked if we could write a report. Neither of us knew anything about writing reports, but said we guessed we could learn and were informed that we would both be assigned to the General Investigation Section and that our boss would be Martin J. Peters.

A couple of Investigators were waiting around outside the ADDI's door to learn where we would be assigned, and when we told them we would be working for Mr. Peters, they expressed their sympathy. At the time, I didn't know why. I met Mr. Peters, who was a very serious-appearing Supervisory Investigator. He again informed me of the way he expected me to dress and a little bit about the duties of a General Investigator. I spent a little while filling out necessary papers to get my pay started at New York with a promotion from Border Patrolman, GS-8 to Investigator GS-9. I was told to fill out a leave preference on a 3x5 card and give it back to Mr. Peters by the end of the day. I told him I hadn't thought about when I would prefer to take my leave and would like to talk it over with my wife before I made a preference. He informed me that he expected that card to be submitted to him by the end of the day.

I hastily filled out a card and handed it to him and told him I guess I would take a couple of weeks' leave in June and a couple more over the Christmas holidays. He looked at me and the card and told me that everyone wanted leave during June and December and that at New York City, leave was assigned on the basis of seniority. As I had ten years in the Air Force, several months as a civil service civilian guard, and five years in the Border Patrol, that suited me fine. I told him that was fine with me, that if anyone in his section had over 15 years' federal service, then they would get their choice; and if not, then that's the dates that I preferred. He said no more to me about leave. It turned out that it would make no difference in the long run, but that was my introduction to the General Investigation Section.

I looked around me and discovered that I would not be entirely alone, that a former Patrol Inspector from Brownsville named Bailey was already in New York; and one of my classmates, Jerry Donnely, was also assigned to the same General Investigation Section. At noon, Mr. Peters told me that for the rest of the day I would be working with

Jerry. He also explained that there were not enough desks for everyone to have an individual desk, so I would be sharing a desk with an Investigator named Weitz. Weitz was not in the office that particular time, but he would turn out to be a very helpful and friendly Investigator.

That afternoon Jerry and I hit the streets of New York with 12 inches of snow that had fallen the previous day. I remember we walked up and down Mott Street in Chinatown, and at the end of the day, I was just about frozen. My shoes and feet were soaked up to the knee. My pants were wet above the knee, and when I went back into the office, Mr. Peters saw my condition and exclaimed, "Oh, didn't you wear your rubbers?" Jerry was a little better prepared. He had knee-high overshoes and had adapted in his few short months at New York to the way of the native New Yorkers. He had purchased his narrow brimmed hat with a feather in the side, wore his suit, carried a briefcase, and I learned that was the typical dress for all of the Investigators and that inside their briefcases some carried a sandwich for lunch, a map of the City of New York, and their rubber overshoes.

As I only had one suite that I was wearing, I had to ask around, and I learned that almost every Investigator was involved in some kind of sideline and could advise you where to buy anything. One of them advised me that rather than buy expensive new suits, he knew a little shop where I could get a used suit or two and save a bunch of money. It seemed like a good idea, and I ended up at a little Jewish Haberdashery that sold me two used suits at a price I could afford. At noon, before going out into the snow, I had the opportunity to go to a bank behind our Immigration office at 20 West Broadway, and accompanied by an Investigator to vouch for me, the bank had cashed my travel check. I'd also called my wife at her hotel, and she asked me if I wanted her to check me out of the Holiday Inn and move into the hotel with her, as her room was a bit cheaper than the one I was in. That suited me fine. I was glad to hear from Jerry and learned that she had traveled from Knoxville, Tennessee into Manhattan, New York without any problems. She taxied over to the Holiday Inn and paid my bill and waited for me at her hotel with a surprise.

We had not lived in a place where it had snowed for many years, but she remembered making a snow cream. As I remembered when I was a child, my mother made snow cream out of fresh snow, some sugar and vanilla flavoring. She had found a deli that sold the necessary ingredients and had gone to the roof of the hotel to gather some fresh snow and mixed up some snow cream for me when I got home. The mixture had been setting in the container for a while before I got there, and some of it had a chance to melt. We looked into the pitcher, and it was covered with a black film of soot on top where the snow had melted and the soot had risen to the top. Our snow cream wasn't fit to drink. We learned that the snow in New York was so contaminated that no one ever ate it.

The twentieth day of March was my first day in New York City as an Investigator. The next day I met Abe Weitz, with whom I would share a desk. I spent most of the morning reading the Investigators Handbook, meeting a few more Investigators who came in and out of the office. At noon I was given my first case, which was concerning a Greek crewman who had been in the United States for almost seven years.

I didn't know much about a file, so Abe was real helpful in pointing out what material belonged on the left hand side of the file, what material belonged on the right hand side, and what to look for. This particular case was a "bag and baggage case" in that the man had already had a hearing and had been ordered deported, but had not reported for deportation. At that time, we received information from the Social Security Agency informing us where people with a certain Social Security number were employed. Our request for information had been returned with them showing an employment for this Greek crewman in Brooklyn. Investigator Bailey, who shared a desk nearby, told me that he had a car assigned to him for that afternoon and that he knew where the restaurant was located in Brooklyn and would take me over there if I wanted to go.

We proceeded to go to Brooklyn to the restaurant where the seaman worked. He was named Ionis, which I learned was John in Greek. I don't remember his last name. We approached the manager of the restaurant and asked if Ionis was on duty, and he, not knowing Ionis' background, told us, yes, that he was on duty and that was him, and he pointed him out to us.

There was a man with a bright red jacket and black silk pants working as a waiter, and before he knew what was happening, I told him that I was an Immigration officer and that he was under arrest and had him handcuffed. I took him back to the office, sat down to write out a little apprehension report, showing that I had apprehended him just like we did in the Border Patrol, and was promptly told that I was doing it all wrong. First thing Mr. Peters asked me was, where was my Warrant of Arrest? I told him that we didn't use Warrants of Arrest in the Border Patrol. He very quickly told me that I was no longer in the Border Patrol and that at New York City, when we went out to arrest a person, we would get a Warrant of Arrest in advance. Bailey came to my defense and told Mr. Peters that we were not sure we would be arresting Ionis and had no time to get the Warrant of Arrest after we found that he was there. I then learned how to fill out the proper reports, and Mr. Ionis was eventually deported back to Greece, just before he had been in the United States for seven years and could have applied for suspension of deportation.

 A few days later, I thought I was prepared to go out and work the field on my own without someone else taking me. Mr. Peters had issued me a pocket full of subway tokens, which were also good for use on the buses. He had assigned me several cases, all located in the Bedford-Styvesant area, which was a formerly Jewish neighborhood, but in recent years had been taken over by blacks and a lot of people from the West Indies, Jamaica, Trinidad and other islands, who were living in Bedford-Styvesant. My first cases were the very simplest kind, called "locate cases" and involved relocating or verifying the departure of an alien who had been granted the opportunity to leave the United States voluntarily by a certain date for whom we could not verify the departure.

 Every morning I would have several questions to ask my desk mate, Abe. And Abe would very patiently give me a lengthy explanation of everything asked him. In fact, his answer went beyond the question I had asked, and he would realize that he had lost my attention and abruptly say, "Enough said." Abe was a GS-9 Investigator who had been one of the Investigator Trainees we had seen at Port Isabel in the fall of 1962. I learned that most of the Trainee Investigators had already been promoted to GS-11, and some of them were even GS-12's assigned to the Fraud Section. Investigators in the Fraud Section had appealed to the Civil Service Commission to be upgraded from GS-11 Field Grade Investigator to

GS-12 and won their appeal. So everyone in that section was a GS-12.

There was one other Investigator assigned to our squad under Mr. Peters who was still a GS-9, and I wondered why he had not been promoted to a higher grade along with most of the other trainees form the class of '62. I learned at our squad meetings that it must have been a personality conflict and that Mr. Peters had an intense dislike for Investigator Weitz. It was evidenced when he would read a memorandum telling us something the regional office had sent down via memorandum to be dispensed to the Investigators. When Abe would find a point he didn't understand or didn't agree with, he would interrupt Mr. Peters by saying, "Now, Marty." You could see the redness come out of Mr. Peters' collar, go up around his ears, across his forehead, and he would almost get apoplectic every time he was interrupted by Abe saying, "Now, Marty."

Another thing I learned was that Mr. Peters was reluctant to let the investigators use an Immigration car. If we were going to use a car, we had to fill out a 3x5 card listing the justification of how long we wanted to use the car and what cases we would be working and why we needed the car. I also learned that he did not want to issue pistols to Investigators. This seemed strange to me since we had a weapon assigned to us in the Border Patrol, which we kept with us all the time. In fact, some of the men had bought their own and had received permission to carry their own pistol as a service weapon. I believed that in New York, especially, we might need the weapon for our own protection. Once again, I was told when I requested that I be issued a pistol to fill out a 3x5 card and to submit my reasons why I thought I needed to carry a pistol in New York City. I inquired, and Abe told me the reason behind Mr. Peters' reluctance to issue the pistols. It seemed that one of the Investigators had been working his cases on public transportation and had gone to sleep on the bus. When he awoke, he had realized he had just passed the stop where he wanted to get off and yelled at the driver to stop the bus and let him off. The bus driver had told him that he would stop at the next stop and he could get off there. The Investigator told him, no, to stop and let him off right then and there. When the bus driver refused, he had pulled a pistol and forced him to stop the bus so he could get off between stops. It was determined who the Investigator was, and as a result, instead of punishing the Investigator who had threatened the driver, all Investigators gave up their weapons and would only be issued a weapon on an individual basis if Mr. Peters decided one was needed.

During that first week, when I was becoming oriented to New York City, Jerry had not been idle. She had been checking the paper for apartments and had looked at a couple before finding one she liked in the Astoria section of Queens. Since she told me she had found one she liked, would I take a look at it, I told her if it suited her, it certainly suited me. The following weekend we left the hotel and moved into our new apartment. The apartment was not supposed to be available until the first of the month, but Jerry learned the Yankee ways in a hurry. Someone told her to give the building superintendent a few dollars, and we could move in early. I retrieved my car with the U-Haul trailer from the parking lot. It had remained somehow undisturbed for a week. Maybe the twelve inches of snow that fell that week on top of the earlier snow kept the vandals at bay. Astoria turned out to be a good section of the city to live in. I learned the city was ethnically divided, and Astoria had been the Greek section of the city. I learned that the Jewish and Italian families lived in Williamsburg. The West Indies and blacks lived in Bedford-Styvesant, where my casework was located. The blacks and Puerto Ricans gravitated into Harlem, while the South Americans congregated in Elmhurst, and Dominicans lived in Corona.

During my first week as Mr. Peters gradually assigned me a caseload, I had time to accompany my desk mate, Abe, on his cases in Williamsburg and go with other Investigators to Brooklyn. They would go through Bedford-Styvesant and help me make my few stops, and I realized how difficult it would be to work the Bedford-Styvesant area using public transportation. The second week I believed that I needed the use of a car, and one morning I filled out my 3x5 card requesting that I be authorized the use of a car for that particular day, turned the 3x5 card in to Mr. Peters, who gave it a cursory glance and said it did not contain enough justification for him to authorize the use of a car. No one had asked me to accompany them into the field that day, so I sat around the office reading the Investigator's Handbook, looking over the few files that I had, then filled out another 3x5 card and gave it to Mr. Peters. He looked it over and again rejected it, saying it did not have enough justification. I went back to my desk, fiddled around awhile longer, took a coffee break, turned in my third request for authorization to use a car, and by then, the morning was gone. And evidently Mr. Peters decided I wasn't going to leave the office without the car, so he reluctantly okayed the use of a car.

Things went fairly well as I got into the swing of being an Investigator in New York City. Each time I used a government car, Mr. Peters cautioned me about being careful, and his concern was justified within the first month. I had asked Jim Gennette to go with me to Brooklyn. I was driving when I turned down a one-way street that still had snow and ice on it; I realized I had made a mistake. The street I had just turned down was one-way with cars parked on both sides, and there was a solid sheet of ice. There was no opportunity for me to guide the sliding car into the curb to stop it. I simply had to steer it down the street, between the cars, into an intersection where a car was stopped for the red light. I slid right into the back of the car, causing slight damage to the other car's trunk. The first thing I thought of was, well, here I go again, another "Dear Chief" memo explaining this accident.

The occupants of the car I had just hit turned out to be a priest with a teenage boy as a passenger, and I was lucky that I also had Jim Gennette as a passenger. I filled out the necessary accident report, wrote my memo, and time passed by until one day Mr. Peters came to me and asked, "Bruce, what about that other car in that accident you had?" I explained to him that there had only been the government car and one other car. He told me that the priest in the other car was claiming damages to the front fender of his car, saying that my car had bumped him into another and caused damage to the fender. Jim verified that there was no other car involved. I don't know if the government ever paid for the repair to the priest's front fender or not. Although I was only responsible for the small dent in his trunk, it's my guess that the service paid him everything that he asked for.

I enjoyed working with Jim Gennette on the few occasions that we worked together. We had something in common. We had both had Roland Lomblot as a Station Senior in the Border Patrol. I had the opportunity to ask him if it was true what we had heard about

Dear Chief

the way Roland ran his station at Falfurrias, Texas, and Jim confirmed that whatever we had heard about Roland was probably correct.

In April, after I had been in New York City only a month, fate would determine when I would use my annual leave. I received a phone call from my brother-in-law in Hiawassee, Georgia saying he had bad news. My father was dead. I used emergency annual leave to attend his funeral and spend a few days with my mother. Upon returning to New York City, I felt the anguish of having to return to that place, which I felt every time I left the city and returned, even if I was only away for weekend reserve duty.

As the weeks went by, I learned the subtleties of working in New York City. We were expected to work a couple of hours overtime each day, and before the end of the shift, we were required to call the office and tell Mr. Peters where we were working and what case numbers we were working on. He would also ask, "What is the number of the phone you are calling from?" One of my buddies told me to always say I was calling from a pay phone and I didn't know the number because it was torn off of the phone. This was an acceptable answer as the number was missing from most of the phones and, in fact, it was hard to find a pay phone in the city that did not have the speaker torn off or had not been broken into for the coins to be stolen.

It was hard to get used to the callousness one encountered in the city. I remember seeing the first wino with his throat slit and how the people were stepping over or around him as he lay sprawled on the sidewalk and a non-caring policeman telling them to move on. I remember another callous situation that occurred one Sunday. That weekend, on Friday, I had gone directly home without going back to the office on Friday evening and neglected to fill out my time and attendance report, which Mr. Peters expected to be on his desk so he could look at them the first thing Monday morning. I decided to go back to the office on Sunday and prepare the paperwork so he wouldn't be looking for me on Monday morning. I was riding the subway between stations in Manhattan when the train stopped. It was not unusual for the train to stop before reaching the station in weekday rush hour traffic. But it was unusual for one to stop between stations on Sunday. I was in the second car form the front of the train, and a few people came back from the first car into the second car while the train was stopped.

I was curious as to why we had stopped, so I went in the first car and noticed the front door to the train was standing open and the engineer was not in the cab. I looked over the front of the train just in time to see a transit authority policeman and the train conductor pulling a body from underneath the train. He was laying parallel between the tracks, and one person had one arm and one had the other. They pulled him from beneath the train and lifted him up into the first car where I was standing. I asked the policeman, "Is he dead?" The policeman just shook his head and said, "I don't know." I knelt down beside the man lying on the floor of the train while the conductor got back into his cab and started the train moving. The policeman stood over me watching, but I could not detect whether there was a pulse or whether the person was breathing or not. I noticed that there were no bruises or marks or mangled limbs, and it was possible that a person lying between the tracks could have the train pas over him without being hit. The policeman then told me to go back to the other car. I did as I was told, but I watched to see what he and the conductor would do with the man lying on the floor. In a few minutes, we arrived at the next station. The body hadn't moved. It appeared lifeless, but the policeman didn't know, and I didn't know, so I watched to see what they would do. The train stopped with the front car at the very far end of the station platform. The front car door opened. The policeman got the man by the feet. The conductor got him by his arms, and they carried him out of the train and laid him on the concrete platform of the station. The passengers boarded. The policeman and the conductor boarded, and the train sped away. I don't know until this day if that person was dead or alive, or if anyone was notified that he was lying on the station floor. To me, it was just another example of New York callousness.

The investigative work at New York City consisted of every type conducted by I&NS Investigators. It was divided by type, with each type assigned a grade of Investigator, ranging from subversive through criminal, which was called "CIN," standing for criminal, immoral, and narcotic. Then Fraud, then General Investigations, then what the Border Patrol had called "city scout" was known as "Area Control." Coastal Control was the type of work performed by

Inspectors boarding ships and looking for stowaways, control of deserted crewmen, and was the smallest unit. The Area Control work was considered the basic type and was performed by mostly GS-9 Investigators with GS-11 Team Leaders and a GS-12 Supervisor. The General Section, to which I was assigned, did locate cases with a few cases considered more difficult and called "dual action cases" assigned a few dual action cases so we could gain experience. The fraud Section, as I mentioned earlier, had recently been upgraded to GS-12 after appealing to the Civil Service Commission who agreed that their work was of a difficulty commensurate with a GS-12 grade. All of these sections had a supervisor. Then there was the Assistant District Director and Deputy District Director, and all the problems we encountered were presented at this level before ever reaching the District Director, who was a diminutive person whom we seldom saw unless we happened to ride the same elevator. District Directors were such supreme beings that you never got to know them. P.A. Esperdy was no exception.

    With a lot of assistance and advice from my desk partner, Abe Weitz, and what I was learning from working with the other Investigators, I was getting into the swing of things at New York City. It took me a long time to realize that the ten closings Mr. Peters wanted each month could be cases placed in what we called "pending inactive." That meant we would do our agency checks and interview someone at the previous known addresses, and if we had no further information, we would place the case in "pending inactive." This didn't seem like a desirable thing to do, and I held off on them as long as I cold. I believed that those people were still out there, or possibly had departed, and we could either find them or verify their departure. But Mr. Peters kept a close look on my cases and told me that some of them world be wasting my time and to go ahead and put them in the "pending inactive" category.

    I learned that an older investigator, Ted Mort, was working the same area in Bedford-Styvesant that I was working, so we teamed up and used a car to work as a team in that area. Ted claimed he grew up in Brooklyn and knew the area we were working, so he always insisted on driving. I didn't know anything about the area, so I sat in the passenger's seat with my city map open and tried to help Ted find the addresses we were looking for. He was going by memory, and I was going by what was printed in the map, which showed the one-way streets. I was constantly telling Ted, "Ted, we have to go two more blocks in order to get on the right direction," or "Turn here, Ted." He paid very little attention to me, and we were constantly having to make unnecessary distances to get to the address we were looking for. Ted also drove very slow, and when I mentioned it to him, he was afraid, he said, that children playing in the street would dart out in front of him. He also didn't look very far ahead of the car and would come up behind the cars that were double parked, and then cars passing on our left side wouldn't let us get back into the stream of traffic, and I fidgeted all day long, every time I worked with Ted.

Ted's career extended back several years, and the highlight that he talked to me most about was what they called "The drive of '54." In 1954, Immigration Officers congregated at the far reaches of the Rio Grande Valley and worked their way toward the border, rounding up thousands of illegal aliens in the process.

Ted lived on Long Island, beyond the reaches of the elevated train, so it was quite a commute for him to come to work. Each day he drove to the last stop on the subway system, parked his car, and rode the subway to our Manhattan office, where we met, got a government car and went back to Brooklyn to work. At least three times when Ted got off duty and went back to retrieve his car, it had been stolen. Evidently some teenagers just wanted to joyride and would leave his car somewhere within a few blocks from where they had stolen it. The last time I remember his car being stolen, we thought it was gone for good. He searched the area for several blocks around where he had left the car, but couldn't find it. It was several days later when he received a call from the police department saying the car had been located in a parking garage and would he please come and retrieve it.

One morning I came to the office and found a typewriter that was not being used, and thought I would do a quick one-paragraph report for a verified departure that I had been fortunate enough to learn about through the previous day's investigation when relatives of an alien I was looking for told me the date and flight number my subject had departed on. I then went to our microfilm records section, checked the departure for the airline they had told me about, and sure enough, there was a copy of her departure record. I was going to type the report myself and save the three weeks' delay that was usual for reports we sent to the stenographic pool. As I typed the report, Mr. Peters saw me and in a few minutes came over to my desk, looked over my shoulder and said, "What are you doing?" I told him that I was doing a little short closing report, verifying the departure of an alien. He reminded me that our reports should be dictated, then turned in to the steno pool where a stenographer would listen to the tape and type the report, and we would eventually get the typed report and be able to close the case.

I have mentioned that our agency reports were a part of our investigation and consisted of a form requesting information from the Social Security Administration to see if the alien had applied for a Social Security card, and if so, we might be able to get a new address. We also did postal checks, and the form going to Social Security was filled out in longhand and submitted to the steno pool, where, after another three weeks' wait, we would get the typed form back and would then send it to the SSA. This seemed like duplication of effort to have a stenographer do the work that we had just done in longhand, and I mentioned to Mr. Peters that someone should suggest that we print the information legibly and submit it directly to Social Security without going through the typing pool. He discouraged me, saying that that had been thought of and suggested many times over the years and was not acceptable.

I couldn't understand that rationale and read up on the proper procedure for submitting a suggestion. I learned that it could be submitted directly to the involved agency without going through my supervisor, whom I knew would turn thumbs down on my idea. I prepared my memorandum suggesting that they accept legibly printed information requests. After a few weeks I was told that the suggestion was being favorably considered and I would hear from them again. After a few more weeks, the suggestion was adopted, and I was awarded a check for $50, less $6 tax for my suggestion. This was very encouraging, and some time later I had another, what I considered, good idea, worthy of a suggestion.

This suggestion involved bypassing the records section that received all incoming mail, including replies from other agencies. They then checked the alien number to see if the case was assigned to an investigator, and if so, they would then deliver in the daily distribution the returned agency checked forms. This entailed thousands of hours of clerical research, and I believed that the investigator could somehow identify himself, and the mail could be brought directly to him. Then, if he no longer had the file, it could go back to the records room, and the file clerk could place it in the file on the shelf. I suggested that we use a letter for the section of investigation that we worked. In my case, General Investigations would be "g", Fraud would be "f", and so on, for each section, followed by a slash and the Investigator's initials; so on the outgoing correspondence on the right hand corner, I would put "G/BS." Then when the incoming document was received in the mailroom, they immediately knew that this went to General Investigations, and it would come to me. Once again, I was not received warmly with this suggestion, but I submitted it anyway. After another lengthy wait, I again was informed that the suggestion was acceptable. I received another award for this suggestion in the amount of $50, but this time they didn't deduct the tax.

  Christmas holidays came, and we were having somewhat of a Christmas party. We got together in the Investigation Section, and our Supervisors wished us a Merry Christmas and warned us to have a safe holiday, that they wanted us back for the coming year, and we got a visit from the District Director, who gave us a very unusual Christmas message. It was obvious from his comments that he had not been pleased with the Investigators of the Fraud Section being upgraded by the Civil Service Commission to GS-12, and he left us with a comment that something had happened in the Immigration Service that never should have happened. Promotions were something for the Service to approve or disapprove and the way it had happened should never have happened, and it was up to the Supervisors to make sure that it never happened again. That was the strangest Christmas message I had ever heard.

  We GS-9 Investigators learned that there had been other appeals to the Civil Service Commission in offices such as New Orleans, where the Gs-9 Investigators had been upgraded to GS-11. We thought being in the biggest office in the Service, having a heavy caseload, that we also deserved upgrading form GS-9 go GS-11. We discussed the situation and decided that many of us would appeal. Almost all GS-9 Investigators signed the appeal, and then it was up to us to prove to a representative of the Civil Service Commission that our work indeed entitled us to an upgrade. We were given a specific date to have our justification prepared and meet with the Civil Service Commission representative. I just barely had a year at New York, so I was probably one of the least qualified to be upgraded, so I looked to the other Investigators who had more experience than I to lead the way in preparing a justification. Mr. Peters kept an eye on what we were doing and told us that he could not help us on our appeal, but he wished us well.

Probably the best qualified Investigator that I hoped would give good advice and be justified in an upgrade so the rest of us could ride in on his coattails, was not interested in our appeal as he learned that he was being promoted back to the Border Patrol and gave us no assistance.

Some of the others just weren't willing to put out the effort to write a valid justification, and when the date for our meeting with the Civil Service representative came, I bore the biggest burden of proving that we were justified. I based my justification on the fact that we had hundreds of cases on people who entered the United States without a Visa and were on their way, usually, to Canada. These were called "transients" without Visas, and we abbreviated it TRWOV, and called them "Trwovs." One of the General Investigators had more of these cases assigned, and we had what was called "Dual action cases," but we only had a few of them. We were assigned those for our training, according to our Supervisor. The Civil Service representative listened to my story, looked at my cases, and said we would learn of his decision later on, as his decision came back to us through official channels. When the decision came, it was no surprise to me that we were not upgraded. We were not even given a decision on what percentage of our work was at the higher level. The decision simply stated that our request was unjustified. So much for the Civil Service appeals process.

After I had been in New York for a year working almost exclusively the Bedford-Styvesant area, I noticed that there were newer Investigators. Some of them had come off the street, as we called it. They were retired New York City policemen who had retired at an early age with 20 years' service on the Police Department, and as they were from New York, they wanted to be Investigators for the

Immigration and Naturalization Service and were hired as Investigator Trainees. I approached Mr. Peters and told him that I believed that I should be given a little better area to work, as I had been there longer than these Trainee Investigators, and surprisingly, without saying anything, he just started assigning me cases outside the Bedford-Styvesant area. That way I got to work with different Investigators, and there was always something I could learn, either something I wanted to remember to do to assist me, or in some cases something I would learn not to do.

  When I did my cases I was always alert to encountering other illegal aliens. Chances were good that an alien from South America coming to visit other aliens from South America would be living with other illegal aliens. Some of the older investigators I worked with were only interested in learning a name so they could put it on their report, and they never asked the person they were interviewing their own status. They would just ask, "You're a citizen, aren't you?" and the person would say, "Si, Senor." I went a step further and often irritated my older partner. Instead of suggesting that they were a citizen, I would ask to see their documents, which resulted in locating several other illegal aliens. The procedure was usually to look at their passport, since most of them had entered as tourists or students and simply neglected to go home. We would then take the passport and give the alien a business card with an appointment date to come to the Immigration Office for processing by the Area Control Squad. We would put the passport in a large manila envelope the Area Control Supervisor kept for that purpose, with a slip of paper attached showing the date and time the alien would be in for processing. This worked out pretty good for everyone, as we didn't have to spend much time writing the apprehension report ourselves. On one of the cases I worked, I was unable to locate the alien and was putting the case in pending inactive status. I got back the typed report from the typing pool and submitted it to Mr. Peters for his signature, so he could count the case as statistically closed. As usual, he was going over it with a fine tooth comb. I had searched the request for the extension of stay, and found where the subject had been granted an extension of stay. On the form was the information where the person had been staying. They had written in Spanish "primos." Mr. Peters read the report, handed it back to me and told me that he didn't believe I had completed it, that he couldn't find any place in the report where I had interviewed the Primos family. I got a chuckle out of this, and I explained to him that primos was Spanish for cousins. She had indicated she was staying with cousins. Mr. Peters got a little red around the ears as he sometimes did, mostly at the monthly information meetings, and I thought even Mr. Peters still can learn something.

As my caseload was extended further and further away from Bedford-Styvesant, I worked with other Investigators. One of the Investigators I really enjoyed working with in the Manhattan area was Investigator Zoukas. I went with Zoukas to an area near Central Park, looking for an alien from Jamaica. We went to the apartment building and found an elderly lady who was the building superintendent. Mr. Zoukas asked her about the person we were looking for, and she replied that she didn't know who we were talking about "dear." Mr. Zoukas "deared" her right back and said, "Yes, dear, you must know who we are talking about because he's still getting his mail at this address." She insisted, "No, dear, there's no one like that living at this address." And we could see that she wasn't going to tell us anything. As we reached the ground floor, started to depart the building, a black man was just entering the front door. He saw us, made an about face and ran down the street just as hard as he could run with Zoukas in hot pursuit, right on his heels. This happened so suddenly that I hardly realized what was going on and was some distance behind as we raced down the street. About a block and a half from the building, Zoukas finally overtook the guy, grabbed him by an arm, and they were going around and around in the middle of the street when I caught up and grabbed the man by the other arm.

I didn't know what we had just caught, and the man was very indignant, saying, "Who are you and what do you want with me?" and so on. Zoukas explained to him that we were Immigration Officers and believed he was the person we were looking for, and asked him for identification. The man claimed that he was not carrying any identification but he was a United States citizen from North Carolina. I was a bit concerned that we had actually apprehended a United States citizen, but as the man continued in his protestation that he was not the person we were looking for, he finally said, "Tell me what is going on here, Mohn." When I heard that man pronounced with an "o" as Mohn instead of man, I was sure happy and told him, "Well, Mohn, you sure aren't from North Carolina." Since he had no identification, Mr. Zoukas told him that we would probably have to take him down to the Immigration Office and take his fingerprints as a way of positively identifying him. He got in the car with us, in the back seat. We started towards the Immigration Office, and after a few minutes, he spoke to Mr. Zoukas calling him by his last name. Zoukas turned around and looked at him and said, "How do you know my last name? I didn't tell you." He then said he wanted to tell the truth, that he really was the person we were looking for, and that one day he had come to the Immigration Office to get forms to request an extension of stay, and that he had seen Mr. Zoukas, who was red-headed and very memorable, and that he had heard his name, but Mr. Zoukas had not seen him.

One of the things I liked about working with Zoukas was, although he was a conscientious Investigator, he took a lunch break every day. We would usually get a hero sandwich at a delicatessen, then drive several blocks into mid Manhattan, where all of the women were coming out of the office buildings on their lunch breaks. We would sit in front of one of those large office buildings and enjoy the sight as we ate our sandwich and drank our soda pop. Zoukas explained that it was stressful working in Manhattan and that we needed a few minutes of therapy.

I understood that stressful comment, as it was more than a joke, that if an Investigator stopped for a pack of cigarettes or a cup of coffee at a delicatessen, when he came back outside, his car would have been towed away by police or stripped by vandals. We usually worked in teams of two, and we really needed three: two to go inside, and one to stay outside and watch the car.

I also worked a lot with Richard Cheadle. Richard was enthusiastic about our work and enjoyed checking Chinese restaurants. One of the restaurants that we checked had some illegal aliens who hid in the cellar, and some who ran out the door and were pursued by Richard while I apprehended those that were trapped in a basement. Richard said that the one he brought back at the end of the chase had run two city blocks holding a bowl of rice that he never put down and never spilled a grain of rice during the chase.

On another occasion, we checked a Chinese restaurant and found four Chinese who did not have their alien registration cards in their possession, pretending to be legal residents. We put the four of them in the car, told them we would have to take them to their residence to see the registration card and make sure they were legal and proceeded on to the first address. I went inside with the alien who, sure enough, was a resident alien. I examined his card and warned him that he was required to carry it. We went on to the next spot. This time Richard went inside; same thing, he saw the card, the alien was legal and was warned that he was required to carry the card. We then went to the third address. This alien also was a legal resident, but since he spoke English and the remaining Chinese did not speak English, he agreed that if we would take him back by the restaurant, that he would go with us to the fourth address and be our interpreter. I stayed in the car while Richard accompanied the fourth alien to an upstairs apartment.

It seemed that they always lived on the sixth floor of an apartment building with no elevator. The three were gone for what seemed to me an extraordinary amount of time. Then I saw the Chinese that I had checked last come running out of the building back to the car saying in a breathless voice, "Come quick, you come quick. He wrestling with boy. You come quick. He wrestling with the boy." I jumped out of the car and ran up the six stories of stairs and found Richard at the head of the stairs, hanging on to one arm of the boy who was hanging on to the stair railing with his free hand. Richard would then grasp the hand he was holding to the banister with, and it would take all his strength to break that hand loose. The alien would then catch on with the other hand. When I reached the head of the stairs, we quickly subdued the young man and put handcuffs on him.

Then Richard told me that he was an illegal alien who had jumped ship and who wanted to be released and had offered Richard $50 as a bribe to let him go. Richard stuck the money in his pocket, but had no intention of accepting a bribe or letting the alien go, then tried to take him back downstairs to the car. The boy thought that by keeping the bribe money Richard should let him go and was resisting with all his power.

We returned to the office, called a U.S. Attorney about the attempted bribe, and he decided there was not sufficient evidence since I had not been in the building and been an eyewitness to the attempted bribe, that we would not prosecute the alien. We would just go ahead and deport him. We thought nothing else about this case for several weeks. Later I was in the detention facility in our building and saw the alien was still there. I inquired as to why he had not been deported. I was told there was pending investigation, as the alien had alleged that the Investigators who caught him had stolen his $50. As the money would not be needed as evidence, the District Attorney had suggested that Richard donate it to the Immigration Welfare Fund, and the investigation was terminated once Richard showed the receipt.

Although I preferred to work with a partner, I still had to do quite a bit of my work alone. Some of this was in the Elmherst area, which was convenient to Astoria where I lived, and I could leave the apartment and go directly to the area. I wanted to work by subway or elevated train, whichever the case might be, and then proceed to the office later in the day. I also did quite a bit of work to get my overtime on the way home. One of those locations in Elmherst where I had to check an employment was a grocery store. I figured that the grocery store would employ more than one illegal alien, and the one I was looking for was long gone. In anticipation of what would happen, and since I was by myself that day, I went to the store manager's office, which was in front of the checkout registers in a little cubicle to the side of the building. As I approached his office, I noticed the curious stare from the checkout and bagboys. I told the manager I would be right back. I rushed out the entrance round the side of the building and reached the back door just in time to grab one Colombian as he ran from the building. I then went back with my alien in custody. I verified what I already knew, that the person I was looking for was no longer there, and proceeded to do as Mr. Peters had told me that I could do: that was to take an apprehended alien to our office on the public transportation system. When I got there and told the other Investigators in my squad what had happened, they teased me and told me that I was the only Investigator they had ever known who could surround a building by himself.

Elmherst was becoming a gathering spot for aliens from every South American country who would get together in the local bars where they all claimed to be Puerto Ricans. They would get a big laugh when another South American would enter the bar, and someone would say, "Here comes another Puerto Rican." Then everyone would hee haw!

Another time in Elmherst while working by myself I decided to enter a small employment office, which was on the second floor on a street lined with small street-level shops where the owners sometimes stood in the doorway. I climbed the stairs to the second floor to the employment office. The receptionist wanted to assist me. I told her loud enough for the people in the office to hear that I was an Immigration Officer who just wanted to look around at the people she was hiring. My real purpose was to see who would make a hasty departure from the office once they heard the word immigration, and I wasn't disappointed. Two or three of them immediately headed for the door, and I followed them downstairs and thought I might be able to catch a young man who was carrying a large package. He saw I was coming down the stairs behind them, and he started down the street as hard as he could run, with me hot on his heels. He was like the Chinaman Richard Cheadle chased for two blocks who refused to put down his bowl of rice. He refused to put down his package. It only took about a block to catch up with him, and as I came escorting him back with one hand on his belt, the shopkeepers all were calling to each other, "Look at that, look at that, he caught that boy." Three or four of them began applauding, saying, "That's the way to go." I knew they had no idea that I was an Immigration Officer chasing an alien. I'm sure they thought I was catching a shoplifter. The young man who had given himself away by running when he heard the word immigration turned out to be an illegal alien from Colombia. The bulky package he was carrying, which weighed almost nothing turned out to be a lampshade.

One day Mr. Peters called Investigator Meyers and me into his office. He told us that he had a request for assistance from the Australian Consul's Office, and that we should go to the office and talk to the Consular Officer and see if we could assist him. We found the Australian Consul. He talked to us and explained that there was a woman, a citizen of Australia, who had become stranded in New York City with no money and that they had been giving her a weekly handout until the money they had to give her was exhausted. She was unwilling to leave New York City. They said that she would be in their office within a few minutes. In fact, she was already waiting in the outer waiting room. They pointed her out to us so we would know what she looked like. The Consul also requested that we wait until she had left the building before we took her into custody, so it would not appear that he had anything to do with having her removed from the United States.

We got a look at her so that we could identify her. We followed her out onto the street. She immediately entered a building next to the Consulate building. The building she entered was about 10 to 12 stories high. We followed her into the building, saw that she was getting on the elevator, and we rushed to get into the elevator with her. She punched the top floor button, and we were curious to see what she would do. So we rode up the elevator with her. She was carrying a rather large handbag. We got off the elevator, and she searched for an exit to the roof. There were other people going to the roof as well. She took a small camera from her bag and stepped to the edge of the roof as if she were taking pictures. She then stepped up onto the ledge, and just as she was tilting forward, Investigator Meyers grabbed her coattail and pulled her back onto the roof.

She was a very despondent person. The Australian Consulate had given her fifteen dollars and told her that was the last money they could give her. We proceeded to write an apprehension report and proceed with deportation proceedings against her, and then forgot about her. It was up to the Deportation Section to see that she was sent back to Australia. We learned about two weeks later from our Immigration Office in Frankfurt, Germany that there was a lady in the airport from Australia who had gotten off a plane and had been sitting in the airport terminal for three days. They wanted to know what we could tell them about her. I could only hope things turned out well for her.

As I worked more and more in the areas outside Bedford-Styvesant, I thought conditions were improving. Mr. Peters was now letting us sign for our weapons for a two-week period. He was authorizing overnight use of the car for periods as long as a week at a time. I was still leaving the city one weekend each month for Reserve Duty at McGuire Air Force Base in New Jersey.

Other things in the United States were changing. For instance, as America was more and more involved in the Vietnam War, it became unpopular with the American people, and there were anti-war demonstrations in the major cities and in Washington, DC. Several Investigators from New York City and from other cities were sent on detail to Washington to assist the U.S. Marshals in guarding the White House and the Pentagon. My good friend, Richard Cheadle, was one of those facing the demonstrators at the Pentagon. The demonstrators became violent and were throwing everything they could get their hands on at the people guarding the Pentagon. When Richard came back from his detail with a patch over one eye, he explained that he had been hit in the eye by a steel pipe thrown by a demonstrator. I thought Richard would be displeased with what had happened to him, but instead he decided that Secret Service work would be more interesting to him than what he was doing in the Immigration Service. His application for employment with the Secret Service was accepted, and I would lose one of my best working companions.

    They replaced Richard, and I began working more and more with a retired New York City policeman, who I though was the best of the bunch that Immigration had hired. Jack Stearn and I became constant working buddies, and we worked all over the city, including trips outside of the city to Upstate New York. Anything outside the city limits was considered Upstate. We also worked the Long Island area. Jack was one of the most energetic Investigators I ever knew. In fact, he almost ran me into the ground. When we would be going to a sixth floor walk-up, Jack would take the steps two at a time and leave me panting along behind him before we reached the sixth floor. He really believed, as I did, that the most important work we could do, since we could not prevent illegal entry of aliens, was to apprehend those that were already here. I believe with concerted effort in apprehending aliens and enforcing their departure, we could do away with most of the casework. If we could catch them before they married and filed application for their benefits, we could eliminate some of the marriage fraud, and we wouldn't have so many locate cases, after they have requested and been granted voluntary departure, and then refused to leave.

    One morning on arriving at the office, Mr. Peters called me into his cubicle to inform me that I was being sent to the Journeyman Investigators School at the Border Patrol Academy at Port Isabel, Texas. As any opportunity to leave the city was welcome, I immediately saw this as a chance for my wife to visit her family in Mississippi while I attended the Academy. I told Mr. Peters that I would like to drive from New York to Port Isabel, and he informed me that no one had ever driven from New York to attend the Journeyman school, that they always flew. I insisted that I be given an opportunity to drive or I wouldn't go to the Journeyman school. After some bit of reluctance, Mr. Peters agreed to let me go. I could only claim the time as travel time that the other Investigators used to travel by public carrier. I stated that was all right with me, that I would use a day of annual leave before the day of travel, and another day of annual leave while returning to New York.

Jerry and I put our Chihuahuas in the car and headed south, she to Greenville, Mississippi, and me to Port Isabel, Texas. I knew from my previous Border Patrol work at Harlingen and attending the academy at Port Isabel, that it was about 26 miles from the end of nowhere, and I didn't want to be stranded out there with no transportation.

Since I had to go through Harlingen, Texas to get to Port Isabel, I stopped at the Border Patrol Office to see who of my old Border Patrol buddies were on duty. I visited with them for a little while and met three other Investigators who had flown into Harlingen and had caught a cab down to the Border Patrol Office to ask for transportation out to Port Isabel. I bundled their luggage into the car, and the four of us climbed aboard and reported to the academy.

There were Investigators from all over the United States. One of them was my former Border Patrol friend from Harlingen, Robert McCord, who had left Harlingen on the same weekend that I left Harlingen in 1966. He was going to San Francisco as an Investigator while I was going to Stockton, California on a transfer. I was also glad to meet the other Investigators, whom I would work with later at other stations.

I don't remember very much about the Investigator school, except there was a lot of beer drunk, although I didn't drink beer, and a lot of singalongs in the evening after classes, as there was nothing else to do. It seemed like the more the guys drank, the better their singing sounded. One of those playing the guitar was Paul Haggard from the Chicago office. Some of those singalongs lasted late into the night, and I thought I might as well participate because there was no way to get away from the noise.

After attending the Journeyman Investigator School, I began to think about promotion to Grade 11 Investigator. The year 1969 would be bad for Investigators as far as promotions were concerned. The promotion system had been changed. There was no longer a highly recommended list, and a recommended list, and those who were not recommended. Instead, the service changed to a grading system in which each Investigator, based on his appraisals, was assigned a numeric score. One of the New York Investigators who was displeased with his appraisal and his score went to the president of our union, the AFGE, to complain about his yearly appraisal. The AFGE president was Ed Kavizangian. Ed went to the Civil Service on a complaint that the appraisal system was unfair and requested that promotions be suspended. The service, it appeared, was only too glad to comply with his request that the promotions be suspended for that appraisal year, and there would be no promotions until June of 1970 as a result of what I consider this stupid action. During 1969, I did get two more chances to get away from the city for a while. I used my military leave that year to attend the Non-Commissioned Officers Academy at Norton Air Force Base in California, and in the fall, the service started an operation along the border to deter entrance of illegal aliens and try to intercept some of the narcotics that were being smuggled across the border. I, along with several Investigators, was detailed to El Centro, California. I had never worked the border in the desert area, and this would be an interesting experience for me.

When we arrived at El Centro, I learned that the Border Patrol didn't think highly of the ability of the Investigators, even though we had all previously been in the Border Patrol. They teamed up one Border Patrolman to work with an Investigator and kept a couple of us at the office as processors.

They left two of us working in the office as processing officers to write apprehension reports on anyone who was apprehended. However, there were very few apprehensions, as the border was closed down. The word got out into Mexico that everyone was inspected thoroughly, vehicles were being searched thoroughly, and it was reported in the Mexican newspapers that the line of the vehicles waiting to enter the United States stretched twelve miles back into

Mexico. I had very little to do as a processing officer. Ward Leis was the other person they chose to stay in the office as a processing officer.

After a couple of days, I had almost nothing to do, so I asked the Station Senior, Fred D'Albini, if I could take a car and get out and do a little outside the office. I promised to stay in radio contact so I could hurry back to the office if I was needed for processing. Fred told me I could get away from the office from time to time. He told me he didn't believe that I would find any illegal aliens in the El Centro area because there were so many legal workers who used their alien registration cards to work in the United States, but who preferred to live on the other side of the border where it was cheaper to live in Mexico. But, since I wanted to get out of the office, I began scouting around, and the first two people I apprehended were picking dates beside the highway. I stopped to talk to them and discovered that they were illegal aliens, or at least they claimed to be undocumented aliens. In reality, they may have border crossing cards, which they used to cross the border at the inspection point and then sent back home. That way, if they were apprehended, they could simply claim to be illegal entrants and be sent back immediately to Mexico without losing their card. Anyway, everyone in the office was surprised that I had made an apprehension.

The Station Senior and I got to be very well acquainted and became better friends. He saw that I was really interested in enforcement, and he even invited me to go along with him a couple of times to look for a sign of illegal entrants along the railroad tracks leading up from the border.

I was just a jack-of-all-trades while I was on detail. One day they told me that I would be coming to work on the evening shift and that I would work with a Customs Officer. The reason for this was that Investigator Haggard from the Chicago office had located a stash of marijuana. It came about that his partner, one of the older PI's, had taken Paul down to the border where the border was divided from Mexico by barbed wire fence and pointed Paul towards Arizona, which they call the East Desert, and told him to drive a Jeep along the drag way by the fence. He then proceeded to seat himself in the passenger's side, got comfortable, pulled his hat down over his eyes and dozed. He told Paul to just keep driving until he came to the ricer, which was the state line between Arizona and California, and then to turn around and come back.

A few miles out into the desert, east of Calexico, Paul noticed some tracks across the drag way, and he turned to follow them into the United States toward the highway, which was Interstate 8. He noticed some scuff marks in the sand, and the tracks then turned around and angled back into Mexico. He stopped the Jeep, kicked around a little bit in a pile of sand and found four G.I. Barracks bags full of marijuana with about a hundred pounds in each bag. He then woke his partner, the sleeping PI, and showed him what he had found. The PI then called in the discovery to the office at El Centro. They in turn notified the Customs Service, who stated that they would handle the case from there.

I was to act as a Liaison Officer with a Customs Officer. I would take my walkie-talkie radio so that we would have communications with the Border Patrol. I joined the Customs Officer in his civilian-type vehicle, and we went screaming up the Interstate at ninety miles an hour to the site where the marijuana had been found. On the way, he told me the plan was to leave the marijuana bags overnight at the place where they were found. Then they would apprehend the person who came to retrieve it the following morning. It seemed that the plan was to stake out the cache with Customs Officers, as they believed it would be the following morning before anyone came to retrieve it, as he told me that was the way it always worked. When we reached the place opposite the cache, we swerved off the highway down into the brush several yards, and there we met the stakeout officers and a few other Customs Officers there with their civilian car. They had a fire going and were heating coffee. One of the officers had a chrome-plated .45 automatic pistol that he was firing at an old 55-gallon drum that was on the highway right-of-way. They knew each other, and the owner of the pistol told my partner that it was a real fine weapon, wouldn't he like to try it. They shot a few more rounds, which I thought would warn anybody within miles that we were at the site of the marijuana cache. We discussed the plan of operations. The two men on stakeout would stay at the site. They had a night scope set up in the brush where they could plainly see the site, even in the darkness. My partner and I would proceed eastward about a mile to a roadside park where we would wait just in case anything happened, and if the smuggler who had the marijuana made a run for it, we would be out on the highway and be able to intercept him.

As it proceeded to get dark, the Supervisor of the Customs Officers was on the radio saying he was going to come out to the site. One of the men told him the shoulder of the road was very soft and sandy at that point and just to stop on the side of the road and not to drive out into the desert. The Supervisor acknowledged, but evidently had ideas of his own, because the first thing he did was spot their fire and swerve off of the road and get stuck in the sand. It took considerable effort to get him unstuck. Then the Customs Service Officers put out their fire, settled down to await the smuggler and did the one thing that I could see was correct and helpful. They drug a camouflage net from one of the cars, threw it over the car they had hidden in the brush, and the vehicle just disappeared from sight. You could be ten feet away and still not know that a car was hidden there.

My partner and I proceeded on to the roadside park and had uneventful evening until 10 o'clock that night when we received a radio message that a car had parked alongside the cache, and a man and a woman were sitting in the car. They continued to set there until the men began to get inquisitive about why they were there, and they decided that the man and woman could not be the narcotic smugglers and asked me to radio a Border Patrol vehicle and have one of them stop and ask the man and woman if they needed assistance. The man in the car said no, that his car had just overheated, and they were sitting there waiting for the engine to cool off before proceeding. Evidently this inquiry by the Border Patrolman was enough to send them on their way, and they departed.

My shift ended at midnight, and the next day I was curious to find out what had happened. I came to work again at the same time and teamed up with the Customs Officer whom I had worked with the preceding day. I learned from him that the narcotics had been dug up and transported into their office, that the stakeout would be continued another day. The same routine was followed the second day, and sure enough, about the same time the second night, the same car with the man and woman pulled up to the same place and stopped. There were no longer any narcotics for them to recover, so there wouldn't have been a cache even if they had tried to find it, since it had been moved.

So the Customs Officer, once again, asked me to contact he Border Patrol and have them check the car. Another Border Patrolman came out to the spot, checked the identification of the man and woman, found out their names and that they had a San Diego address. He then proceeded to explain to them that this was a spot where illegal aliens often entered and walked out to the highway and met someone who would transport them to Los Angeles or other places. When they opened their trunk for him to make an inspection, they trunk disclosed nothing but a shovel, not even a spare tire. So it is easy to guess who would have been apprehended as marijuana smugglers if things were handled just a little differently.

Anyway, the interception of 400 pounds of marijuana at that time was considered a significant find, and the Sector Chief let it be known at the next day's meeting before going on duty that he would be recommending the Border Patrolman for a commendation for the good job he had done. Paul Haggard asked, "But what about me, Chief?" The Chief said, "Well what about you?" The Border Patrolman then had to admit that Paul had been the one who really found the marijuana and had done a good job. The Chief decided then that this incident was all in a day's work and there would be no letters of commendation.

I had to admire Paul for another reason, also. When we first arrived at El Centro, we had been given permission to use several of the old Border Patrol vehicles that were awaiting delivery to the General Service Administration for disposition. These cars had high mileage and were old enough to be turned in and replaced with new vehicles and were called "dead lined vehicles," but they would still run. We were staying at motels all over town and using the old Border Patrol vehicles to get back and forth to work. The Chief had decided that we should all move into one motel, which was across the street from the Immigration Office where we were in walking distance. Several of the Investigators complied with the Chief's desire and moved into the motel closest to the office and gave up their dead line vehicle that they had been using to go back and forth to work. I was staying at a motel closer to town and not within walking distance to the Border Patrol Office, and turning in the dead lined vehicle would have caused a hardship on my roommate, Bill Schaub, and me. A couple of the other officers also had no desire to leave their motel where they were getting very good rates and move into a very expensive motel nearer the office. They requested to be given permission to continue the use of the dead lined vehicle during Operation Intercept. The Chief was hard nosed about turning the vehicles back in, and gave us a couple of days to move.

Paul Haggard decided that there was no reason that we should not continue to use those vehicles and contacted his Senator. He explained the situation and asked his Senator to contact the General Services Administration, who it seemed was not aware that the Chief had told us that we would no longer use the vehicles because they belonged to the GSA. The GSA Administrator was only too willing to cooperate with the Immigration Service and Operation Intercept and stated, of course we could use the vehicles as long as we needed them. At the following briefing before our tour of duty the next day, the Chief said that he was glad to be able to tell us that he had arranged for us to continue the use of the dead lined vehicles.

Bill and I had been afraid we would be without transportation, but an Investigator from Los Angeles had solved the problem for us. He was one of those I had met at the Journeyman Investigators School, and that friendship paid off. He had driven an unmarked station wagon from Los Angeles over to El Centro, and at the first opportunity had then brought his private vehicle over to El Centro and loaned us the station wagon so we could go back and forth to work. This was also an unmarked vehicle and was useful in going to lunch or any other activities when we were off duty.

One day when we were both off duty, Bill decided he would go back to his Border Patrol station where he was stationed before becoming an Investigator, and he drove up into the mountains between El Centro and San Diego to a place called El Campo and another town called Tamecula. It was a scenic trip and something for an off-duty Investigator to do to enjoy being on detail in El Centro.

I really learned to like the desert country. I even went to the airport and got checked out to rent an airplane. I had renewed my student pilot's license, and after a check ride, the plane owner was willing to rent the plane at $20 an hour. At that price, I could only afford a few hours' flying time, and I used it to fly along the border and as far as the Salton Sea. The last hour I used the plane, I taxied out to the end of the runway, as there was no control tower to advise on permission to land or take off. I checked the wind direction, did a 360-degree turn on the taxiway at the end of the runway to make sure there was no traffic. As the sky looked clear, I taxied onto the runway, opened the throttle, and just as I was lifting off, I heard someone on my radio saying he didn't see them. I never did see a plane, and I wondered if someone else was approaching that I had not seen. Anyway, the airplane owner was very concerned and said that that was the last time he was renting his airplane for $20 an hour.

As the end of Operation Intercept neared, we New York investigators were looking forward to going home. I had had a successful detail. I had apprehended a few other illegal aliens. In fact, I apprehended the same one twice. I first found him picking cotton at the end of the field where the cotton-picking machine was working. A lot of cotton is mashed down or missed at the end of the row, so this fella was picking at the end of each row to give the machine room to turn around. He claimed to be an illegal entrant, and I wrote an apprehension report, and he was sent back to Mexico. A couple of days later, I was telling Ward Leis about apprehending the alien. Ward suggested that he might be back at work and we could go back to the field and check again. Sure enough, as we approached the field, I recognized him. This time, there would be no quick return of the alien to Mexico. He would be issued a Warrant of Arrest With Order to Show Cause and sent to the Alien Detention Facility. There he would be reinterviewed by a screening officer, who might determine that the person had really used a border crossing card to enter rather than enter without documents as he had claimed.

As Operation Intercept came to a close, I was told that I would be one of the last to leave. One of my last days of duty was in the west desert with the Training Officer, Tom Gaines. Tom was a famous pistol shooter in the Border Patrol, and it was a pleasure to spend the night in the desert with him. He really came prepared to spend the night. We would be working at a place called the Cattle Pens Corral. Even though the fence had long ago been torn down, the spot kep0t its name so it would be easy locating. Tom had brought some charcoal and two steaks, and we cooked those and had a real good meal. The next morning, we heard a noise from the direction of Mexico, even thought the border is not marked by fence; we knew a vehicle was coming across the desert from Mexico. We intercepted a camper-type pickup with one occupant. The man said he had been gathering rocks and wasn't sure where the border was. As he had been in Mexico, we told him this was not an inspection point, that he could not enter and would have to go back to the highway and follow it to Mexicali and enter at the port of entry.

A little while later, we heard the sound of an airplane coming from Mexico. There was a small single engine plane, and evidently the pilot knew that we were on the little hilltop. He skimmed along so low that he was below the skyline and tilted a wing slightly so that we could not read his registration number. Operation Intercept had not been very successful in their attempts to stop anyone from entering from Mexico. They had been successful in following one single engine plane that crossed the border and then turned eastward, and our intercept plane, which was a twin engine Beechcraft, had overtaken him and landed right behind him at a little airport in Yuma, Arizona. The pilot went into the manager's office and wanted to complain to the airport manager that he was reporting a plane that had been following him too closely. As he was questioned by the Immigration pilot, it turned out that he was a citizen of Australia who had a valid passport and claimed that he was prospecting along the border. His small plane had been stripped of everything except the pilot's seat. There were no drugs located in the plane, but he had behaved so suspiciously that the Border Patrol pilot asked for a ground search along his route to the airport. Sure enough, about a mile from the airport, the Border Patrol discovered another barracks bag full of marijuana that he had obviously dumped from the plane as he was approaching to land. But the marijuana could not be legally connected to him, so he was home free.

Another interception was made by pure chance. The Border Patrol has a person known as the Air Detail Officer who does Liaison work at airports along the border, and by chance, he was at one of the local airports when a small plane landed and taxied up o the office inquiring about obtaining fuel. The pilot told the airport attendant, within hearing of the Immigration Officer, that he had just come from Mexico and that he needed fuel. The Air Detail Officer then identified himself and stated that since the plane had just come from Mexico, he would have to do an inspection of the plane, and he found a load of marijuana.

Dear Chief

During the period Operation Intercept was maintained, there was also a crash of a plane in the desert. The plane crash was located, and trackers followed the two pilots. One was slightly injured and was located immediately, very close to the plan. The other was tracked for some distance before he, too, was apprehended.

People who were better equipped could cross the border with immunity. Some portable radar sets were brought in and spaced along the border to assist in locating aircraft. These radar operators were reporting contacts with highflying jets such as the Lear jets that were flying higher and faster than anything the Border Patrol had to intercept. Them. In fact, it would have taken a military fighter plane to intercept those planes which were headed into interior cities and disappears from radar, headed towards Denver or Omaha or other interior cities. Operation Intercept had literally shut down the border. There were so many complaints from Mexico from the civilian population and from the Mexican government that Operation Intercept changed its name and became Operation Cooperation. In my opinion, it had limited success.

I was not anxious to get back to New York City, but I was getting anxious to see my wife. However, I would make one more apprehension before I left El Centro. This came about as a result of a joy ride I had taken in the rented plane. I had spotted a herd of sheep in the west desert near the Naval Air Station and noticed that there were two sheepherders and a small trailer. I decided to go back on the ground and check the immigration status of the sheepherders, as most of the sheepherders were Portuguese Basques. They were contracted to the Cattlemen's Association to work on a specific sheep ranch. When I located the sheep on the ground, I questioned the two sheepherders and found one of them to be out of status. He had been contracted to work for a rancher in Colorado and had broken his contract and moved to California and found work from someone else. I wasn't sure how to proceed with this apprehension, but I took him back to the office and Mr. D'Albini was behind me one hundred percent. He said we will lock him up if you want to. One of his other Seniors was saying, "There's nothing you can do with a sheepherder. We never apprehend sheep herders." Mr. D'Albini decided we could apprehend sheepherders, so we decided that we would issue him an Order to Sow Cause and schedule him for a deportation hearing.

As I was preparing the apprehension report, the owner of the sheep came into the Border Patrol office as mad as a wet hen. He added a little profanity for the Border Patrol and wanted to know what he could do. I tried to calm him down. He wanted nothing to do with the Border Patrolman in the green uniform, but since I was in civilian clothes, he was willing to talk to me. I explained to him the procedure we were using and that there would be some time before the alien deportation hearing and that in the meantime he could take him back to the camp if he would assure us that he would bring the alien back for his appointed hearing at the proper time. He assured me that he would take him anywhere that we told him to go at the proper time, and before leaving the office, he had calmed down, was very grateful to be having the alien released to his custody and shook my hand and thanked me. The Border Patrolman in the room called him and S.O.B. and said, "Look at that. He won't even speak to us, but he shakes the Investigator's hand." I will never know if that sheepherder ever got deported.

Things continued to change at New York, even our names were changed. We would now be known as Criminal Investigators. Mr. Peter's squad had been split into two squads with a GS-12 in charge of each squad. Mr. Peters would now be in position to appeal to the Civil Service Commission to be upgraded to a GS-13, as he was supervising two other GS-12's. His appeal was successful, and he was upgraded to a GS-13. I continued to work with Jack Stearn who was in the same squad as me. I really learned a lot from Jack. The first thing I learned was how to get in and out of the parking garage in the basement of our building. There was an electric power garage door, and one would open the door by pressing the button at the inside of the wall. The door would rise. You then drove the car through the door, stopped outside, got out, walked back and pressed the close button on the outside of the building. Jack told me that he knew how to do that without getting out of the car and walking back to close the door. He was going to demonstrate. He opened the door, got in the car, drove up to the doorway, reached out and pressed the close button, and then was going to drive the rest of the way out of the door before the garage door could close. Jack may have been successful at doing this many times, but this particular time he wasn't fast enough, and the descending garage door scraped the trunk of the car as we drove out from under it.

There was no real damage to the car, just a few little scratches to the paint, which we didn't bother to report. No one wanted to be making an accident report on something so frivolous. In fact, the cars looked like New York taxicabs with dents in the fenders and doors on almost every car, but accident reports had not been filed on them. We accepted them in whatever condition they happened to be in and were glad to get anything that would run.

Jack drove just like the New York taxi drivers. His experience as a policeman had really taught him how to get along in Manhattan. We rode all over the city and many miles out on Long Island and upstate as far north as Newberg, New York. We were working in Newberg one morning when we saw a sign on a new restaurant just opening in a Newberg mall. The Chinese restaurant had a sign saying, "Grand Opening 11 A.M." As this happened to be the day of the grand opening, we were curious about who the employees would be. We were circling the mall at about 10 o'clock when we saw five Chinese walking toward the rear entrance of the restaurant. We stopped to explain to them that we were Immigration Officers and would like to see their immigration documents. All five of them claimed to be legally immigrated aliens who had left their alien registration cards in their apartment, which was a large room on the upper story of the mall near one end. We left the car, walked with the five of them back up the stairs to their apartment with Jack near the front and me bringing up the rear.

The first person in the apartment went right on through the room into the bathroom, and by the time we got the other four in the apartment, we realized that he was making an escape through the bathroom window. Jack went through the window right behind him. I stayed to check the four that remained behind, and one of them turned out to be a seaman who had jumped ship. The other three were legal. I got the one that I had apprehended into handcuffs and into the car and then went looking for Jack. I spotted him at the front of the mall on the roof. He motioned me to come back around to the back where he could come through the apartment and down the stairs. He said the alien had jumped from the roof and got away.

We circled the mall and saw several people standing in front of the laundry at the point where the alien had jumped. We stopped the car, and someone said that he was over there behind a laundry cart. Sure enough, there was the alien, dressed in his white kitchen garb, crouched behind the canvas cart that was used to haul laundry in and out of the laundry. He had sprained an ankle or broken it and was unable to run and was attempting to hide. We put him in the car and decided that we better take him to a local police station where we could use their telephone to call our office and report to Mr. Peters. I had apprehension reports with me, so I would do an apprehension report for the two aliens while Jack made the phone call. We had only been in the police station a few minutes when one of the policemen arrived with another Chinese person in white kitchen garb. He told us, "I knew you fellas must be in town because I caught this fella running down the street about a half mile from the restaurant."

He said he would do us a favor and take the person with the injured foot by the Public Health Service office if we wanted him to. We said that sounded like a good idea, and in a little while, he was back with the alien and the doctor's report that the x-rays showed the person had, indeed, fractured his ankle, and the doctor had given him a shot for the pain. He said that there was no immediate hurry that the alien's foot could be put in a cast within the next 24 hours. We told Mr. Peters by phone what had happened and that we would be bringing the three aliens back to the office in New York. Mr. Peters wasn't too happy with the situation, and wondered if we couldn't just leave the injured alien there. We told him, no, that too many people had seen us apprehend the alien. We couldn't just turn him loose, so we brought him back to the office and then took him to the Public Health Service where they put a cast on his foot, and everything was accomplished very satisfactorily, I thought.

There was another instance where I went to place an alien into detention sometime later, and saw the alien was still there wearing his cast. I inquired about him through the Detention Officer. He told me, once again, that an investigation was being conducted because the alien alleged that the apprehending officer had pushed him off of the roof. We were successful in convincing our supervisor that the alien had jumped off the roof on his own accord and had not been pushed off the roof. That was just one of the things that kept working with Jack so exciting.

Another time, we were working together on Long Island, and it seemed that every pizza parlor had an illegal alien, either a Colombian or an Italian working in it, and that every shoe shop had an illegal Italian working in the shoe shop. Most of them were aliens who had entered without Visas claiming to be in transit to Canada. These people are easily disposed of, as the airline which brought them was responsible for their custody and for transporting them out of the United States. When we located one, or in this case, we located several, we transported them to Kennedy Airport, prepared our apprehension report, put them back into custody of the airline security, and they were on the first available transportation, transported on to Canada or back to Italy.

I also enjoyed working with Ed Halcrow. Ed was a GS-11 Investigator who had transferred to New York City, and his cases and my cases were in the same area, so we teamed up quite a bit. Ed was a likeable, easygoing fella, and I was trying to help him familiarize himself with the area in Brooklyn. I told him about a particular Greek restaurant where I usually stopped for a coffee break and that I usually checked the kitchen help when I was there, and they often had an illegal alien. I learned from previous apprehensions at the restaurant to choose a seat near the back where I could see the back door. And this visit was no exception. We seated ourselves inside the back door. Someone recognized me from having been at the restaurant previously, and I saw someone dash out the back door. I left Ed sitting at the table with the coffee. I pursued the person down the street for two blocks. I was slowly gaining on him until he turned around a corner and was out of sight for a moment. When I rounded the corner, he was no longer in sight. I started looking at the entranceways into the building, and about halfway down the block I found him crouched in the basement entry under some steps. I took him into custody and discovered that I was not carrying my handcuffs that particular day. I had learned working at Stockton that if there was a possibility of an alien running, you had better keep some sort of hold on him. The best way was to take him by his belt and the seat of his pants and walk him along on tiptoes. That way, you could lift him off of his feet if he attempted to run.

As I walked the alien back towards the restaurant, I sure wished Ed would come around the block in the car, but he didn't. We arrived back at the restaurant, and Ed was calmly finishing a second cup of coffee. When I mentioned to him that I might have needed some help, he said, oh, he thought that I could handle it, there was just one alien, and I could take care of it.

Another day, Ed and I were returning to the office through the Astoria section of the city, which is an industrial section. We spotted a person so out of place that we just had to stop and talk to him. This was a black man in a bright blue suit with a white shirt, a red necktie, and carrying an umbrella. We circled the block and stopped in front of him, and when we were close enough, we could see the scars on his forehead, which were his tribal markings, and sure enough, he turned out to be an African looking for work.

This reminds me of the term which has become popular referring to illegal aliens as undocumented workers. That certainly was not applicable to most of the aliens encountered in New York City, as they had entered with a passport with a Student Visa or a Visitor's Visa, in most cases. It might be applicable to a certain percentage of the aliens who entered from Mexico and had already found work and might be undocumented workers, but I always prefer the term illegal alien. As I mentioned, many of them have Student Visas, which brings up the question, why in the world does the American Consulate Officer issue a Visa to a 40-year-old alien who does not speak English and claims to be coming to the United States as a student. There is no way such a person can be a bona fide student, yet they are admitting thousands of them from every Consulate office around the world. Most of them have no intention of attending school, and they apply for a Student Visa because Student Visas don't cost them anything for the application, whereas a Tourist Visa might cost them a little money.

The experience I gained from working with Mr. Peters was probably the best I could have gotten anywhere. Mr. Peters expected our written reports to be thorough and he tried to install a little motivation into every Investigator to at least reach his unwritten limit of production. However, we had one Investigator who never reached the expected minimum, and each month at our training meeting, Mr. Peters would point out to this individual that he had again fallen short of what was expected of him. The Investigator was never at a loss for an answer and always claimed that he had an excessive number of hours during the month, working liaison with the mayor's office or some other such excuse.

I was usually fairly conscientious, although I was not perfect by any means, but I had always believed in giving a day's work for a day's pay, including overtime. I knew there were some people who never worked the overtime. They just called in and claimed it for pay purposes. Overtime was somewhat of a sore spot anyway. The FBI received up to 25 percent of their pay for overtime. We Immigration Officers felt that we were being shorted, that we worked just as many hours, yet we were limited to 15 percent. Our union attempted to gain equalization with the other agencies and started documenting all the criminal work that we did. In fact, almost every alien we apprehended had violated one of the criminal statutes. We were successful in having our title changed from Investigator to Criminal Investigator. The changed title didn't feel too appealing to me. Was it that we were investigating criminal cases, or were we criminals ourselves? However, that was the new title. We would be stuck with it, and our overtime pay was increased to 25 percent.

I found myself in Brooklyn alone one evening at time to call in and report the cases I would be working on during my overtime for that day. I noticed when I went into a bar to use their public telephone (since the ones nearby on the street were broken), that the bar was occupied by all blacks, but I went ahead and made my call and decided to use the men's room while I was inside the bar. While I was inside, two black men who had been sitting at the bar decided they would follow me into the men's room. They stopped in the doorway and looked me over. The larger of the two was the spokesman. The shorter, or the smaller of the two, was his little echo. The larger guy said, "Hey, man, you're in our world, you kinda light to be in our world." Sir Echo said, "Yea, baby, you in our world." As a precaution, I zipped my pants and made sure that my coat was unbuttoned, and when I turned to face them, I made sure they could see that my hand was only a few inches from my service revolver. Their eyes got a size larger, and they backed out of the doorway and let me leave the place without further incident. At that moment, all of those times I had filled out the 3x5 cards requesting that I be issued a service weapon felt justified.

There were a few incidents, but I don't remember anyone seriously harmed while I was in New York. One of the older Investigators who had been brainwashed into the New York system of working alone using public transportation was in the Bedford-Styvesant area when some teenagers began taunting him and teasing him and wondering why he was in that area. In a few minutes, the group had become a gang which surrounded him and were threatening to take away his clothing. He was getting concerned when he noticed a school bus coming down the street. He managed to get off the sidewalk and into the street and waved his hands in front of the school bus, and when the bus stopped, he managed to convince the driver to let him on and get him out of that area.

I could have stayed in New York the rest of my career, but I would never get used to working alone. At one of Mr. Peters' training sessions, he told us he had noticed that we Investigators were spending too much time in the office, that our work was out on the streets and that's where we should be, except when writing reports. He banned us from the office and told us that we should stay in the field. That didn't suit too well, as we thought we knew when we needed to be in the office and when we needed to be in the field, and there was a minor rebellion. Nothing was said, but during that month we just didn't turn in any reports. We stayed in the field, and the unit's production dropped almost to zero.

I don't know what the other Investigators were doing, although I have some ideas because one of them was with me when we went to see a New York Mets baseball game in the afternoon, one of the few times I really goofed off on duty. I happened to see one of the GS-11 Investigators who was promoted to Supervisory Investigator later on during that time, and he was at a city swimming pool on Long Island having a swim when he was supposed to be working. New York City was a big place, and if anyone worked hard, it was through devotion to duty, and if anyone wanted to goof off and only meet the minimum requirements, there was no way in the world a supervisor could keep up with what he was doing.

When Mr. Peters' section was split into two squads, Jack and I found we would still be in the same squad and would be working for

Oscar Colton. Oscar was a real nice person and easy to work for. In fact, some of the people who had been there longer and knew him better called him Prince Igor. I was not comfortable in calling Mr. Peters anything but Mr. Peters. We had another Supervisory Investigator, who had been promoted because of affirmative action, until he was promoted beyond his capacity. Occasionally when we would call in at the end of the shift, Mr. Colton's number would be busy, and the other Supervisor would pick up the ringing telephone. I would tell him my name, and before I could give him my case numbers that I was working on, he would reply, "We don't have anybody here by that name." I would explain to him again that I was in Mr. Colton's squad and would be working overtime. Eventually, Mr. Colton might get the message, but most often he would not. It appeared to me that this person who had been promoted to a Supervisory Investigator position had been promoted not on ability but on filling a minority employment objective. He would be promoted to still higher positions.

The year under Oscar's supervision was going as well as a year could go at New York City. Jack and I were still working together, more than any other. Mr. Colton realized that we could give him top numbers of case closings and still apprehend a large number of illegal aliens. For each illegal alien we encountered, Jack, would show two hours of area control duty, while I didn't feel comfortable with claiming two hours, so I only claimed one hour for each apprehended illegal alien.

I hadn't thought anything about receiving awards since I had left Harlingen, but as the time approached for the annual recommendations for Superior Performance Awards, Mr. Colton found the way of recommending both Jack and me, and I eventually received a Sustained Superior Performance Award. I also learned through union activity that our personnel folders were now available for our inspection in the presence of our Supervisor. Our personnel folders had been previously guarded better than some of our state secretes, so I was curious to see what was in my personnel folder. I spent the necessary memo to the Central Office in Washington, and a few weeks later I was informed that my personnel folder had arrived and I could review it in the presence of my Supervisor. The first thing I saw when opening the folder was two pages of recommendations by

Mr. Colton to justify my SSP Award. I was curious to see what SPI Lomblot had written about me while I was stationed at Harlingen. So I thumbed through the pages of the personnel folder to the period of time during my stay in Harlingen, and nowhere in the folder was a single word of recommendation, which Roland had told me he had submitted. I was a little disappointed, but not too surprised.

One day Mr. Peters called a meeting of the General Investigation Section and informed us that the following day we would be detailed across the river to the Newark, New Jersey office. He explained that they had the same problem in the pizza parlors in New Jersey as New York City had. There were illegal Italians in almost every pizza parlor, and we would make a hush, hush raid on the pizza parlors at a given time after the parlors had opened the following day. We drove over to Newark, and I teamed up with Bob Hollowell, an old ex-Border Patrol classmate, and we positioned ourselves to be able to sweep down on the first on his list of pizza parlors at the appointed time. We swooped and nothing happened; all was calm. We didn't find any illegal Italians at the parlors. In fact, it looked like they might be working a bit shorthanded, so we went to the next parlor. The same things occurred until we reached the third on our list, and there we found an illegal Colombian who did not speak Italian or English and somehow had not gotten the word. It was obvious the word had been given. Once again, the telephone had been quicker than the automobile. But whose tip was it? Was it from our side of the river or, more likely, from the Newark office? Bob and I then took our Colombian into custody, wrote an apprehension report and spent the rest of the afternoon going from jail to jail, looking for a place that was not overcrowded and had room to lodge him overnight. It would have been simpler if I could have just taken him with me and put him into the detention facility at the New York office, but the Hudson River was the dividing line between two districts, and things just didn't work that way.

Talking about the Italians reminds me of a story of three Italian immigrants who had just arrived in New York City and didn't have any money to their names, so they were just standing on a New York street corner, admiring the beautiful women and the fancy cars that drove by and wishing. They got on to the subject of making love and asked if you could make love to any woman in the world, who would you choose? The first one of them to choose stated that he had always thought Sophia Loren was a beautiful woman, and if he could make love to any woman in the world, he would choose her. The second said, well, he had always believed that Raquel Welch was the most beautiful, and if he could choose anyone in the world, he would choose her. The third thought a while, and they prodded him until he finally said he would choose Georgia Peep O'Leen. They looked at each other and had never heard of Georgia Peep O'Leen and asked, "Who in the world is that?" He told them she must be surely the world's greatest lover. They said, well, how do you know she's the world's greatest lover? He said, "Well, her name is in all the papers." And right beside them in a newsstand was the day's headline story: Three men die laying Georgia pipeline.

One of the administrative steps in eventually deporting an alien from the United States is the issuance of an Order to Show Cause, or OSC, as we refer to them. At New York, we were occasionally assigned to the processing desk that issued the OSC's, which were notification to the alien of a hearing, asking why he should not be deported from the United States. These aliens were usually represented by an attorney. In New York there were several of these attorneys who specialized in immigration work. Probably the best known of these was Hy Abrams. It's amazing how aliens learn of these attorneys who specialize in immigration work. They occasionally are needed, but usually in the preliminary application process, when an alien is attempting to prolong his visit in the United States by obtaining an extension of his permit to be in the United States, a lawyer was not needed. But thousands of them did pay unnecessary money to these immigration attorneys for things they could handle themselves if they were only more familiar with immigration procedures.

One day, Mr. Peters called me into his office on a Friday evening, just before quitting time, handed me a file, told me to check a car out over the weekend, and advised me that the file he was giving me already contained a Warrant of Arrest, and that I should proceed to the address in the Bronx and serve the Warrant of Arrest and take an alien into custody. I asked Jim Genette to accompany me, and we proceeded into one of the worst areas of New York City.

We found the address. We entered the building by edging our way between five or six black men sitting on the steps who gave us the eyeball and obviously wondered what are those two white men doing up here and followed us into the building. We knocked on the apartment door, and the subject we were looking for was home and let us into his apartment. A few other people had congregated in the hall outside. They were very curious as to what we were doing, and we could hear angry mutterings. The alien in question stated that he had an immigration attorney working on his case and was scheduled to come to the Immigration office the following Monday morning. I considered Mr. Peters' instructions to serve him the Warrant of Arrest and take him into custody. We probably could have affected his arrest and gotten him out of the building, but by that time there were between 15 and 20 people crowding the hallway outside and into his doorway. I thought the minute we tried to remove that man from the building we would be in deep trouble. It was my judgment, since the alien stated he was coming to the Immigration office the following Monday morning with his attorney, that it would be the best course of action just to take his passport, give him a business card instructing him to see me at the office, and get out of that building if we could. I knew I would have to explain to Mr. Peters on Monday morning why I hadn't taken the alien into custody. I worked my way into the office on Monday morning to arrive about five minutes after the time I had set for the alien to appear with his attorney. I was glad to see the alien and Attorney Abrams waiting for me. The situation had worked itself out very satisfactorily.

The annual appraisal and promotional scores were issued to each Investigator. They were not made public, but Investigators, out of curiosity, compared scores with each other. Mine showed that I had a very good promotional score. The thought of promotion after a year of a suspended promotion list was appealing. However, I decided not to apply for one of the vacancies announced at the New York office. I believed my score would be high enough to be certified to some other office for promotion. In June, the promotions came, and twenty Investigators were promoted to Grade 11, and twelve Grade 11 Investigators were promoted to Grade 12. Mr. Peters was somewhat surprised that I was not one of the twenty Investigators promoted to Grade 11.

Then one day he called me into his office and stated that it might not be any of his business, but he had noticed that I did not apply for a promotion at New York City and wondered if there was some reason. I told him that I believed that my promotion score was high enough to be certified to some other office and that the way I read the vacancy announcements, if I applied and was accepted at New York, then I would be committing myself to another two years at New York City, and Didn't want to spend two more years at New York City. Mr. Peters said no, that was not correct, it only meant that moving allowances could be used every two years and had noting to do with accepting a promotion. I couldn't argue with Mr. Peters, but I was curious. He said that he believed that I had a misunderstanding of the promotional system and maybe I should write a memorandum to the Central Office for clarification. I thought about that for a couple of days; then I decided rather than write a memorandum, I would just use a day of leave and travel down to the Central Office in Washington and talk with someone.

I took the train and enjoyed the ride from New York City to Washington, DC. I arrived at the Central Office without an appointment and asked to see Mr. Green. The secretary stated that Mr. Green was out of town on a detail, but Mr. Casey was in. Mr. Casey agreed to see me for a few minutes. He was very cordial. We talked, and he asked me what was my ambition, what did I want to be in the Immigration Service? I told him I might tike to some day go back to the Border Patrol and be a Chief Patrol Inspector. He seemed a little surprised and thought that surely I would rather be a District Director someplace. I told him, no, that I would be very satisfied with a lower grade and continue to do something that I really enjoyed doing. He then asked a secretary for my promotional folder. Then he told me it was out on certification, that he could not tell me where I would be promoted, but with my score, there was a very good chance that I would be promoted and that one of the places that I might go was to San Francisco, California. He also stated that I had a correct understanding of the promotional system, and my choosing not to be promoted at New York City indicated that.

I went back to New York very pleased with my trip to the Central Office. Patiently, I awaited some word, and in a few weeks I learned that I had indeed been certified and selected for a promotion to GS-11 Investigator in San Francisco. There were two vacancies announced there, and Bill Leis had applied for the other vacancy and was also selected. Bill and I had a going away party together, and I was pleased to be going back to California.

I knew my wife, Jerry, was anxious to leave New York, even though we had moved fourteen times in the past seventeen years. Leaving New York and moving to California would not be easy. The move would be just as eventful as moving had been when we came from Stockton to New York. I got the estimates from the moving companies who knew exactly how much my moving allowance would be, and that was the estimate they gave me. However, they tacked on an additional charge, an elevator charge, as I lived in a sixth-floor apartment. I could see I was going in a hole with this move unless I found an alternate method. The best alternate seemed to be to rent a Ryder truck and make the move myself. I received the same amount in advanced travel expenses that I had received coming to New York. That was a check for $1,200. I hired the building janitor to assist me, and for two days we loaded furniture onto the truck. At last, I was ready to go.

We thought of how to move the old car, which was by now a typical New York car with sideswiped right hand side and various dents. The Ryder Company would not rent me a tow bar. They said they were short of tow bars and didn't want their tow bar to end up on the West Coast, that any tow bars they rented had to be returned to their office. Jerry decided that she would, once again, follow me. As I drove the truck, she would drive the car. She vowed this time that she would not get in front of me and become separated. I checked the route we would travel and saw that we would leave Queens, cross Manhattan on to the George Washington Bridge.

The appointed departure came. Jerry had put a few things in the Ford, along with our two Chihuahuas. We proceeded to leave Queens, and as we crossed Manhattan, we turned on to Sutton Place, one of the most exclusive streets in New York City. As I approached a parked car in the right hand lane (which, by the way, was double-parked and illegally parked in front of an apartment building that was being renovated or remodeled), I swung into the left lane to go around the double-parked car. In my rear view mirror, I could see Jerry attempting to swing into the left lane to follow me, but as she did so, a car zoomed up on her side, blew his horn, startling her, and she swerved back into the lane she was in and ran into the rear end of the double-parked car. I quickly came to a stop, rushed back to see if Jerry was all right. At first it looked like her teeth were broken, but it was just paint from the steering wheel. When I realized she was all right, I then turned to face a man who had run out of the building. He was cursing and threatening Jerry, and as I stepped between him and Jerry and told him to shut up and was tempted to take a poke at him, a policeman arrived on the scene and pushed him back against the wall of the building. The radiator of the car was busted, so without a tow bar, it looked like it was the end of the line for our old Ford. As Jerry was only shaken up and not hurt, we looked at each other, decided that there was nothing to do but to continue in the truck. I told her that the old car had been a good one, but it was eight years old, and we had gotten full benefit from it; we would just leave it there and never look back. She said that suited her just fine. A policeman and a couple of the construction workers helped me push the car over to the curb. I left the switch keys in it, so if there was anything they wanted from the car they were welcome to take it. We boarded the truck and said "Adios" to our old Ford, "Adios" to New York City, and didn't look back.

CHAPTER FIVE: SAN FRANCISCO

By taking a couple of days' delay en route, Jerry and I would attend the National Pistol Championships in Jackson, Mississippi. We spent a couple of days with Jerry's cousin and her husband in Jackson. The first day, he and I went fishing and had good luck fishing in some private ponds. The second day he told me to take the family car rather than drive the truck out to the pistol range. Jerry went with me. I was shooting in the lowest classification, being the Marksman Class. In fact, I never did get rated higher than a Sharp Shooter, but still, I was there to enjoy the tournament. Since I was not a member of the New York team who did attend, I just shot as an individual.

When the firing was over and Jerry and I were ready to leave, I discovered that I had locked the switch keys in the trunk. There were hundreds of law enforcement officers of every kind—state, county, local, federal—and no one could open the trunk to the car. But a highway patrolman finally said by calling in the vehicle identification number to the dealer in Jackson, they could send out another key. This was accomplished, and we were finally able to return to Jerry's cousin with the car, even though I was somewhat embarrassed. We then proceeded to cross the southwest, headed for Novato, California. I knew that my friend, Bob McCord, who had been stationed at Harlingen, Texas, had stated that Novato was a good place to live, and several Investigators who worked in the City of San Francisco lived in Novato. We also wanted to go back through Stockton, California and visit the friends who had shared the duplex apartment where he had last lived in Stockton. That was Dave and Marie.

We did visit them, and when we were ready to leave their house, Jerry wanted me to put her overnight case in the back of the truck. She had kept it underneath her feet for several days on the trip from New York. We were nearly to our destination, so I placed her overnight case at the very rear of the load in the back of the truck. We said our goodbyes to Dave and Marie, drove through the little town of Lodi, California, and decided to stop and get some grapes at a roadside fruit stand. I dismounted from the truck, walked around behind the truck and noticed that the door had not been securely locked, and the bouncing had caused it to open slightly. I noticed that Jerry's overnight case was missing. It obviously had bounced out of the partly opened door. We immediately retraced our route, looking on both sides of the street and in the street for Jerry's overnight case. But there was no sign of it. We traced the route a second time, more slowly, looking on the side of the road, in the weeds, anyplace that the overnight case could have possibly landed, but it wasn't to be found. Obviously, someone had immediately spotted it and picked it up. Even though it was tagged, there was never any report that anyone had found it. It contained two government checks, my advance travel check in the amount of $1,200, s smaller check for about $60 from the Air Force Reserve, a few dollars cash, and Jerry's jewelry. The most important thing to her, although not a large value, but having a sentimental value, were the cameos that I had sent her from Italy. The first order of business when I reached the San Francisco Office would be to write a "Dear Chief" memo to the Central Office Payroll Section, advising them that I had lost my advance travel check. But first, we must continue to Novato.

We arrived in Novato only a little better off than when I had arrived in New York City. I had some pocket money, but without the advance travel check, I would not come close to having enough for a deposit on the house we were to rent and the first month's rental, as well as the deposit on utilities. And I would have to borrow from the credit union to make a down payment on a new car. I was an Investigator in need. The McCord's, Bob and Barbara, proved to be friends, indeed. They literally took us in and treated Jerry and me like family. Bob would take me into San Francisco to work the following morning. Jerry would look for a house, and that evening Bob and Barbara decided they could loan me enough money for the security deposit and first month's house rent. Bob would be going on an out-of-town detail, so for a couple of mornings after that, I would ride to work with Tom Smith, whom I had met the first day at the office. I had also met my Supervisor, Billy Glazner.

I did not receive very much of a warm welcome like a new Investigator might get at his new duty assignment, and it would be some time before I learned why. I would eventually learn that there were two Investigators at San Francisco who had not been promoted and who might have been promoted if Leis and I had not applied for the two vacancies, and there was some resentment and feeling that we had taken their jobs. It turned out that Glazner had also told the people in his squad that these two New York Investigators were real hot shot producers, and his squad members had better get to work if they were going to keep up with the new men. That was the reason for the suspicious looks we got when we reported for duty.

    I made arrangements for the purchase of a new car, checked the newspaper ads for San Francisco and talked to a dealer at a Chrysler dealership. I made him an offer on one of his cars, and he advised me that he couldn't accept my offer. I had very little time to a look around and ended up going up to the little town of Petaluma, near Novato, and purchased a new Ford. A few days later, I received a call from the Chrysler salesman asking if I was still interested in purchasing the car. I advised him no, I had already bought one. He wanted to know what kind, and I told him that I had bought a Ford. He asked if I didn't mind telling him how much I had paid for it. As I was satisfied with my purchase, I went ahead and told him exactly what I had paid, He said, Oh, I could have put you in a Chrysler for that price. I reminded him that he had his chance, and that was the last I ever heard from this Chrysler salesman.

    I was told that my first duty would be with the Area Control Squad, as all new Investigators assigned to San Francisco would be doing a tour while familiarizing themselves with the city and surrounding area in the Area Control Section. I met my partner, Investigator Veblin, who was assigned to work the East Bay, that was Oakland and the surrounding small town suburbs. We might even get as far south as San Jose. The first day or two, Veblin told me to be ready and he would be picking me up at five o'clock in the morning. Then, after a couple of days of picking me up, he told me to keep the car overnight and to pick him up at five o'clock in the morning. Once again, five o'clock seemed awfully early to be going to work, just as it had seemed to be in the Border Patrol. But that was the way we did it. Each morning, we would cross the Richmond Bridge into the East Bay and head for the bus station in Oakland, but that was the daily routine: start at five in the morning and go to the Oakland bus station. We did catch a few illegal aliens, and I tried to remember the places we were going to, which were usually greenhouses. They grew a lot of flowers in the Bay Area, and there were also numerous construction sites where we could usually manage to find a couple of illegal aliens in housing construction.

To me it seemed we were going to work about two hours before the illegal aliens started moving around and were putting in a lot of miles relative to the number of apprehensions we were making. The Bay Areas was not completely familiar to me. I had lived in Hayward, California a couple of months while I was in the Air Force. I had also visited San Francisco five or six times and had done the usual things that a tourist does. I had visited the Golden Gate Bridge, Fisherman's Wharf, had attended the ball game at Candlestick Park, and had ridden the cable cars.

After three weeks of area control with Investigator Veblin, they decided that I was familiar enough with the area to work on my own, and that suited me fine. I then reported to the General Investigation Section for an assignment of a caseload, which was the same type of cases I would be working as a GS-11 that I had worked as a GS-9 in New York. About the only difference was there would be more Philippine nationality cases and less British West Indian cases. There would also be some South Americans, but mostly Mexican.

I continued to work with Tom Smith as much as I could. One day Tom asked me to go with him to check someone into the San Francisco jail. He said there was something he wanted me to see. When I got there what he wanted me to see were about eight to ten transvestites that the police had rounded up the night before. By the time we saw them in the middle of the morning, the next morning, their beards had begun to grow. They had on fishnet type stockings, with hot pants, tight shorts, and some of them were wearing wigs, and some of them had tried to let their hair grow long and bleach it, and the bleach had turned it a bright orange color. Their makeup was smeared, and they were a miserable-looking bunch.

Tom also asked me to go with him one day to apprehend some aliens at a dairy farm in Marin County. People working in dairy farms go to work very early to do the milking. Then in the middle of the morning, they are through with the milking and were all congregated in the little house beside the barn. We drove into the parking lot. Tom said he would take the back door if I would take the front. I didn't know how many people would be inside, but we could hear them speaking in Spanish. Tom knocked on the back door, and a voice inside asked in Spanish, "Who is it?" Tom answered, "Immigration," and there was a deathly silence for several seconds. Suddenly the door flew open, and three people came running out. I grabbed one in each hand as they ran by me. Of course, the third one was into the pasture and into the bush. The two I grabbed weren't really trying to fight me, but they were struggling to get away, and one of them eventually broke loose. I continued to hold on to one of them. I had him by the wrist with both hands, and he was pulling as hard as he could. We ended up going around and around, with me hanging on. Tom then came around from the back door. I don't know how many people had gone out the back, but there was a dirty footprint squarely on Tom's chest. They had knocked him down when they ran out the back door, and all of them had gotten away. To say the least, Tom was a little bit irritated.

We carried the little slapper-type blackjack. The next time the alien I was holding onto made a circle, Tom slapped him across the head with his little blackjack, and that really made the alien mad. He began to struggle more fiercely, but I was still hanging on for dear life. As we swung around within Tom's reach again, he hit him again with the blackjack. This time he hit him harder, so hard in fact, that the little slapper came apart, and what was left of it bounced off the alien's head and struck me across the upper lip. This time he had hit the alien hard enough to take the fight out of him, and we ended up with one apprehension. Of course, the others had run away, and the dairy farmer was really upset. He was almost pleading and complaining that he couldn't get legal help, he had to use illegal aliens, that nobody else would stay out in the remote area where his dairy farm was located. He had tried over and over, he claimed, to get people to work by calling the employment office in San Francisco. He said that if the employment office sent anyone out there, they would only stay a day or two and be gone, and we were putting him out of business. I had heard that story many times in the Valley and didn't pay much attention. Our reply was the same one as always, that if he didn't use illegal aliens we wouldn't be there to catch them, and no one would be disturbed. I filed the location in the back of my mind to check again later.

Another time Tom wanted me to go with him to apprehend someone in the Mission district. As we traveled along the street, I asked Tom if he had a photograph or anything of the alien we were going to be looking for, so I would know who to look for. He said, yes, there was a picture in the file, and he dug it out and showed it to me. The person was extraordinary in that he had a long thin nose which one would recognize anywhere. Two or three blocks before we reached the address, I told Tom, "Stop, stop the car. Your alien is right there on the street." Tom couldn't believe that out of all the hundreds of people on the streets of San Francisco, I had spotted the one he was looking for. When we stopped and I jumped out of the car, I told him to go around the block, that I would trail the alien until he circled the block and got in front of the alien, then when we had him between us, we would apprehend him. It worked out perfectly, and the alien was more surprised that we had found him on the street than Tom was surprised that I had seen him.

Tom also introduced me to the jailers at the Marin County jail and the Sonoma County jail in Petaluma, California. If we were working overtime and apprehended an alien too late to deliver to the detention and deportation section in San Francisco, we would house him over night at one of the county jails. This would come in handy during the entire time I worked in San Francisco.

The area where my cases were located was the northern part of California. I would work from San Francisco all the way to the Oregon state line, and the remote part of our area was so far from the office it would require an overnight detail. I sorted through my caseload and prepared for a detail that would take me to Red Bluff, over the mountains through Lassen National Park to Susanville, California, then to a little place called Eagleville, then to Alturas, Redding, California, into Eureka, which was on the coast, and back down to San Francisco. I thought it would take me three days. I stopped in Red Bluff to check with the Postmaster to see if there was any record of the people I was looking for still receiving mail or having left a change of address. While I was in the post office, I noticed two Mexicans buying money orders to send back to Mexico. I tried to engage them in a conversation in English, but they gave the answer in Spanish, no speak English. I then switched to Spanish and identified myself as an Immigration Officer and asked them for their immigration documents, and they didn't have any. I took them into custody, and to my surprise, I found that I had locked my keys in the car. It was a bit embarrassing to stand around the car with two aliens in handcuffs, watching me attempt to get into the car to recover the keys. With the help of a coat hanger from the Postmaster's office, I finally got the door open. I proceeded to prepare a request to the sheriff's office to keep the aliens in custody and an apprehension report, then advised my Supervisor that I was leaving them in jail in Red Bluff while I proceeded on with my detail.

The trip across the Lassen National Park was very impressive. Northern California is beautiful country. Susanville is a little college town, and I was looking for two Iranians who supposedly had come to the United States to attend college, but like most of them, they had no intention of going to school. The Student's Visa is just a way of entering the United States. I had no luck getting any leads on where they may have gone and proceeded on to a little town called Cedarville, where I spent the night in what must have been the oldest hotel in California. It could have come out of a movie set.

The following morning, I went on to Eagleville, which consisted of a service station and a general store. I then went on to the ranch where the two aliens had been working when they were apprehended by the Border Patrol. I don't know why the Border Patrol didn't take them on with them when they found them, but for some reason the rancher had persuaded them to leave the aliens for a few days to help him complete his haying. He had promised that he would send them back to Mexico, and the Border Patrolmen had agreed. There was no record that they ever returned to Mexico, and on that basis, locate cases were opened on them.

The farmer seemed honest enough when he told me that he had personally taken the aliens to Reno, Nevada and put them on the bus after he purchased their tickets so they could return to Mexico at San Ysidro. They had documents to turn in at the border to verify their departure, but the documents had never been turned in. It's possible they took the documents with them to Mexico, but it is more likely they got off the bus in Los Angeles or some other place the bus stopped before returning to Mexico. Anyway, the rancher said that he had watched them board the bus and asked me why I was picking on him anyway. Why didn't I catch the aliens that the other rancher had just a few miles up the road? I assured him that we did not intentionally overlook any illegal aliens and that if he would tell me where they were, I would make an attempt to find them.

Luck was with me to a certain extent. As I approached the ranch he had told me about, a wagonload of hay was stopped beside the road, and two illegal aliens were unloading the bales of hay. I took them into custody and gave them a chance to go into the bunkhouse and gather up their personal belongings. I noticed that there was a third bunk in the bunkhouse with clothes hanging beside it, but no one in sight. I took the two aliens that I had apprehended and started across the mountains to Alturas. I was driving an old Chevrolet with automatic transmission. Something happened to the transmission, and the car would not shift to high gear. I could only drive in low gear and could not reach the speed of more than 20-25 miles per hour. I proceeded over the mountain, which was 5,000 or more feet high to Alturas, and I called the office and told Mr. Glazner that I was having car trouble and would probably need some assistance. He said he would send someone to help me, and the person he sent must have really flown because a few hours later Tom was banging on my motel door. By then it was dark, and I figured Tom would want to get a night's rest before starting out with me the next morning. I told him about the two aliens I had apprehended and that I felt sure I had left another one at the ranch. He said, well, let's take his car and go back to the ranch; if we didn't pick him up no one would probably ever find him.

Back across the mountain we went. We pulled into the yard in front of the bunkhouse. There was a board fence around the whole place, and when we climbed across the fence, I jumped down on the other side into what was a calf watering pail or tub and really skinned my shin. Dogs began barking after all the noise we were making. I felt sure the illegal alien would wake up and run into the night, but he was still sleeping as sound as a baby when we finally convinced him to open up for us. We gathered him and his belongings and headed back to Alturas for the rest of the night. The following morning we gathered up our three aliens, put them in the back seat of my car, and Tom was going to drive along behind me in his car in case the one I was driving completely gave out on me. We eased our way back across the National Park, finally reached Interstate 5 but were still some 60-80 miles from the San Francisco office. We started down the highway, and something snapped inside the transmission of the car I was driving. The thing changed gear, shot right up to 60 miles an hour, and it never gave a bit more trouble on the way back to the office. We arrived at the office, and Billy said he didn't believe anything had been wrong with the car. He felt like I just wanted Tom to come help me out on the detail. I never convinced anyone that something really had happened to the car's transmission.

I soon had enough work to justify a day in Stockton. I was anxious to go back to Stockton to see how the Border Patrol station had changed since I was there last. When I dropped in, a PI named Smith was alone at the station taking care of the paperwork. He told me they were still having trouble with the farmers, and they even saw crazy Miller occasionally when they worked the Modesto area. He said Miller now carried a German Shepherd dog around with him in his pickup, and whenever he saw a Border Patrol, he would stop and tell them, "Be careful, boys. This dog is trained to attack."

I planned another detail to Redding, California, and across the coastal range of mountains to Eureka, then through Ukia, on the way back to San Francisco. I found another couple of illegal aliens in Ukia to bring back to the office with me. As I walked down the hall to the Area Control section to leave the aliens I had brought with me, I heard some of the men in my section saying, "There goes Sims again with more wets. He thinks he's still in Area Control. Anybody can catch wets." That's true. Any Immigration Officer can catch illegal aliens. But it seemed to me that they had forgotten the part of our mission that says to apprehend those that are already here. I thought to myself, if they are so easy to catch, why do they always come back to the office with an empty car?

I had only been in San Francisco a few months when the District Director, Mr. Fullilove, retired. I hated to see him go since he was the one who had chosen me to come to San Francisco. The new DD was Mr. Williams. He had not been in San Francisco but a few days when he came by my desk and asked me if I knew the location of the French Consul's office. I told him that I did know where it was. He then told me to get a car and take him over there. The most direct route from our office to the Consul's office was through Chinatown, which was a congested area with narrow one-way streets.

Dear Chief

As we proceeded through Chinatown, I noticed a telephone company truck was parked on the right hand side of one of the one-way streets with these caution cones placed out on the street, but the street was wide enough to ease by the parked truck. The car in front of me made it by the truck with no problems. I eased over to the left hand edge of the street and started by the truck, but just as I drove even with the truck, the truck started backing up with its wheels cut into the street, and the front end of the truck banged into the side of the car I was driving. Mr. Williams jumped out of the car, said a few unpleasant words to the truck driver and told me he would catch a taxi on over to the French Consul's office, for me to go ahead and make out an accident repot, and if anyone said anything about the accident, just let him know. I did the paperwork, and no one ever said anything about that accident, but that was just one of three minor accidents I would have in a short period of time.

After the second accident, the Regional Office became interested and even sent an Investigator to check me out. I don't know if they thought I was an alcoholic or on drugs, or just what, but two fender benders was too many. The third was a little more serious than the first two. It wasn't as much of a fender bender as the other two had been. There was just a little bit of damage to the trunk of a car. We had both been stopped at a stop sign and started moving, when the car in front suddenly stopped again, and I put a very slight "v" shape dent in his trunk lid. It was so minor I started not to even report it, but then the other driver found out that I was driving a government vehicle, and I could see the dollar signs ringing in his eyes like a cash register. Then he told me that he would have to see his private physician. I went back to the office and completed the accident report forms and also wrote my Dear Chief" memo explaining the accident. I told my Supervisor that I believed the driver of the other vehicle intended to make trouble for the Service and asked him who he was assigning to do the accident investigation. I winced when he told me the person he was assigning, and I realized that he was inexperienced and had never done an accident investigation before. Billy thought it was not as serious as I thought, and the man he was assigning could handle it all right.

I kept checking with the Investigator to see how he was progressing with the investigation and urged him to go to the man and get a picture of his vehicle to show that it was only a slight "v" on the trunk of his car and there had been no personal injury. It was at least a week before he got around to getting the picture of the damage to the vehicle. By that time, the "v" was no longer visible, and the damage was a half round indentation in his whole trunk about the size of a basketball. It looked to me like he had deliberately backed into a telephone pole to show the damage more severe than it actually had been. In a couple more weeks we began receiving bills from the other driver. He submitted a bill for the damage to the car and weekly visits to a chiropractor. Each week we got another bill. Things went along until his claim had reached $1,800. Someone in authority then decided that we better pay the man before the bills got any higher.

Shortly thereafter, an Investigator came to the San Francisco office from the Regional office. It was obvious that he was not doing an accident investigation, but was really investigating me. He must have found that I was not on dope and did not use alcohol. He wanted a sworn statement from me. I was reluctant to make a sworn statement, as I advised him that I had set forth the details of the accident and the conditions in my memorandum, and that I was willing to swear that the contents of the memorandum were correct; but I didn't see any need for further sworn statements. He threatened me for being uncooperative, but his threats came to nothing more than a memorandum from Slick Martindale saying that I was at fault in the accident and that I was being reprimanded for my carelessness. He further added that if I chose, I could reply to his memorandum. I wrote another memo to Mr. Martindale, expanding the details I had given in the first memo and explained that the accident was a result of my foot slipping off of the brake pedal and letting my vehicle push forward just enough to put a dent in the other vehicle while we were both at a stop sign.

My memorandum to Mr. Martindale was not appreciated, and after a response saying that I would still be reprimanded and further correspondence was not necessary. I put the accident behind me, but I believe that the interest of the service had not been served and my personal interest had not been served. I was becoming convinced that the Immigration Service did not take care of its own; when one was the least bit in the wrong, we would be hung out to dry. I was fortunate that I had no other accidents as long as I was at San Francisco.

I was working alone a lot of the time, although I preferred to work with a partner when one was available. I still teamed up with Tom Smith often, and we occasionally would ask an Investigator to accompany each other when we thought we needed a witness or the job was too big for one person. I intended to go back by the dairy farm that Tom Smith had taken me to, and I asked Gary Murphy to accompany me. We arrived in the middle of the morning after the milking had been completed. I warned Gary what had happened before, how the aliens had burst out the doors and all but one had gotten away. I told him to keep his foot on the door so they couldn't swing it open at the back while I again went through the front. This time when I knocked on the door, all was quiet for a few seconds, then a question in Spanish came, "Who is it?" I answered that it was Immigration. In a few seconds someone timidly opened the door, and I eased my way in. I noticed that there were six aliens sitting around just finishing eating their breakfast. No one made any attempt to get away. I told Gary to come on in, that the back door was open, and I noticed that as he came through the back room, the kitchen part of the shack, that he picked up a kitchen butcher knife and put it where it would be out of reach. I looked around the front room and saw a shotgun standing in the corner, so I got between the gun and the seated aliens. I kept the gun with me while we rounded up their belongings and threw their boxes of personal things in the trunk of the car. Then we crowded the six aliens into the back seat. They had to sit in each other's laps for the six of them to get in the back. By then the rancher was on the scene. He paid them some, if not all, of the money he owed them. He said the shotgun was his, so I returned it to him, and we headed for the office in San Francisco. Those would be the last six aliens I would catch at that dairy farm. Some weeks later, I drove by again just to look over the situation. We found the barn was deserted, there was no one living in the shack, and sure enough, the farmer had gone out of business. That was the only time in my career that I know for sure that the Immigration Service actually put someone out of business.

I would return the favor and go with Murphy on one of his cases. The particular case he asked me to go with him was to arrest a woman from one of the South American countries. He had found where she was working and obtained an arrest warrant for her. She was a clerk/typist for some sort of organization. We arrived at their office, and a receptionist identified her for us before she realized we were Immigration Officers and intended to take the woman away. We went to her desk, and Investigator Murphy advised her that he had a warrant for her arrest and that she would have to accompany us. She was reluctant and didn't want to get out of her seat. By then, several employees were gathered around to see what was going on. The so-called director or manager of the office didn't think that we could take her, began questioning our authority to be there, and I could see a situation was about to develop where we might have a hard time getting the woman out of the office.

Murphy let everyone know that we intended to take the woman, but would cause her no harm. I snapped my handcuffs on her wrist and told her to come along. The people in the office then realized that we were going to remove her, so they lined up on the way to the front of the building. Everyone was putting their two cents worth about what they thought about the Immigration Service. One of them was right along beside us with a camera, and said he was taking pictures. I never saw any of them, but he pretended that he as taking pictures and said that we would hear from him or his attorney because he had everything recorded. True to his word, we heard from him the next day. When I arrived at the office, someone wanted to know what I had been into now. I asked him what he meant, and he said there are pickets outside the building, picketing the office, and their signs have your name on them. I didn't want to agitate the pickets, but I went to a place where I could see, and sure enough, there were about a dozen of them walking back and forth across the entrance to our office building. One of the signs said, "Who is Bruce Sims?" It was funny how they had remembered my name, but hadn't remembered Murphy's name. I certainly didn't think I was important enough to deserve picketing.

I have mentioned that I lived in Marin County and would occasionally leave an alien overnight in the Marin County jail. Marin County also was the location of another better-known prison. One day I worked late on the East Bay and was crossing the Richmond Bridge back to Marin County with one alien in custody that I had intended to leave at the Marin County jail. I had answered his question about what was going to happen to him, and told him that he would have to spend the night in jail and that tomorrow he would be transported to Livermore to our detention facility and then be put on the bus going back to the border. As we crossed the bridge, the alien asked me in his best Spanish a question that sounded like, "Vamos a San Guentine?" I didn't understand him and had him repeat the question, and he again asked me, "Vamos a San Guentine?" Then it struck me. We had just passed under a large green highway sign showing directions to San Quentin Prison, and he was scared, thinking I was going to take him to San Quentin.

Since I was keeping the car overnight, it was now my turn to help a new investigator get settled in. Dick White had transferred to San Francisco to fill a GS-12 vacancy in the Fraud Section. He thought he wanted to live in Marin County, and the Supervisor told me to do whatever was necessary to help him get settled in. For two days I took Dick to real estate office, to different addresses that he had seen in the paper in the real estate ads. We looked at several places until the end of the second day. A very attractive lady real estate agent felt sure that she had just what Dick was looking for, and he told me that he would not need me a third day, as she would take him to the sights he was interested in looking at. Sure enough, he bought a beautiful home beside the golf course. Dick was an easygoing and likeable fellow. He let it be known right away that he had not come to San Francisco to compete with anyone, that he had just accepted the promotion in order to get his "high three" as we called it. Retirement pay is based on the average salary of the three highest years of service, which is usually the person's last three years. True to his word, Dick would only stay the three years that he said he was going to stay before retiring. He fit right into the scheme of things at San Francisco and would be one of my poker-playing buddies.

I thought sometimes that he was too easygoing, especially one morning as I was going to give him a ride into the office and wanted to check an address in San Rafael, California. I was also going to give another Investigator a ride into the office. We went by the address, and sure enough, an illegal alien answered the door. When we checked the occupants, we found two men and a woman to be illegals. I took the precaution of handcuffing the two men together. I figured the woman would not run away and leave them. Then I told Dick that he could watch them and let them pack a few things they could take with them while I went on across the little town of San Rafael to pick up the other Investigator.

When I got back to the address, Dick was standing on the front porch waiting for me, and sitting in a chair beside him was an elderly man. I didn't see the three other aliens anywhere. I asked Dick, "Where area they?" and he said, "This is him." I asked, "What do you mean, this is him? Where are the other three that I left with you?" Dick explained that someone had knocked on the door, and when he went to answer the door, the two men and the woman had run out the back. The man knocking on the door was a friend of theirs who was wanting to get a ride to work with them, and Dick had taken him into custody, but the other three were gone with my handcuffs. I was a little perturbed with Dick. I thought he could have been more careful, but what was done was done.

We went on to San Francisco, and late that afternoon there was a call from the San Rafael Police Department. The desk Sergeant asked if one of our Investigators had lost a set of handcuffs. They got me to the phone, as I had told them about the incident at the office. I told him, yes, that I had lost a set of handcuffs, but there were two men attached to them. He told me that I could come back and get my handcuffs because when they found them the two men were still attached. Some woman had seen someone behind her house in a little brush-lined ditch. She didn't think the people had any business back there and had called the police. They located the two illegal aliens still wearing my handcuffs. The woman was still with them, so I recovered my handcuffs and the three illegal aliens. That would not be the only set of handcuffs I would lose.

By now, I was used to the routine of being an Investigator in the General Investigation Section. It was time to enjoy my work. I had all weekends and all holidays off, and it was a daytime job. I also was enjoying myself off duty. I had started playing softball with the team in the Novato City League. I was also attending a few pistol matches and would be attending other matches while on duty representing the office as part of the pistol team. We had a real Master Pistol Shooter at San Francisco who had come to us from

Arizona. That was Jerry Jackson, who was a National Combat Pistol Champion. He anchored the team, and I was the lowest qualified shooter on the tam, but we still managed to win a few trophies, both as a team and as individuals, in matches in the Bay Area. Jerry would repeat as Federal National Champion again in 1973. I would also attend the National Championship Matches in Jackson, Mississippi in 1973, but I would not attend as part of a team. I managed to take my vacation during that time of the year and would shoot in the marksman classification.

I didn't think I had done very well and didn't stay around at the end of the tournament for the award ceremony. I was only competing against other federal employees in my class. By the way, I never advanced further than sharpshooter. I returned to California not knowing I had won anything and was really surprised a few weeks later when a large package arrived for me. The package contained two trophies, one from the sponsors of the match for a first place in one of the individual matches, and a smaller trophy which I valued more highly because it was from the National Rifle Association informing me that I was the First Federal Marksman. So San Francisco office had two champions, Jerry Jackson in the Masters Classification, and I was the marksman Champion. Jerry got quite a bit of coverage in the local press for his Federal Championship, and I got a small paragraph in the local Novato paper. Jerry Jackson was the most dedicated pistol shooter I had ever known. He trained the hardest, the most conscientiously and deserved to repeat as Federal Champion shooting on the Border Patrol Team.

After about a year in the General Investigation Section, the Assistant District Director, Roland Fleagle, came to me and told me that the Area Control Section needed a GS-11 Investigator as a Team Leader and asked if I would be interested in working in that section, as I had been in the General Investigation section in New York and for a year in San Francisco. I believe I had learned all I was going to learn and told him I would be pleased to go to the Area Control Section. He said that Billy Brunskill would be busy as the Training Officer for the Trainee Investigators. All during his absence, I would be in charge of the Area Control Section.

There was an older Investigator already assigned to the Area Control Section, but he would have no objection to my being in charge. He was Dale Sparr. I would end up working quite a bit with Dale and appreciated his dedication and hard work. Dale's Spanish was not the best of any Investigator's; in fact, he would quite often in questioning an alien just throw out the infinitive form of a verb, rather than conjugating the verb and asking a perfectly conjugated sentence. It would some times end up like, "Donde obtener sus papeles?" In fact, when questioning a female with a birth certificate, she got so disgusted at his Spanish that after a few minutes of his questioning, she threw up her hands and said, "Okay, okay, I confess, that's not my birth certificate." She admitted that she had bought it from a vendor in Mexico. I recognized the woman as a bartender/waitress who worked in a bar in the Mission District who had been questioned once before by an Investigator I was working with, and he had accepted the validity of her birth certificate and told me she was 'okay.'

  I was also working with Dale one day in San Jose, California, when we found ourselves at a stoplight behind a pickup with five passengers in the back and the driver and one passenger in the cab. The passengers looked like typical illegal aliens, and I was wondering how we would get the pickup stopped without the aliens jumping off and running away. At the next stoplight, Dale solved the problem by jumping out of our car and jumping into the back of the pickup with the passengers who were too startled to move. I could see he was talking to each one of them as we proceeded to the next red light; he held up five fingers indicating to me that all five were illegal aliens, and we pulled away. At the next stoplight, he began pounding on the roof of the pickup truck to get the driver's attention, who didn't realize that he had just acquired an Immigration Officer as his sixth passenger in the back of the truck. When he heard the pounding on the roof, he pulled over to the side, and I stopped behind them and immediately went forward to assist Dale in securing the illegal aliens. I also checked the passenger in the front of the pickup and found he was also an illegal alien. We secured them in our car, and the driver, who was very surprised, continued without any passengers.

  Dale eventually retired. He had in enough time to retire any time he chose to, but he had a minor accident on the Bay Bridge, and rather than face an investigation he decided it was time to retire.

  Tom Smith was also working in the Area Control Section. His primary responsibility was doing the jail checks in the Bay Area, but he would still have some free time to work with me on Area Control. He asked me one evening to accompany him on the way back home. He said that he knew of a house in San Raphael where an alien was living. Tom asked me to go to the back door, and he would knock on the front door. The occupants of the house were having supper, and I discovered that there was no back door for me to watch. I could see someone get up from the table and answer the knock at the front door. I also saw a second person leave the table and go to the other end of the building, and I could hear him going out the side door. I ran around the end of the building just as fast as I could. The man had a fairly good head start, but it was downhill, and as I chased him, I could tell I was gaining on him. He would occasionally look back, and I was right behind him. After about two blocks, he made the mistake of looking back just as we came to an intersection. He crossed the intersection while looking back over his shoulder and ran off of a small embankment and fell down. By the time he scrambled to his feet, I jumped off the small embankment, and the alien turned around to face me. I thought he would surrender, since I had caught up with him, but he tried to run again. I grabbed onto his shoulder and spun him around and swung at him with my fist.

Instead of hitting him with my fist, I struck him with my elbow. I gave him quite a clip on the chin, and he went back to the ground again. This time he lay there several seconds, and I began to be worried, thinking I had really injured him. Then in a few seconds he began to moan and tried to get to his feet. I slipped the handcuff on him before I helped him regain his feet and marched him back to the house where Tom was still waiting for me. Tom was a little bit surprised that I had caught the young man and said he figured we had seen the last of him.

Many of these young aliens we were apprehending in the Bay Area had been smuggled for amounts ranging from three hundred dollars and up. They were three hundred miles away from the border and were determined not to be apprehended. They would resist arrest, or at least run at the least opportunity. Tom had learned through his experience dealing with these people that it was important to keep them well secured when in custody. Tom usually had two or three pair of handcuffs, if not hanging from his belt, at least in his briefcase, and I was soon to follow his example.

We had vehicles with screens between the front seat and back seat, and we had removed the window handles and the back door handles, but the back door could still be opened from the outside. There was not a real good way of securing a person in the back while we went inside to look for others. I tried handcuffing one hand to the alien and one hand to the ring in the seat safety belt. I had returned to find an empty car on more than one occasion. Someone had opened the door while we were inside the building and cut the seat safety strap, and the alien had disappeared. After this happened a couple of times and I had lost a couple of sets of handcuffs, we had to come up with a better way of securing aliens. Our solution was to buy a short piece of chain with a large ring at one end and bolt the chain to the floor where the safety straps were bolted. Then we could attach several sets of handcuffs to a ring and to aliens seated in the back. Then it didn't matter if somebody opened the door for them from the outside; they still weren't going anywhere. This worked out pretty good for several months. We would often overload the sedan, and since we didn't have panel trucks available to us, we would either transport as many as we could haul back to the office in the sedan or call by radio and advise Mr. Brunskill that we had more aliens in custody than we could haul, and would he please send a Detention Officer to meet us with a panel truck.

We learned that we could save time by carrying a clipboard with several blank forms, and while we were waiting for the Detention Officer to drive the sixty miles from San Francisco down to San Jose, we would have the apprehension report written. He could then transport the aliens directly to the detention facility at Livermore without ever having to take them to San Francisco. If a panel truck was not available, we would often have someone guard some of the aliens while we took a carload to the county jail in San Jose, and we would leave them in the drunk tank and then return to San Francisco with an empty vehicle. That way we could work our way back, and usually load the vehicle again somewhere on the way. The only problem was the delay in getting assistance. Mr. Brunskill was very deliberate in his actions and would sit at his desk and smoke his pipe and think about problems before giving an answer. Very often we would wait and wait and never hear from him until we called him a second time to ask if the Detention Officer was coming or not, and he would tell us he was still working on it. After I had worked for him for several months and annual appraisals were due, he stated that one of my faults was that I made decisions too quickly. When I was the Acting Supervisor and someone called me, I tried to give them an answer as quickly as possible; so if that was his only criticism of me, then I could certainly live with that.

It was my impression that Mr. Brunskill was not too happy in his job as Supervisor of the Area Control Section. He had come to San Francisco after a tour in Germany, and it was his impression that he would be given the OIC job in one of the San Francisco sub-offices, either Sacramento or Las Vegas.

Whenever I could, I liked to take the whole section as a task force and check some of the larger nurseries, construction sites, or the racetrack. These were places where we needed all of our officers to surround the business, and we would load all of our sedans and the panel truck if we could get one to accompany us. During the racing season, we liked to check the racetrack at Belmont where we found grooms and stable boys, and of course, they ran all over the place. We also checked housing construction sites in the South Bay, and there were several nurseries scattered all over the Bay Area. I have seen aliens literally run through the walls of the nurseries. Some of the walls would be sheets of plastic, and some would be glass. It was difficult to catch all of the aliens. I'm sure we never did, and for that reason we had to return to the same sites fairly frequently, because they would very quickly replace the ones we had apprehended.

One of the places we checked fairly often was a business that arranged dried flowers. The aliens could see us the moment we pulled into the parking lot, and they would be running and hiding and crawling under cardboard boxes and under the flower cuttings. You would just have to feel around underneath the stuff and find them hiding. Occasionally, your hand would touch a thigh or a breast even, and how we would laugh about having to drag the aliens out of their hiding places.

One of the places where I took my whole section to check was a laundry in Mountain View, California. We had the owner's permission to check all of the employees. They said they really didn't want to use illegal alien help. They weren't exploiting the aliens. They paid them as much as they paid the citizen or legal workers. We checked the laundry, and they were hiding in every place imaginable. I knew some had gone into the ladies' room, so after we had all of the ones assembled, I told one of the managers to warn the women in the ladies' room that a man would be entering in three minutes. After the three minutes' warning, she accompanied me into the ladies' room, and we found a half dozen women hiding. Some were just standing in the stalls, and you could just see their feet underneath. Others were standing on the seats, trying to stay out of sight, but it was to no avail.

One of the filthiest places that we checked was a tanning business where they turned sheepskins and cattle hides into leather. The place was filthy with drying hides. There were also rats where the hair was removed, and the floor was covered with salt. It was generally a dirty place to go to, and you had to just dig them out of the hiding places and actually take some of them off of the roof, as they would run upstairs and go through the ventilation windows out onto the roof. But it was all exciting, and I never got tired of it.

After conducting one of the group operations, then we would split up and work our way back to the office. One of the places where I liked to stop on the way back was the Copperpenny Coffee Shops. There were several of them in the Bay Area, and we could usually stop at a different one each time. We would have a cup of coffee, which would give us time to look at the dishwasher and busboy, and most times we would then decide to check their identity. Time after time we would take one or two aliens with us after our coffee break. Some men were a little embarrassed about stopping at a restaurant or café and having lunch or a coffee break, then checking the kitchen help. I was never embarrassed about this, as I believed they should not be using illegal aliens. I didn't believe the owner or manager's complaint that he couldn't get anyone else to do these jobs. In my experience, there was always someone looking for a job.

Another one of my duties in the Area Control Unit was assisting in the maintenance of the District's vehicles. Our beautiful and efficient secretary, Denise, kept up with the scheduled maintenance inspections and had a status board showing the mileage of each vehicle, but someone had to make sure that the radios were taken to the radio shop and that the vehicles were taken back and forth to the garage. Also, our vehicles were not new vehicles when they came to us. They had been used for a year by the Border Patrol before they acquired new vehicles and gave their year-old vehicles to us. They were all light green and white, the Border Patrol colors, which were unsuitable for investigation work, so it was up to me to take the vehicles over to Earl Scheib for a cheap paint job. Tan or light brown were the most frequently painted colors, but I decided that we could spice up things a bit, and I had one painted chartreuse and another was a grey color bottom with a cream top. These two certainly didn't look like government vehicles, but the ones that were painted a solid color were not fooling anybody. In fact, in the Mission district one day, when I returned from checking an address, a young boy about eleven years old was on the roof of the car telling some younger street urchins, "This is a police car." He was pointing at the hole in the roof that had been plugged by a rubber plug where the roof-mounted radio antenna had been removed and I had replaced it with a fender-mounted antenna.

I was keeping a car overnight most of the time except on weekends. It was hard to justify having a car on Saturday and Sunday, so I usually checked one out on Monday morning and turned it in on Friday at the end of the shift. The request for overnight use had to be signed by my Supervisor or Mr. Fleagle, the ADDI. He knew when I had a car and would frequently see me near the end of the day and tell me he wanted a ride home with me that evening. I was usually pretty conscientious about carrying passengers, as we had been accused of using the government cars as a taxi or a carpool for the people living in Marin County to get home, and I would usually tell him, "Well, you know I'm going to work overtime on the way home; if you want to go with me, fine." He would say, "Well, let me get my pistol," and he would take his pistol out of his locked drawer that he kept it in during the day, and we would look for illegal aliens on the way home.

There were a couple of restaurants that I checked periodically, and I would occasionally go by the nursery that Tom Smith had taken me to. This was located in a narrow valley with steep hillsides. The only way to approach it in a vehicle was directly up the valley; and if they were watching, the illegal aliens could see the car turn off the highway almost a half mile from the building where they were working in the flower shed. Mr. Fleagle was with me one evening when I checked the place, and sure enough, as I approached within a couple hundred yards of the building, the aliens saw me and started running out the back and up the sides of the hill. I sped up to get there and tried to cut some of them off before they could get up the hillside. I was successful in grabbing a couple and throwing them in the back seat of the car.

Mr. Fleagle got out to check the little warehouse where the flowers and shrubs were being arranged. There was usually someone who didn't run, so Mr. Fleagle checked those who stayed behind. I continued on beyond the shed, and the owner's dog ran out and grabbed the car by the wheel and it sent him for a flip. The owner came out and thought I had injured his dog. He bent down to see about it, and the dog snapped him and bit him on his wrist, hard enough to bring blood. To add to those troubles, we had run off and caught part of his help. I continued chasing one in the car that I could see running in the road ahead of me. He stepped over an irrigation pipe. I didn't know exactly what these pipes were made of, and I ran over it with the car. It turned out it was made out of paper-thin aluminum, and I smashed one joint of his irrigation pipe as flat as a pancake. I caught that alien and then brought back the ones I had caught, and the man was fuming mad. He cursed me and called me every name he could think of. I just stood there and thought, well, maybe I deserved part of it by hitting his dog and smashing a joint of his pipe.

After awhile, he kind of ran down and started repeating what he had said before, that he was going to sue somebody for damages. Mr. Fleagle hadn't said a word; he just stood there and listened. Finally, he asked the man, "Don't you have homeowner's insurance?" The man hesitated a minute and said, yes, that he did. Mr. Fleagle said, "Well, that should take care of it," and we got in our car and left before he had time to think about it any further. I always thought that was pretty fast thinking on Mr. Fleagle's part.

I enjoyed working with the old man. In fact, we had a nickname for him. One of the boys started calling him the "Old PI," because of his Area Control work with me. We didn't call him that to his face, but my wife eventually asked him one day if he knew what his nickname was. She said, "The guys have started calling you the 'Old PI,'" and he grinned, and I believe he really liked his nickname.

Dear Chief

Despite the warnings we received about giving our buddies a lift home in a government car, the four Investigators who lived in Petaluma, California, continued to give each other a ride. One of the four nearly always had a car overnight so the other three, to keep from being so obvious about it, would wait on the street corner about a block away from the office while the one with the car would come by and pick them up and give them a ride home. Petaluma was just a few miles north of Novato, and the Old PI and I would occasionally find ourselves in heavy traffic, riding alongside the Investigators on their way home to Petaluma. In instances like that, we just pretended we didn't see them and gave no indication of recognition. Some things were just better left unseen.

I enjoyed visiting and talking with the Old PI about his Immigration experiences. His wife, Lettie, and Jerry were good friends, and he hosted the poker party occasionally. My Wife, Jerry, and I had continued to visit with Bob and Barbara McCord often. Bob and Dick White and I were regulars at the poker party, which I enjoyed. The stakes were small, and no one ever won or lost any big money. It was just a chance to get together and shoot the bull about what was going on at the office, but the poker parties were about to break up. Bob had decided he would apply for one of the vacancies in Chula Vista for Assistant Chief in the Border Patrol. It would be a promotion to GS-12, and fortune would smile on Bob. He was selected to fill the Assistant Chief vacancy, and Assistant Chiefs were upgraded by the Civil Service Commission to GS-13. All Bob had to do was spend a year in grade, and he was upgraded to GS-13 and would go on from there to be promoted to the Regional Office and eventually return to a sector as a Chief Patrol Inspector. I was happy for Bob. It isn't very often that one of the good guys gets the breaks.

I thought things were really going well in the Area Control Unit. By working together as a task force, we had increased the number of apprehensions from what they were before I went into the section. We would get a little break. The sub-office at Las Vegas only had two Investigators. The OIC felt that that was not enough for a good operation. He requested five men be detailed to Las Vegas for a week. I took four of my Investigators, and we flew over to Las Vegas. The OIC, Jim Walsh, was glad to see us. He told us the first place he wanted us to check would be Western Linen Company, a large laundry where we would probably apprehend fifty aliens. I was a bit skeptical, as I had never found fifty aliens before in one place. We asked for further assistance from the Police Department and the Sheriff's Office. They surrounded the place while we went to the door. Mr. Walsh talked to the owner, who was reluctant to let us in, but was not willing to personally prevent us from talking to the illegal aliens. So we went in and found aliens hiding in every conceivable place. They were in dirty clothes hampers, they were in machines, they were under machines, they were on top of machines, and we did catch almost fifty. When we thought we had found every one and were ready to leave, as we exited the main part of the plant, I said, "Boys, there's one more we better take with us." They said, "Where, where?" I said, "On the wall over our heads." The building had steel beams supporting the metal roof, and one of the aliens had climbed one of those beams and was hanging on to the wall just under the roof. We had walked under him several times without looking up and seeing him. We had transportation waiting, one of the Sheriff's buses. We marched them outside, and as we were about to leave, one of the female Deputy Sheriffs, who was quite a large woman, came marching a little Mexican about half her size back up to the bus, holding him by the back of his shirt and almost lifting his feet off the ground. She was smiling from ear to ear and said, "I got me one; he climbed over the fence, but I caught him."

  Things were hectic for the first three days, but we still had time to visit the casinos on our off duty time. By the end of the week, things had slowed down, and we were just catching a couple here and there. We stopped one morning at the International House of Pancakes restaurant. There was an illegal looking young man mopping the floor. He bumped our table but didn't say excuse me. We could see another one or two in the kitchen. I told the boys I was sitting with, "When we get ready to leave, we'll have to take this young man with us." The investigator across the table could see into the kitchen better than I could and said, "If we take him, we'll have to take the other two that I can see in the kitchen." We finished our breakfast, paid our bill, and I told the cashier that we were Immigration Officers and this was also a business call, that we would also have to check their kitchen help. About that time the day shift came on duty, and another group of illegal aliens arrived. We ended up taking seven illegal aliens from the restaurant. We left the waitresses almost in tears. They were lamenting, "Oh, what will we do now?" Then they were deciding someone will have to wash dishes and someone will have to do the busboy's job, and we had really made a dent in the alien population of Las Vegas.

By the end of the five-day detail, we had pretty well checked all of the businesses we wanted to check and were going to addresses where aliens had been reported to be living. We were a little too late in most cases. There was evidence that someone had departed hastily. There was unused food in the kitchen, half eaten meals on the table, and no one to be found. When we asked the neighbors what had happened, they said, "We don't know, but a carload of them loaded up last night and left in a hurry. We think they were going to Los Angeles." They hadn't taken long to get out the word that Immigration was cracking down on illegals in Las Vegas, and they were looking for someplace that wasn't hardly so hot.

There was one more item of business to tend to while we were there. Walsh told me about a bar that constantly hired illegal aliens and had become a trouble spot for the Police Department. Jim had good relations with the Alcohol Control Board and the Governor of Nevada, and the Governor had promised him that if one more illegal was apprehended at that bar, he would pull their liquor license. Jim asked me to go by at night one night while we were there and see if there were any more illegal aliens. We went by, and sure enough, we did apprehend one more illegal alien, and that was justification for closing the place. Jim thought we had done a good job on the detail. My men and I enjoyed the five days. I had been to Las Vegas to visit the casinos several times previously and usually ended up losing money, but this trip, at the end of the five days, I had more money than I had arrived with.

There was always something exciting happening in Area Control. One morning I found myself alone passing by a Laundromat in the edge of Chinatown. I glanced inside and saw two young men who certainly looked like illegal aliens. I decided they should be checked. I went in the only door to the Laundromat with my ID card in my hand. One of the boys was talking on the telephone. I could hear them speaking Spanish. The other one was just standing over his shoulder. The minute I identified myself and told him this was an

Immigration check, I needed to see their Immigration documents, the one on the phone dropped the phone without hanging it up, and they both charged towards the door trying to get past me. I was not able to hold on to both of them. One managed to squeeze by, and the other one, although he was not a big person, certainly was strong, and he was really resisting. We were wrestling around enough so I could not get my handcuffs on him. Finally he slipped on the slick floor and grabbed my coat pocket and ripped the pocket right down to the hem of the coat. It was damaged too severely to ever be repaired. He ignored my order to be calm, continued to struggle, and I was a bit angered that he had torn my clothing. He continued to resist, so I walloped him across the head with my handcuffs, which cut a little bit of a gash but took the fight right out of him. I handcuffed him and marched him the couple of blocks to the office.

    I asked my supervisor about the damage to my suit. It was not an expensive suit. He referred me to the Deputy District Director, Mr. Pullin, who informed me that he doubted that the Regional Office would have any money to replace my torn clothing. Nevertheless, I prepared a memorandum giving the value of the suit and stating that I believed it was still worth half of the original cost and requested reimbursement. The men in the office were very curious and kept asking me what progress I had made with my request. It was divided in opinion whether I would be reimbursed or not, and those who doubted that I would be were surprised when a few weeks later I received a check for the amount I had requested.

    It was time to get more cars from the Border Patrol. This time we would be receiving three cars from the Chula Vista Sector. I took two Investigators with me, and we flew to San Diego. A Border Patrolman met us at the airport and drove us to the Sector Headquarters. I hoped I would be able to visit with Bob McCord, but he wasn't working that day. I was pleasantly surprised to see a familiar face. It was Assistant Chief Gillman, "Uncle Al," who had been our Station Senior at Harlingen, Texas. He showed me the vehicles we would be driving back. They were equipped with red lights and sirens. The sirens were under the hood, and the red lights were mounted in the grill. I persuaded him to leave the siren and the red lights on the vehicles. We started back to San Francisco. I drove as far as Los Angeles. It was getting late in the evening, and I decided that was far enough for one day and found a motel to spend the night.

One of the other Investigators had a relative in Los Angeles and had told me that he was stopping to spend the night with the relative. I wasn't sure what the other Investigator was doing. I checked the local paper and saw that the Los Angeles Dodgers were playing the New York Mets that night, so I went to the baseball game. The Mets were one of my favorite teams ever since I lived in New York. I finally got to see a World Series Game when the Mets played the Oakland Athletics. The next day I continued on to San Francisco.

There is a mountain between Los Angeles and Bakersfield that is called the Grapevine. As I came off of the mountain on to the lower level Valley, I was passed by a man in a Porsche sports car. He was going at a rapid rate of speed, and I wondered if we had to chase someone in the cars we had gotten from the Patrol, which were eight cylinder Ambassadors, would we be able to catch him. I speeded up until I was going ninety miles and hour and still wasn't overtaking the sports car. The car I was driving was very steady with no shimmy and still had more power, so I mashed harder on the gas pedal until my speedometer registered 106 miles per hour, and I was just eating the sports car alive. He glanced in his rear view mirror and saw this car with the green and white markings overtaking. He quickly slammed on his breaks and slowed down to the legal speed limit, and I flew by him and didn't slow down until I was well ahead of him and out of sight. Those cars proved to me that they had plenty of power. After those cars came back from their Earl Sheib paint job, they looked nothing at all like government vehicles.

Ii was during my assignment to the Area Control Unit that a young lady, whom I shall call Norma, came to the Immigration Office. One of our Area Control men had apprehended her uncle. She came to see what was going to happen to him and asked if there was anything she could do to assist him. I explained to her as best I could the procedure when an alien is apprehended. I told her that in his case, a Warrant of Arrest and an Order to Show Cause had been issued, and he would be having a deportation hearing before an Immigration Judge. She wanted to know what would happen to him at the hearing, and I explained to her that if he had a return trip ticket to show the Immigration Judge and told the Judge he was willing to leave voluntarily at his own expense, he would probably not be ordered deported. We talked a bit more. I told her that her uncle's case was now in the hands of the Deportation Sections, and there was nothing more I could do. She told me that she was like her uncle, a citizen of Bolivia and assured me that she was a student in a legal status and was going to school. She stated that she was willing to do anything to help her uncle, and I caught the emphasis on the "anything." She departed, and I didn't think much about her or her uncle. A few weeks later, Norma showed up at the office again and came to see me. There was really no reason for her to come to see me a second time, but she said she just wanted to thank me for being so nice to her. She told me that her uncle had gone back to Bolivia and that I would be welcome to come by where she lived for tea or coffee if I wanted to. This time I paid a little more attention to Norma, and my curiosity was aroused. I noted that she was short with long black hair down to her waist and had a nice smile. Her visit would change my life considerably.

It came at a time when Jerry had been saying she was going back to Mississippi. I told her, "Fine, go back to Mississippi," and took her to the bus station in San Francisco where she caught the bus. She would be in Mississippi for three weeks before she said by phone that she was ready to come back and asked me to come get her. During those three weeks I would be burning the candle at both ends. As soon as Jerry was on her way to Mississippi, I went by the address Norma had given me. She had no phone, so I just dropped by one evening after work, unannounced. It was on my way home. The house she was living in was a multi-story house with a car garage and apartment at ground level. Norma was living in the apartment by the garage. She was home and seemed glad to see me. I found out she was twenty-six years old. She told me that the man who owned the building was seldom home, and he gave her the garage apartment for taking care of his house and feeding his dog while he was away. Norma was not at all reluctant to get closer acquainted. She knew I had not stopped by just for coffee, and that suited her. We quickly found ourselves on the couch enjoying each other's company. Sex just seemed to be a natural part of life. In fact, looking back, I realized that it was a very casual thing, not very emotionally involved. It was just something she could give a friend.

The first week that Jerry was gone I visited Norma again, and we decided to enjoy our weekend with a drive up to Lake Tahoe. Before the week was out, however, I discovered that she had a sister living with her. I don't know where her sister was the first evening I visited, but after that, when I arrived, she would go upstairs. I took both of them on the round trip to Lake Tahoe. It was a very scenic trip, the lake was beautiful, there was some snow on the ground, and they seemed to have a good time. I bought lunch, and they both ordered a steak. I ordered my steak medium; they wanted theirs cooked rare. When their steaks arrived, I think they were surprised that rare was not cooked very much. Rather than sending their steaks back and have them cooked more, they only ate about two bites of the leanest part, and the rest was wasted.

During week number two, I still found time to visit Norma as often as I like, but one evening I got there before she arrived home from her classes in Oakland. She claimed she was late because she had missed her bus that she usually took. She was also accompanied by a young man. She told me his name, but I really didn't care what his name was. It was an inconvenience. He was also slightly embarrassed and claimed that they had intended to study together, but he wouldn't be staying and made a hasty retreat. The family Norma was living with decided to move. The next thing I heard from her she was furnishing me a new address in Oakland.

Getting from San Francisco to Oakland was an inconvenience, not nearly as handy as working some overtime and stopping by her house on my way home. I did, however, get over to Oakland, and she and her sister had moved into the main house. There was no separate apartment for them. When I was there, the family was on vacation and left her to take care of the dogs. They had left her a little money to buy dog food, and she had bought the most expensive cans of dog food and dry dog food that she could buy. She had used up all the money they had given her, and although the family had been gone a few days, she had run out of food for herself and her sister. She claimed that the money she usually received for her school expenses had not arrived, so I bought a few groceries. Since the family would be away over the weekend and her sister now had something to eat and could take care of the dogs, I asked Norma if she could come to the house with me and spend the night on Saturday night. She agreed, and I took her to my house in Novato. I should have known that the neighbors always had curious eyes and never missed a thing that was going on in the neighborhood. I had taken no precautions to conceal the fact that I arrived at home with a woman in the car. I'm sure the neighbors noted that she didn't leave until the next day.

A few days later, I received word from Jerry that she was ready to come back to California. She asked that I come and get her, and I was certainly ready to. I took some annual leave and went back to Mississippi. We returned to California, and the first day that Jerry was home and I went back to work, the neighbors (she would never tell me which one) had wasted no time in telling Jerry about me bringing a woman home with me. When I arrived home from work that day, she knew all about it, and she asked abruptly, "Who was the woman?" There was no use trying to deny what I had done. I was an adulterer. No one forced me to do what I had done. It was just a weakness in my character. There was nothing to do but confess the whole affair and ask for Jerry's forgiveness. It was a tearful scene. Jerry had to make up her mind whether she wanted to forgive me and continue to live with me or to take some legal action. She decided that she would forgive me, but the trust she had had in me was destroyed, and things would never be the same between us again.

I had told Norma I was bringing my wife back from Mississippi and that our affair was ended. There were no sad goodbyes, and I would hear from her only once more. A few months went by, and she called me at the office to let me know she had met and married a man in Oakland who would file a petition for her so that she could remain in the United States. She said that he was not disappointed that she had a ten-year-old daughter in Bolivia and was willing to petition for her, also. I suppose things worked out for her in the long run the way that she wanted.

I believe things were going well as far as my duty was concerned in the San Francisco office. We were making record numbers of apprehensions, but I was due for a surprising and unexpected change in assignments. One weekend, Mr. Fleagle told me that I was to report to the District Director's office the following Monday morning I went to see Mr. Williams, the District Director. Mr. Pullin, the Deputy District Director, was in Mr. Williams' office. The two of them were expecting me. As soon as I entered the office,

Mr. Pullin started the conversation by telling me that he had heard that I had installed a length of chain in the back of the cars in which we were securing aliens, and that I had several pairs of handcuffs. I told him that was correct, that we were making lots of apprehensions, that we needed several pairs of handcuffs to secure the aliens as we apprehended them, and that the chain had worked out quite well as they were no longer able to escape when we were away from the car, even though someone might be willing to open the door for them from the outside. He told me that the first thing I would do was to take the chain out of the car, turn in the extra handcuffs that I had got from supply, and I would only keep the one set I had been originally issued.

I looked to Mr. Williams for some sign of support. I explained that the length of chain with the "O" ring end in the back of the car was for the security of the aliens, and the extra handcuffs were needed because we were making numerous apprehensions, and that I felt they were necessary for the safety of myself and my partner. Mr. Williams surprised me by saying, "Well, Bruce, if you think you can only handle one alien each in safety, then apprehend your two aliens and bring them back to the office." That must have been the signal for Mr. Pullin to terminate that part of our discussion. He then told me to come with him into his office which adjoined the District Director's office. Once again, he continued by telling me he had heard that I had left the red lights and sirens on the cars we had obtained from the Border Patrol. I told him he was correct. He informed me that I would have them taken off immediately, and that I was reassigned to the Fraud Unit. I was surprised at the abruptness of this change of assignments, but it would prove to be a good move for me. I had not heard of any of my Investigators misusing the red lights and sirens. I don't know what prompted Mr. Pullin's actions, but I couldn't resist before leaving his office in telling him that I had always believed he supported his Investigators, and I was disappointed in this lack of support. His last comment was that no one had ever accused him of not supporting his Investigators, but that is the way my assignment to the Area Control Section ended.

After complying with Mr. Pullin's order to remove the red lights, sirens, and chains from the vehicles, I reported to Mr. Charles Hoffman for duty in the Fraud Section. Charles Hoffman looked younger than his years. Some of the Investigators who had been assigned to the Fraud Section for a long time called him Chuck, but I was never comfortable with calling him Chuck. I always referred to him as Mr. Hoffman. The Fraud Section was considered a bit more prestigious an assignment than the General Section. There were four Grade 12 Investigators in the Fraud Section doing the harder cases. One of them was Richard White, who would be retiring soon. Richard was true to his word when he told us he was only going to do three years, and then retire. When the three years were completed, Richard sold his nice home by the golf course for a tremendous profit and moved back to North Carolina.

The area we would be working was, in fact, a larger area than I had worked in the General Section. One of the Grade 12 Investigators was named Francis Leo, who was of Chinese descent. He was a very likeable person, always smiling and was willing to answer the many questions I had about fraud cases. The first case that Mr. Hoffman gave me concerned a Filipino woman who was suspected of having obtained her legal residence through a fraudulent marriage. The case was nearing the deadline for her permanent residence to be revoked. I made the case fairly quickly by going to her residence about six o'clock one morning. Unexpectedly, I rang her doorbell, and I could hear the movement inside. She told me to wait a minute, and it was obviously noise of someone trying to hide. I looked around and saw that two people had been eating breakfast. I asked her where her husband was, the one who had petitioned for her to become a resident of the United States. She claimed that he had just left, going to work. I advised her that I had been on surveillance outside her apartment and no one had left going to work. I told her I suspected that there was another man in the house, and the noise I had heard was the person hiding, and it would be better if she told him to come out of his hiding place, and we would talk about her case.

After some hesitation, she told the person to come out of the closet where he was hiding. The person proved to be her former Filipino husband. In order for her to come to the United States, she had divorced her husband in the Philippines, married an American who had petitioned for her, and after receiving her resident's identification card, she had left her American husband. The former Filipino husband had entered the United States as a visitor and had

Dear Chief

taken up residence with his former wife. It was her intention to divorce the American husband. She could then remarry her former Filipino husband and file a petition for him to join her as a resident of the United States. It didn't work out that way for them.

Another problem the Immigration Service had which resulted in a fraud investigation was imposters obtaining alien identification cards. Usually a sharp-eyed inspector would detect that an impersonator was attempting to obtain a card, but in many cases, one or two duplicate cards had been issued before the inspectors realized that a fraud was being perpetrated. The case was then assigned to an Investigator to attempt to locate the impersonators and recover the cars that had been issued and prosecute the offenders, if possible.

There were also cases for investigation of schools which furnished forms I-20 for foreign students to attend and businesses who petitioned for foreign professionals, but the majority of our work would be fraudulent marriages between Filipinos and United States citizens. One of the imposter cases that I was only partially successful with concerned a Mexican woman who had immigrated to the United States, and subsequently, applications began appearing in her file requesting duplicate alien registration cards. The woman had long hair which hung over one eye in a Veronica Lake fashion, with only part of her face visible. The photo attached to the application for the duplicate cards could easily have been mistaken for the original person because each of them had their long hair combed over one eye. Two duplicate cards had been issued before an inspector became suspicious and decided that the most recent application was worthy of an investigation before the card was issued. The third photo also had the same hairstyle, but enough of the person's face was visible to see that it was a younger person than the person who was originally issued the card.

Finding a subject in an investigation was sometimes difficult, and getting them to cooperate once they are located was even more difficult. In this case, I finally located the subject and advised her that we knew that the people who had obtained alien registration cards were not her. I advised her that I suspected she was obtaining the alien registration cards and selling them. She protested that she had not obtained any of the cards and had never sold any alien registration cards. I let her convince me that I believed she was telling the truth, but we still had to recover the two cards that were issued. Eventually, she admitted that one of the cards had been obtained by her sister. That was the one who bore the most resemblance to her. The second card had been issued to a cousin when the sister saw how easy it was to obtain a card simply by filling out an application and furnishing photos. The subject eventually told me how to locate her sister, who she claimed had gone back to Mexico and just wanted to use the card occasionally to enter the United States or to work a short period of time. I sent a form letter to the sister's address in Mexico, and to my surprise, the alien registration card was returned. The letter to the cousin was never answered, and I never recovered that card.

Some of the cases were fairly easy to break once it was established that the petitioner and beneficiary were not living together as husband and wife. In fact, some of the petitioners turned out to be related to the beneficiary. Sometimes an uncle or cousin who wanted to help the family relative had entered into a fraudulent marriage and filed a petition. These people would usually agree to withdraw the petition once the investigation was conducted and they saw they were not going to be successful in obtaining permanent residence for their relatives. Most of the beneficiaries had entered the Untied States on Tourist Visas, and the next step was to locate them and have them deported.

If the file contained a Notice of Appearance of an Attorney, we would not question the attorney's clients without him being present. Usually, the Investigator would do a neighborhood investigation and determine if the subjects were living together at the address given on their application. If not, he would try to establish who, in reality, did live at that address, then he would send the attorney an appointment letter asking him to appear with his clients for questioning.

There were several attorneys who worked nothing but Immigration work. Most of them were not looked at favorably in the eyes of the Investigators. We knew that they were charging exorbitant prices for doing simple paperwork that the aliens could do for themselves and pay only a small fee to the Immigration Service. One of the better-known and more highly regarded attorneys had filed the application on behalf of a Philippine gentleman and lady who had become quite famous in the Philippines. She was a recording artist and singer who had made some albums and now used the stage name of Butterfly, or "Papillon." The gentleman she married was about 70 years old. Despite his age, I learned he was still working. I went to the address given on the application where I expected to find them living together, at least for appearance sake until the beneficiary obtained her benefits, but although I went to the address early in the morning, late at night, and several different times during the day, no one was ever home. Finally, I sent the attorney a Notice of Appearance for an interview.

After two set appointments passed and the attorney had not showed up, I finally contacted him on the phone. He told me that the petitioner was not willing to come to the office to talk with me. I advised the attorney what I suspected, since I had attempted to find them together and couldn't, that the marriage was a marriage of convenience, and it would be best if the petitioner would just withdraw his petition. He agreed with me and stated he would have his client withdraw the petition. Several more weeks went by, and the next time I contacted the attorney, he told me that he had talked to his client, who was still unwilling to withdraw the petition or come talk to me at the office, and he sent me a Notice of Withdrawal as Attorney from that case. That left me to pursue the two subjects and question them without his presence, if I could find them. I finally found out where the petitioner was working as a barber at the edge of Chinatown, which is just a few blocks from the Immigration Office. Eventually, I did find "Papillon" at her apartment. When she let me in, the first thing I noticed was that she had a small puppy that she had obviously left alone for long stretches at a time. She had put newspapers down in several spots on the floor, but evidently the puppy was afraid of the newspaper, and it used every spot on the floor except the newspaper for his bathroom. I noticed that she had a large container of water and a large container of puppy chow, so the dog wasn't in any danger of starving, but he had sure made a mess of her apartment. The apartment itself was sparsely furnished, with only a dressing table, a bed, and a large clothing rack with wheels on it. This was the type of rack that I have seen being pushed around through the garment district in New York. It contained several Chinese satin and silk gowns, and evening dresses. There was no indication that a man ever lived at that apartment. I interviewed her, and she claimed that shortly after her marriage, she had been booked on tour to perform at Las Vegas, and once concluding that tour, she was taking shorter engagements in the San Francisco area and in Reno. She would not admit that her marriage was one of convenience, just for obtaining benefits from the Immigration and Naturalization Service.

Finally, the only way to see the petitioner was to meet him at his barbershop, which I did. He invited me to have lunch with him at a fancy Chinese restaurant in Chinatown. We went to lunch and discussed his case. It was obvious that the old man was so smitten with Papillon's beauty and youth that he would have done anything for her. Even though he was not living with her, he would not withdraw his petition. He explained that he knew the vast age difference, and it would seem unusual for them to be married, but he felt that eventually she would tire of her career as a songstress, and they would sometime be able to live together. Since I did not have the cooperation of either one of them as a witness against the other, I could only write a report stating what my investigation had disclosed and recommending that the petition be disapproved.

Within a few months, I was completing as many cases as the other Investigators in the Fraud Section, and I was working a larger area than I had worked as a General Investigator. I have mentioned that one of the GS-12 Investigators, Francis Leo, was very helpful to me in showing me how to prepare my reports and giving me general advice on my investigations. He was one of my favorite Investigators in the Fraud Section. He was always in a good mood, had little funny stories to tell, and I was surprised when one day I would see him looking so downcast. I asked him what was wrong and learned that he was disappointed because he had not been chosen to fill a vacancy as OIC in Hong Kong. I couldn't resist teasing him a little bit. I knew he would have been an ideal person to fill the OIC's job as he was Chinese American and fluent in Chinese language. Naturally Francis wanted to know who had filled the position and found out it was an Investigator named Don Young. I told Francis that was the answer right there, that the person making the selections had seen the name Francis Leo and wondered what would an Italian do in Hong Kong and had chosen a nice Oriental name like Don Young. I wonder what the selecting officer thought when he saw the American Don Young reporting for duty.

Dear Chief

Working the Fraud Section was not as exciting as working the Area Control Section, but I was enjoying it, and I still apprehended illegal aliens occasionally. It seemed like every employment check I made or every neighborhood investigation disclosed another illegal alien, whom I took back to the office with me. I still encountered some sarcasm, especially from the Investigator whose place I had taken in the Fraud Section. If he saw me go by, he would comment, "There goes Sims again with another wet. He still thinks he's in the Area Control Section." He let his resentment be known by telling the other Investigators that I had taken his job. I felt no responsibility. It certainly was not I who decided that either one of us would be reassigned. I never changed my mind about apprehending illegal aliens. It had always been my contention that every Investigator had the responsibility of apprehending aliens who were already illegally in the United States.

After the first rating period, Mr. Hoffman told me that he had been keeping an eye on me for the past few months, that he had not believed I could do the job in the Fraud Section and continue to bring in illegal aliens, but I had proven to him that I could. In the next rating period, he recommended me for an Outstanding Incentive Award, and I was glad to join the group of employees at the San Francisco District Office who received the incentive awards for that period.

One of our best cases was assigned to Investigator Ed Molina. The case consisted of a husband and wife from the Philippines who were admitted to the United States for permanent residence. The woman worked in one of the County Clerk's offices in the East Bay Area, where she had access to birth certificates. She would locate a Spanish surname birth certificate, preferably of a person who had died in childhood or at least was deceased. She would obtain a copy of that birth certificate, then apply for a Social Security Card under that name. With these two documents, the husband would then sell the documents to a Filipino whom they had selected, who in turn would obtain a California Driver's License, and with those three documents could then obtain a United States passport. Ed was working with an Investigator from the State Department.

I am not sure how many of these fraudulently obtained passports had been identified; the number was nearing twenty. Their case had progressed to the point that it was time to make arrests. Ed would need the help of several Investigators, as he planned to apprehend as many at one time as he possibly could. We would all start making the apprehensions at the same time early one morning. On the assigned day, I would work with Mary Lou Listug. She was our first female Investigator at San Francisco. I had worked with her before. Unlike a few of the Investigators who resented a woman becoming an Investigator, I enjoyed working with Mary Lou. She could gain access to houses that I would not be able to. If someone looked out their door and saw a woman standing there, they were much more apt to open the door than if they saw a strange man standing outside their door.

    I met Mary Lou early in the morning at a restaurant hear her home, and we proceeded to look for the three Filipino women whom I had been assigned to apprehend. I had met Mary Lou several times previously at the same restaurant. Usually, her husband brought her there and waited for the Investigator whom she would be working with. I couldn't help but notice there was a little tension. I don't know how many husbands would not resent their wife meeting a man early in the morning and going to work with him. I don't believe Mary Lou's marriage survived her work in the Immigration Service as an Investigator, but I know that she continued to do good work and be promoted in the Service. Mary Lou and I were successful in apprehending the three Filipino females whom we were supposed to locate. They were so confident with their newly acquired documents that they had made no attempt to hide their address or place of employment, and we located the first two at their residence without any problem, and they presented their passports for identification. The third one we apprehended at her place of employment. By the time we arrived with them at about 9:30 at the office in San Francisco, the room was literally lined with the group of Filipinos we were apprehending.

    Ed and the State Department Investigator would be processing and taking statements from the ones we had brought in. I then teamed up with another Investigator to go back to the East Bay and maintain a stakeout on the house that the vendors were living in. Late in the evening, the lady came home. We could see her turn on the lights in the house and occasionally move about in the kitchen. We thought she was preparing supper for her husband, but he must have gotten the word that a number of the persons he had sold documents to were being apprehended. We felt that they would abscond as soon as they heard about the apprehensions. Ed was going to bring a warrant, and we would arrest both of them at their home. Very late in the evening, Ed arrived on the scene without the warrant, but it didn't make too much difference, as the man did not come home. We maintained a surveillance until ten o'clock at night when it was obvious he was not coming back to the house. Ed was unwilling to apprehend the woman by herself, as he felt surely the man would not willingly surrender. As a result, we did not apprehend the man and woman for some weeks. This was a bit disappointing. Their apprehension at one of the airports as they attempted to leave the United States was anticlimactic, but it brought to a conclusion one of the better cases.

One afternoon about three thirty, I wasn't very far from the office when I received a call on the radio telling me a visitor was waiting for me at the office. I parked on the street right outside the door at our office building at #630 Sansome Street, which had just recently been designated a tow away zone after 4:00 p.m. I went inside and up to the office to see what the visitor wanted. It was someone with whom I had left a business card. They had decided they would come see me and wanted to give me a statement concerning one of my cases. I would be required to take a sworn affidavit, which took a little longer than I had expected. By the time I realized I had just passed the four o'clock mark when cars would be towed, I hurried back to the street to find a wrecker had already hitched onto my government car. He refused to unhook the car, even though I explained to him that it was not a personal car but a government car. He told me where I could reclaim the vehicle and drove away.

I went by the garage where he had taken the government vehicle. The owner of the business refused to take anything but cash. He said he had had too many personal checks where the issuer stopped payment before he could collect. This was on a Friday afternoon. If I left the car there would be an additional two days storage fee, but I left the vehicle, and Monday morning I went to see my Supervisor to ask him what I should do about the government car. He thought it would be best if I went ahead and paid the towing and storage fee out of my pocket and forgot about it. I knew I was at fault for leaving the car parked in the tow away zone after 4:00 p.m., but I still believed that it was a government car, and the tow away operator should submit a bill to the government just as he would for any other business owned vehicle. I let another day go by and was called into the Deputy District Director's Office where Mr. Pullin ordered me to recover the government vehicle. I tried to explain to him my beliefs, but he wasn't interested. He told me to go get the vehicle and that was an order.

    I felt a little stir in that stubborn streak within me that I have always had. I told him that I would comply with his order and get the vehicle, but I thought I should be reimbursed and that I would be writing a memorandum requesting reimbursement. He told me that the Regional Office did not have any money for such purposes. Seems like I had heard that statement before. He further added that I could write as many memorandums as I wanted to, but it wouldn't do me any good. I felt that he was probably right; if I wrote a memorandum to the Regional Office, I would get little sympathy. But since I could find no service policy written in our operating instructions, I decided to direct my "Dear Chief" memo to the Central Office. I set forth the circumstances. I explained that I had recovered the government vehicle at my personal expense, although I believed that I should not have been ordered to do so. I included the receipt that showed the exact amount and asked that I be reimbursed for that amount and that the Central Office set forth its policy on recovering impounded vehicles. Of course, every Investigator in the office was curious just as they had been when I requested reimbursement for the torn suit. We waited several weeks. Again, opinion was divided among whether I would be successful. I don't know who was more surprised when I received a check for the amount of my request. We never received any operation instructions setting forth the Service Policy in such matters.

    There were other types of fraud which I want to mention. One of these concerned employment letters, which worked two ways. As part of an Immigrant's Application for Permanent Residence, which he submitted to the American Consul overseas, was required a promise of employment. There were unscrupulous vendors who would sell an alien a promise of employment, although no job actually existed, and some of the so-called employing companies also did not exist. Nevertheless, the alien was usually successful including the employment letter in his packet and in obtaining a Visa. The other way the employment letter worked was for aliens who had legitimate letters, but had no intention of accepting the employment once they were admitted to the United States. This was particularly rampant among domestic help, and American women were constantly coming to the Immigration Office to complain and see what they could do about their maid, to whom they had given an employment letter. Their complaint was that the maid was such a good worker, but after she received her permanent residence Visa she never came back to work for them. I had very little sympathy for these women, as I knew the low salaries they were paying their maids, and their employment letter usually contained an inflated rate of pay and not the true salary they were paying.

This brings me to one of my pet peeves. Resident aliens cannot petition for their brothers and sisters, but they can petition for their parents. Part of the application must be an Affidavit of Support, stating the parents will not become a public charge if admitted to the United States for permanent residence. Many times after the parents are admitted, the son or daughter who petitioned for them would come to the Immigration Office fearing that the Affidavit of Support they had submitted would be binding and they might actually have to support the parent. They would claim some type of unfortunate incident had occurred, such as a fire or an automobile accident, or even that they had a new child in the family, and they could no longer support the parents and wished to withdraw the Affidavit of Support. An untold number of these elderly parents will never be able to find work in the United States, and immediately after entry they start receiving Social Security payments in the form of Supplemental Security Income (SSI).

Our politicians, if they know about this situation, do not show or express any interest or concern. There was no way of knowing how many of these resident aliens are receiving Social Security benefits. Once the parent s are admitted for permanent residence, they can then petition for their other sons and daughters. Admitting one person for permanent residence usually results in the arrival of several other members of the family. These elderly immigrants have no jobs waiting for them, and despite their Affidavit of Support from a member of their family, they will end up on welfare, receiving food stamps and living in public housing.

I once asked one of the officers at the Welfare Office in Marin County, which was one of the most uncooperative offices as far as immigration information was concerned, "What does it take to receive welfare?" The answer she gave me was, "You only have to be poor."

I was nearing the end of my tour of duty in the San Francisco office. I knew Jerry was willing to leave the Bay Area, so I had applied for a vacancy at the San Juan, Puerto Rico Office as a Non-Supervisory GS-12. The last year living at Novato had been a pleasant one for me. I was playing softball in the city league on a good softball team. I had also been the Commander of the local Veterans of Foreign Wars Post and had donated several weekends helping build a boys' club in Novato. Jerry and I had seen some of the most beautiful scenery in the United States in Northern California. We also enjoyed visiting Yosemite Park. On our last trip to Yosemite, I had finally learned how to catch the trout in the river that runs through the park. On previous occasions I had fished and fished, but couldn't catch any of them. Finally, I asked someone who lived near the park why the fish wouldn't bite. He asked me what kind of bait I was using, and I told him. He said what I needed was some hellgrammites. I wasn't sure what a hellgrammite was, but he told me where there was a bait stand that sold them. I bought some hellgrammites and fished in one of the tributaries that ran into the main river. Sure enough, that was what the trout were looking for, and I caught as many as I wanted to catch.

As I approached the point where the tributary ran into the main river, there was a rocky area with a little ledge right at water level. I was surprised to see a fish flopping around on the rocky ledge just out of the water. As I got closer I could see that it was not a trout; it was a small mouth bass, and I thought that bass must have chased a minnow onto the bank and was flopping around trying to get back into the water. As I didn't want to keep the fish, I though I would help it. I stood on the little ledge, squatted down and with one swoop flipped the fish back in the water. It's a good thing my hand was moving because a snake that I had not seen was laying underneath the ledge, and as my hand went down to scoop the fish back into the water the snake struck at my hand, but since my hand was moving it was unable to bite me and flung itself into the river. I was so startled that I fell backwards and dislocated a finger. I thought at first the finger was broken, but I realized that it was just dislocated, and with a good tug, I put it back in place and was none the worse for wear.

As Jerry and I were returning home from the park on a Sunday afternoon, I swung north on Highway 99 near Merced, California. Highway 99 is a four lane divided highway. As I headed north going back to San Francisco, I was passed by two cars going only slightly faster than I was, so it took them several seconds to go past. I glanced over at the two cars and saw that they were both filled with what looked to me like illegal aliens. I counted the people, and there were six persons in each car. Jerry, who is just as adept at spotting illegal aliens as I was, said, "There go two carloads of wetbacks." She has no hesitation in calling an illegal alien a wetback. I agreed and told her I thought so, too. I speeded up a little bit to travel at the same speed they were going. They were obviously traveling together, as each time the lead car passed a slow moving car, the other car stayed right on its tail. Jerry and I began talking about where the aliens could be going. We guessed they might be going as far north as Oregon or Washington to work in the apples. There would be nothing to prevent them from traveling that far. There was almost no possibility of their encountering any immigration Officers. Jerry asked me what I was going to do about the situation. I reminded her that, although I always carried my ID card, it still was a Sunday afternoon, and I was still off duty. She insisted it was still my responsibility, and I knew that it was, so I agreed with her and proceeded to apprehend the two carloads of aliens.

It didn't take long on Monday for Mr. Pullin to hear about what I had done. He called me into his office to say he had heard that I had stopped two carloads of aliens on a Sunday evening. I told him that was correct. He wanted to know how I had done it, but I was determined that I wasn't going to tell him. I knew he though that I somehow used my private automobile to stop them, so I just let him wonder and told him, "We Investigators have our ways."

What had really happened was much easier than I would have believed. After a few miles, the two cars pulled off the road into a small town near Merced. I knew the nearest Border Patrol Station was at Merced. I pulled off the highway and stopped at a service station across the street from the one they had stopped at. I noticed a city police car coming down the street, so I waved at the policeman, and he stopped. I told him who I was and that I suspected there were two carloads of illegal aliens at the service station across the street, and I would like to have some assistance in apprehending them. He was a veteran police officer and told me he wouldn't mind assisting me, but if we walked over to them at that time, they would probably run, and we would only catch a couple of them. He told me there was a Highway Patrol checkpoint only about a mile further up the highway, and that he would call ahead and have the Highway Patrol stop the two cars when they came through the checkpoint. This sounded like a good idea to me. I told him that I would stop and talk to the aliens to make sure they were illegal. We waited until the aliens loaded back into their cars, and I followed them at a slight distance. They came to the Highway Patrol checkpoint, and in only seconds the Highway Patrolmen had them pulled over onto the shoulder of the road. By the time I parked behind their two cars, they had all twelve of the occupants standing around one car with their hands on the roof of the car, and a Highway Patrolman with a shotgun was standing guard over the twelve of them. I questioned each one to make sure he was an illegal alien. Eleven of the twelve had no immigration documents. Only the driver of the lead car had an alien registration card showing he was a legal resident.

Their story was they had been working near Bakersfield until their field labor job was ended. They had then pooled their money to buy the two old cars and were headed for Oregon. I was at a loss as to what to do with them. I asked the Highway Patrolman in charge of the checkpoint if he didn't run into situations like this occasionally. He said, yes, that every once in a while they did. The driver of the lead car had no driver's license. He would not be allowed to drive further. The cars would be towed away. I asked the Highway Patrolman what he did in situations like that. He said they usually called for a paddy wagon and had the people transported to the county jail, where they would remain overnight until the Border Patrol could be contacted to come and get them out of jail. I asked him if he could do that in this kind of situation. He said, yes, he thought that he could. I thanked him for his assistance and went on my way. So apprehending eleven illegal aliens on a Sunday evening turned out to be fairly easy, after all.

Things were changing in San Francisco. My friends were leaving. Bob McCord had been transferred several months ago. Dan Wells, a jim dandy shortstop on our Novato Softball team, also had transferred. Dick White had retired and moved back to North Carolina. In fact, we received a large political advertisement with his picture asking for support as he was running for Representative. A note attached to the poster told us that he didn't make it this time, but he believed he would make it next time. The old PI was retired. Ed McGee, who was also retired, had asked the old PI when he planned to retire. Mr. Fleagle told him that he wasn't really planning to retire. Ed knew that he had about forty years with his former military serviced added to his Immigration service. The maximum amount a person could earn in retirement was 80 percent of the salary. The old PI had that, and he also had quite a bit of unused sick leave which would be computed and added to his length of service. Ed told him that every day he came to work he was losing money. The old PI couldn't believe that until Ed showed him that if he rode the bus back and forth every day, plus his percentage of his salary that was being taken out for retirement benefits, plus buying lunch in the city every day, that he would make just as much staying at home as he did coming to work. The old PI said, "By golly, you know you're right," and submitted his papers for retirement.

I was feeling the urge to move on and was very pleased when I received a telegram notifying me that I had been selected for the Grade 12 Field Investigator's job in San Juan, Puerto Rico. I considered myself a fairly experienced Investigator, having worked in the General and Area Control and Fraud Sections, but I was still short on prosecution experience. There were three Investigators who had specific duties not related to any section. Tom Smith was the Jail Check Officer. It was his responsibility to locate deportable aliens in the City, County, and State Prisons in the Bay Area. Another Investigator, a Grade 13, was assigned to the Attorney General's Strike Force, and Robert Moschorak was the Prosecution Officer. It was his duty to see that the cases for prosecution were properly prepared, that the complaint or information was prepared and the witnesses were available when needed. He would attend the court cases with the U.S. Attorney and supply any information which the U.S. Attorney needed. I went to Bob for some copies of successful prosecutions in the Immigration Service. There's usually nothing new, just whatever worked previously will work again, and we will use the same procedure over and over. He gave me some copies of the forms I thought I would need in Puerto Rico. Jerry was ready to leave Novato, but she wasn't too keen about going to San Juan, Puerto Rico.

CHAPTER SIX: SAN JUAN

The trip to San Juan was not as eventful as our previous moves. We didn't become separated or lose a travel check. We managed to take both cars to Greenville, Mississippi. I pulled a U-Haul trailer with some of the furniture that we didn't want the shipper to ship to Puerto Rico. We would store it in a little storage shed in the backyard of Jerry's mother. We would also leave our second car with our nephew. He could drive it while we were in Puerto Rico. We delivered the newer car to the port at New Orleans, then we boarded a plane what would take us over the southern tip of Florida, within sight of the Bahamas and on to Puerto Rico. We arrived at the International Airport in San Juan and decided on a temporary place to stay.

We decided on the Caribbean Beach Hotel. It was not one of the big hotels in the section of the city called El Condado where there were new hotels with casinos in them. The Caribbean Beach had a nice swimming pool and was right on the north side of the island about halfway between Old San Juan and the airport.

The next day I managed to find the immigration office, which was located in the Pan American Building in the part of the city called Hato Rey. I was surprised. I thought I would not know anyone in San Juan, but I looked around the office, and it was a small office. There were two Supervisors, Grade 12, and there were two Grade 12 Non-Supervisors. I would be one of them. The other was Ed Sullivan, whom I had known at New York City. Although not close friends, I was also acquainted with the two Supervisors, Cochran and Vyse, and Gross whom I had not seen since we were classmates in the Border Patrol. There was an Investigator named Frangie, who claimed to be a New York Puerto Rican, whom they referred to as a "Neorican."

There were four other Anglo Investigators, whom I had not previously met and six Puerto Rican Investigators. The six Puerto Rican Investigators had come to the Immigration Service on transfers from the defunct Sky Marshals Program. As the Sky Marshals Program was phased out, the government was looking for other agencies in which to place the Sky Marshals. The Immigration

Service seemed to be a good place, and they would be transferred to INS as Investigator's Aides. It wasn't long, of course, until the Aides were doing the same job that the Investigators were: apprehending and processing illegal aliens and doing investigative casework. They appealed to the Civil Service Commission that they should have the same status and grade as other Investigators. Their appeal was upheld, and they were entered on an Investigator Trainee Program for their upgrading to a grade equal to other Field Investigators.

The Assistant District Director for Investigation was Mr. Savage. Mr. Savage took me to the office of the District Director, where I met Mr. Longo and a couple of other Supervisors from the Detention Section and Travel Control.

I spent the rest of the day doing paperwork, and Vyse gave me a ride home at the end of the day. He told me that he was keeping the car overnight, and he would pick me up, and we would work together the next day. He told me that we would also go across the island to Ponce, where we would meet the Investigator who operated a sub-office. I learned that the other sub-offices were in the Virgin Islands. We didn't leave until mid-afternoon. I realized that we would not be back by normal quitting time, but I knew we were expected to work some overtime. Vyse said he knew of a good restaurant where we would have supper in Ponce. We went by the office just before closing time. We met Investigator Malave and a secretary. We had quite a bit of time to kill before supper. It didn't take long to see the sites of Ponce. Then we had a good seafood supper. Vyse made no attempt to leave after our meal was finished. It was obvious he was dragging his feet. I began to inquire about when were we going back to San Juan. He told me there were a couple of places that we would be assisting Investigator Malave to check since they were too big for him to check by himself, and we would also have another team of Investigators and a Detention Officer joining us. Before dark, the other team and the Detention Officer, who turned out to be a female Detention Officer who was driving a panel truck, showed up. Mr. Malave rejoined us, and we were ready to go out and check places that Vyse had selected. They turned out to be houses of prostitution. I was surprised to find out that prostitution was not illegal in Puerto Rico.

We teamed up as a task force as soon as it was dark and the places were open for business. There were dozens of women arriving for work. Almost none of them lived at the houses which were just divided into small rooms for the privacy of clients, with a large dance hall and saloon. There the customers could sit and drink while they selected the prostitute of their choice. These places were doing a booming business by dark, and we began checking for illegal aliens. We only checked the women. We didn't bother the male customers.

It seemed like every woman claimed to be legally in the United States, but they didn't have any evidence of their permanent residence. They all claimed they were afraid to carry their alien registration cards or their other immigration documents. They claimed that they would be stolen while they were busy, so they left everything at home. A few of them claimed to be United States citizens. It didn't differ if they were claiming to be a tourist, or a resident alien, or a citizen. If they had no identification, we put them in the panel truck and took them home to see their birth certificate, or alien registration card, or other immigration document. It wasn't long before we had a dozen of them from the two or three places we had checked. I remember the name of only one of the houses. It was called El Reloj, which means "the watch." The plan was, even though I didn't know it, to check the houses in Ponce and then go around the western tip of the island, all the way to Mayaguez, then Aricebo. Sure enough, after we had the panel truck loaded with prostitutes, taking them one by one to their residence to check out their documents, some of them wanted to go to the bathroom. Since there were no bathrooms available, we chose a remote section of the road and told them that if anyone wanted to go to the bathroom, they had to go now. It was an unforgettable sight to see half a dozen prostitutes lined up beside the road, with their dresses up to their hips, taking a pee. This was an unusual day for me, and it was far from over.

Investigator Malave and the Ponce Police, who had been with him, left us, and we continued on around the western end of the island. This must not have been unusual for the Detention Officer, Carmen, for she had brought some food and sandwiches, and somewhere on the western end of Puerto Rico, we had a midnight picnic.

The last place we would check on the way back to San Juan was in Aricebo, where we sorted through and met a group of prostitutes, and the outcome was that after all that work, we only had two who were not in status. We would be issuing Warrants of Arrest and Order to Show Cause and commencing deportation proceedings against them. These two were admitted as visitors. They should never have been issued Visitors Visas, as anyone who had practiced prostitution was not eligible for a Visa. I was to learn that there were hundreds of these people who had been issued Visas and were rotated into Puerto Rico on a three month or six month basis. If they got in trouble and were apprehended by Immigration, there was a lawyer who would immediately come down to the Immigration Office with a briefcase full of money to post a bond for them. He once bragged that he had as many as two hundred women under his control. They were mostly Colombians and Dominicans. He kept up with their immigration documents by retaining their passport and the form I-94, which Immigration placed inside the passport to show the length of time to which the person was admitted. He usually kept up with this very diligently, and as the expiration of their time neared, he would make sure they departed on time to the Bahamas. Then they would send them from the Bahamas to Port Everglades, Florida, where they would be readmitted for another three months to six months.

We noticed that the Immigrant Inspector's stamp, which bore an identification number, was the same on nearly all of the I-94's of the prostitutes. It was daybreak before we arrived back in San Juan, and by the time we did the paper work of the apprehensions, it was eight o'clock in the morning. We showed our duty hours for that day from twelve midnight until eight a.m., and I learned what it meant to be on a variable schedule. Jerry had no idea I would be working all night, and by the time I arrived home she was frantic.

One of the first things that I learned about Puerto Rico was that the prices were much higher than in the mainland United States. Puerto Rico was considered a hardship station, and the tour of duty would be two years. That was true for other government agencies as well as the Immigration Service. To offset the higher cost of living, there was a seven percent cost of living allowance. The seven percent would not come close to making up for the inflated prices on everything except milk, which was controlled. For example, I have seen magazines at the shop at the airport that bore a price of $1.50 for the publisher, marked over and written in with a felt pen, a new price of $3.00. This was true of merchandise in all of the stores all over the island. When asked about the higher prices, the only reason anyone ever gave was that there was a shipping fee involved.

I also learned that the government of Puerto Rico is a Commonwealth, and there was dissention among the people as to whether the system of government should become an independent nation of Puerto Rico or become a state of the United States. Politics would always be as hot as the Puerto Rican weather.

I cold see it was going to take me a little while to learn just where my duties fit into the scheme of things at the San Juan office. I was riding to work every day with either Allen Vyse or Tony Hobert. It seemed that Allen was going to take me under his wing and make me his protégé. It didn't take me long to see that this would not be a good thing, as he had practically Shanghaied me for the overnight trip around the island on my first day of duty. He insisted on stopping at a local bar, which was a gathering place for other agency officers, such as the FBI and the DEA, where he would have several drinks before we proceeded home. I did not drink. I was not a tee-totaller, but I had never had more than a couple of drinks in my life, and it was no pleasure to me to sit around the bar and watch Allen tell war stories while he downed a few every evening after work, so I tried to ride with Tony as much as I could. It was obvious Tony was a real go-getter, and he and I would get along well working together.

Things would get a bit better as soon as my car was delivered at the port where it had been shipped. It's a good thing I didn't have to pay for the car being shipped myself, because I learned the government had paid a $500 importation fee on my car. I would also be in for a rude surprise when it came time to pay my income taxes.

Mr. Savage, the ADDI, was a mild-mannered man who reminded me a good bit of the old PI at San Francisco, and I liked him immediately. In briefing me about my duties, he had told me that our office had a Liaison Officer who, once a month went to the Dominican Republic, to work with the State Department Officers at the American Consul in Santo Domingo, and I would be going on the next trip when it was scheduled. He also talked about the Puerto Rican Investigators assigned to the San Juan Office. He told me that they were good Investigators who knew how to distinguish between illegal aliens and native Puerto Ricans. This was difficult for Anglo Investigators to do. He said if one of the Puerto Rican Investigators told me a person was not from Puerto Rico, that I could believe it, they were not from Puerto Rico. I filed this away in my memory, and it would be influential at a later time.

The day of the trip to the Dominican Republic came. I learned I would be traveling with Mr. Walker, the Assistant District Director for Travel Control, and Investigator Sullivan. Sullivan had a case involving a family who claimed to be derivative citizens. They asked if I had a copy of my birth certificate with me, and fortunately I did have a photocopy of my birth certificate. We arrived at the airport at the Dominican Republic. We were rushed through Customs with a minimum delay and went to the American Consulate Offices.

I was very curious about the operation of a Consulate and the issuance of Visas. I had the opportunity to stand behind the counter where the Vice Consul was interviewing applicants for Visitors Visas. I had always thought that they were too lenient in letting anyone who applied for a Visa into the United States. I was pleasantly surprised to see that this young lady was questioning the applicants very thoroughly. Standing before her were a man, woman, and child, and another adult woman who were applying for Visitors Visas, intending to go to New York City. She asked the man and woman several questions about the other woman, whom they claimed was their maid and whom they needed to go with them to take care of their child. Their application was denied. The Vice Consul told me it was obvious they did not have the financial means of sustaining themselves for a lengthy visit in New York City, and she felt that all three of them would have ended up working in New York and overstaying their time there.

That afternoon an elderly Dominican appeared at the Consul's Office in answer to a request. He was to be interviewed by Investigator Sullivan. I would sit in and assist him with the interview. They wanted to know if we needed an interpreter, and I told him no, that I could conduct the interview myself. They said, "Boy, are we glad to see you, someone who really speaks Spanish." The case was Ed's, but I assisted with taking the statements. The subject of the interview claimed to be a United States citizen by derivation through his father, who was a citizen of Puerto Rico. The father had married a Dominican woman and had lived in the Dominican Republic, and this person was born to them in the Dominican Republic. His interview established that he had not resided in Puerto Rico a sufficient time for his children to also derive American citizenship through him. He was married to a citizen of the Dominican Republic, and his children had been born in the Dominican Republic. Although they were applying for United States passports, it was obvious from the immigration charts which we used to determine citizenship that his children had no claim to American citizenship. Our report to the Consul would recommend that their application be denied. There was one catch, however; the older child, a son, had already been issued a United States passport, and it would have to be recovered. If the owner of the passport was unwilling to depart the United States voluntarily, then we would have to issue an Order to Show Cause and have a deportation hearing for him.

That evening we were taken on a brief tour of Santo Domingo. We met a couple more of the Consular Officers for a good dinner at a nice restaurant, and it was fairly late before we arrived at the hotel where our rooms had been reserved for us. The hotel had a casino, but I only visited it for a few minutes, as the stakes were considerably higher than the casino that I had visited in Las Vegas. The next morning at the Consul's Office they learned that I was traveling on a temporary travel document. I had no United States Passport, but since I did have a copy of my birth certificate, Immigration ID card, and a driver's license, that was all the documentation I needed. They took my picture, and before the day was finished, they had a passport ready to issue to me. The trip to the Dominican Republic was enjoyable to me, but it was of no great importance.

I didn't know how badly Ed wanted to be the Liaison Officer, so the job was given to him. I was interested in seeing that the case I had worked on with him was completed. I told him several times after we returned to Puerto Rico that if he wanted me to, I would help him in locating the person who had received a Untied States passport. He declined my assistance, and I don't know what ever happened in the case.

Housing in Puerto Rico would be expensive. In fact, the pay raise I received for my promotion to San Juan would be used up in the higher cost of living. Jerry had always been lucky in finding a place for us to live. I have always told her if the place suited her, it would certainly suit me. She was just as lucky again at a cocktail party given by the hotel for guests and invited persons, as well as members of a vacation travel club.

Jerry met a gentleman who told her he lived just across the street from the hotel, and his house would be vacant in a few days as he was due to transfer back to the States. He told us the rent he was paying and told us not to let the landlord go up on the rent if we decided to rent the place. It was a convenient location, and we did end up renting the house. We also ended up buying one of the vacation plans. Membership in the club would entitle us to use the hotel swimming pool, and we could also buy many of our groceries at the hotel commissary at a discount. The house we lived in was located in the Isla Verde section of the city in what was about halfway between the city of Old San Juan and the International Airport. I would end up making many trips to the airport intercepting counterfeit or altered documents. They would call me, and I would then determine if the case was one that should be prosecuted, and if so, prepare the paperwork and assist the Assistant U.S. Attorney in presenting the case before the Magistrate. If it was a minor violation or if it was a felony violation, it would be taken to the Magistrate who would find sufficient cause for prosecution and set a bond on the subject, and the case would be tried in a Federal Court.

As there were just two Supervisory Investigators at San Juan, the personnel were about evenly divided between the two of them. Vyse had the Area Control and General Section combined. The other squad was just called a Special Squad and did the casework. It wasn't long before I was again scheduled to accompany Mr. Vyse and his Area Control Investigators on another raid on the houses of prostitution. This time we would only check those in the city of San Juan. There were at least three large houses. The most luxurious of these was the Black Angus. We would be accompanying the San Juan Vice Squad Officers and again, would end up with a room full of prostitutes at the police station. We would interview them and release most of them. In order for them to be deported, we needed a record of conviction. There was never a record of conviction as the prostitutes were allowed to post a fifty-dollar appearance bond. They would forfeit the bond and never show up for a hearing, and there was never a record of conviction.

Things had gone without incident that night, but the next time I was just told to take an Investigator with me and accompany the Vice Squad. I took Investigator Foy, and we accompanied the Vice Squad, who on signal, rushed into the Black Angus with shotguns held at port arms. I was right behind them and was surprised when the police officers began yelling, "Immigration! Immigration!" Some drunken sailor, sitting with a girl at one of the tables, got to his feet saying, "What the fuck is this?" One of the police officers hit him in the face with the butt of the shotgun. That was example enough for everyone else in the bar to stay where they were, but I did not appreciate the fact that they left the impression that the raid was a raid by immigration rather than their own Vice Squad. The following day I told Mr. Savage what had happened, and told him I didn't believe we should be accompanying the Vice Squad on any more raids of the houses of prostitution. He agreed with me, and that was the last one for the time that I was in Puerto Rico.

I would become involved one more time with the attorney who claimed to have two hundred prostitutes under his control. In checking the identification of the prostitutes, Vyse and I had noticed that several of them did not have their actual I-94 in their possession. Instead they were carrying a Xerox copy of the document. Mr. Vyse decided this did not comply with the Immigration law, which stated that an alien must have evidence of his alien registration in his possession. He told me he would show me how to prosecute that type of case. This would be a misdemeanor which would be tried by the Magistrate. We prepared the cases on six of the next group of prostitutes the Vice Squad had brought to the police station and asked us to interview. The case was not successful, as the Magistrate ruled that the girls were not deliberately violating the Immigration law. He stated that they were attempting to comply with the law by carrying a Xerox copy of their immigration document. The attorney was representing the girls, and the Magistrate lectured him on the requirements of the law and made him promise to return the passport and I-94 to each of the girls so they could have it in their possession. There would be other instances in which prostitutes would be encountered in the course of an investigation, but I never went on any more of the large scale Vice raids.

Mr. Savage was gradually assigning me a caseload, but until then I found myself with a lot of time to accompany another Investigator on his casework, or the Area Control Investigators. Many of the aliens encountered in Puerto Rico were from the Dominican Republic, and others were from the British West Indies. They were Black, and if you could get close enough to hear the BWI's talking, you could detect the English accent. The Dominicans were harder to distinguish, as their Spanish sounded just like the Spanish spoken in Puerto Rico. Even the BWI's would try to claim to be Puerto Rican when they were encountered. Investigator Ferrer was one of the best at detecting who was not a Puerto Rican. Each Investigator seemed to have his own little technique. One of the things I picked up from Investigator Foy was his method of sorting out the BWI's from the Puerto Ricans. He would write the word "Hertz" in the palm of his hand with a fountain pen. He would hold his hand in front of the suspect and tell him to spell this. The Puerto Rican would spell the world "Hertz," but the BWI would pronounce the letter "z" as a "zed." That was all it took to get an idea that the person was falsely claiming to be Puerto Rican. It seemed that all the aliens in Puerto Rico wanted to run or fight. One morning, on the way to the office with Tony, he suddenly stopped the car and pointed to a man on the sidewalk and said, "There's a BWI that I have apprehended before." He hurried to get in front of the alien while I was behind him. As soon as the alien recognized Tony, he turned to run, but I grabbed him. He put up a struggle, and ID cards, badges, and fountain pens went flying all over the sidewalk. It was all that both Tony and I could do to overpower him and take him into custody.

Even the women wanted to resist arrest. Another occasion, Tony and I were driving through the parking lot of a department store when he pointed out two large Black women who were carrying bundles on top of their heads in their native tradition. One of them even had an ironing board which she had purchased. It was balanced on top of her head. We approached them and as soon as they saw the two white men in the car, they started running. I jumped out and followed the one with the ironing board, yelling, "Immigration! Stop!" She paid no attention to me and was reluctant to put her ironing board down. She ran almost a city block before I could catch her. The first thing she had done was step out of her shoes and run barefooted like a marathon racer. When I finally did overtake her, she was unwilling to surrender until Tony, who had overtaken the second in the car and had her in custody, arrived on the scene to assist me.

I also worked some with Jewel Gross accompanying him on his casework. We located a Dominican that he was looking for. The man was of small stature, but he refused to be apprehended. We had shown our identification and told him he was under arrest, to come with us. He replied in Spanish, "I'm not going." We told him again that he was under arrest and he must come with us. He again repeated that he was not going. Jewel and I then grabbed him, one by each arm, and the struggle was on. The man was surprisingly strong and was really giving us a hard time. Jewel decided enough of this nonsense, so he took a mace container from his pocket and sprayed the alien in the face with the mace. I was directly behind him, and some of the spray went over the top of his head and struck me. I learned right then not to rely on mace to subdue someone. It only made him struggle harder. It seemed that I was in worse shape than the alien we were apprehending, as my eyes were burning. We finally subdued the alien, but it was because we simply overpowered him. It was not because of the mace.

I had been in Puerto Rico less than two months when I was scheduled to work an evening shift. We had information that several bars in the Santurce Section of San Juan were using illegal aliens as barmaids. One of the bars was supposedly hiring Panamanians. The team consisted of Tony and his partner in one car, and me and my partner in another car. The four of us went to the bar, and the bar maid claimed her immigration document was in one of the rooms upstairs over the bar. We accompanied her up the back steps, and just as my head came level with the second floor, I saw someone dart across the hallway from one room to another. We went ahead and checked the woman's alien registration card and verified that she was legally in the United States. Then I asked about the other person I had seen cross the hall and go into another room. She said she didn't know, so we insisted on looking for the other person.

In one room we found a man sitting on a bed by himself. We finally located the other woman I had seen. She was hiding under the bed in the room she was in, and she admitted that she was an illegal alien with no immigration documents. The man claimed to be a Puerto Rican, so I let Investigators Frangi and Foy talk to him. They talked to him for a long time and were not satisfied with the story he was giving them, even though he was still claiming to be a Puerto Rican. He claimed that he did not have any identification with him to prove his citizenship. His status was further made suspicious by the fact that he claimed he was just visiting the two Panamanian women. Foy and Frangi both agreed that there was something wrong with this guy, that he certainly was not a Puerto Rican.

After talking to him a while longer, I became anxious to move on and asked them, "Well, are we taking him or leaving him?" I trusted their judgment, as Mr. Savage had told me I could. They told the man that we would have to see his identification by taking him to his home to see it. We started down the back stairs, and when we reached the bottom of the stairs, he said, "Wait a minute," that there was no need to go to his residence, that he would tell us the truth, that he was really a citizen of Panama who was in the United States illegally without any type of immigration documents. This admission was good enough for me, so I told him to come along. We then took him and the other Panamanian woman we had in custody to one of the local police station houses in Santurce. I asked if they could hold the aliens for us for a couple of hours while we continued with our investigations. They said they would be glad to.

We were successful in apprehending a couple of other illegal aliens before returning to the police precinct to recover the two they were holding for us. The police desk sergeant gave me a piece of paper and told me, "The man tried to hide this while you were gone." I opened up the folded piece of paper and saw it was a copy of a marriage license. The person listed on the license was a Colombian, so it was obvious why the man did not want to take us to his residence. It probably would have disclosed an illegal alien from Colombia. We went back to our office to prepare the apprehension reports. It would be a long night as we would have to transport the females to a female detention facility about thirty miles from San Juan. Tony would do the apprehension report on the man. The other women would be processed by Foy and Frangi. Tony would also have to take a sworn statement from the man admitting his alienage and illegal status.

Since I was the GS-12 Investigator, I was the team leader and could decide what to do with the aliens we had in custody. The story the man told was strange, but I believed Tony had gotten the truth from him. He told of being raised in Puerto Rico since he was a little boy. He also had lived for some time in New York City, and his billfold contained a number of business cards, addresses, phone numbers, and all kinds of tidbits of information that would show that he had lived in Puerto Rico and New York for many years. In fact, he claimed he had lived in Puerto Rico since he was four years old. He gave a place of birth in Panama, which I would not have thought of immediately. The first place I would have thought of was someone claiming to be from Panama would say Panama City. This man claimed to be born in Colon, Panama. He further claimed that his father was a Puerto Rican sailor who had decided to bring him and his mother to Puerto Rico when he was four years old. He further claimed that he didn't believe his mother and father had ever been married. She had died about two years after she came to Puerto Rico, and he had been raised by an uncle.

It looked to me like this young man had lived in the United States and Puerto Rico for a long time, and he might qualify for suspension of deportation, as the law at that time provided that anyone who had lived in the United States for seven years and was of good moral character could apply for a suspension of deportation at a deportation hearing. The man said he would depart willingly from Puerto Rico if we would give him an opportunity to do so. He further claimed that even though he had no Panamanian passport, he could get a travel document with which to travel back to Panama. I decided this would be the best course of action, to let him depart voluntarily if he was willing to; so I decided to issue him a voluntary departure letter, which is an Immigration Form I-210, with thirty days in which to obtain his travel document and leave voluntarily from the United States. There would be no bond required, and he was free to go once the apprehension report was completed.

As he was leaving the office with his letter authorizing him to depart voluntarily from the United States, I foresaw possible trouble from this young man. As he was leaving he bent over beside the

Panamanian girl we had apprehended at the bar with him, and I heard him, in a low voice, tell her, "Say they hit me; say they hit me." He then left the Immigration Office. The very next day my uneasy feeling proved justified. "The shit hit the fan." He had gone directly to a lawyer's office with the story of how we had beat him and forced him to make a confession. The lawyer believed his story and had gone directly to the FBI to complain that Immigration Officers had arrested a citizen of Puerto Rico and had tortured him into a confession of being an illegal alien. His story was flashed in blazing headlines across the front page of the daily paper. I shall call the young man Jamall.

    The next morning the District Director, Mr. Longo's office, was covered with reporters wanting more information on the Jamall story. The original article in the paper had given Jamall's side of the story as the attorney had told it. Mr. Longo was assuring the reporters that his Investigators were experienced officers and had not put a citizen of the United States in jail. I tried to tell Mr. Longo that we had placed Jamall in detention for a couple of hours, but we were justified in doing so because he had already admitted that he was an illegal alien before we took him away from the building where we located him. Shortly after the reporters came the officers of the FBI. This case was no longer a simple case of establishing whether or not Immigration had located another illegal alien claiming to be a citizen. The case now was an opportunity for the FBI to show that they would take immediate action against federal officers who violated someone's civil rights.

    FBI agents barged into the Immigration Office and announced that they were going to take statements from the four Investigators. I told their leader to wait just a minute, that before he could take a statement a person had to be willing to give a statement. I further told him that we were members of a union, the AFGE, and we were entitled to have a union representative with us before making any statements. He was somewhat surprised, and he didn't know exactly what to do. That gave us some time to regroup and see what defenses we were going to have. I learned that the FBI couldn't even take a leak without first checking with their Central Office and seeing how to proceed. The leader of the FBI team took his men and told me he would be back later. He expressed his surprise that we were not going to cooperate with his FBI Investigation. It wasn't that we were not going to cooperate; we wanted our side of the story to be told, but we just didn't want to be steamrolled.

Bad news travels fast, and it didn't take but a few hours to reach the Southern Regional Commissioner. When an incident like this happens, and Investigators are threatened, there is a common bond between all Investigators who feel that if it could happen to them, it could happen to me. There was sympathy for our case, and we received word indirectly from friends that the Regional Commissioner was sending a real SOB from New Orleans to do an Internal Investigation. Within hours, the SOB arrived at San Juan. He came to the District Office to pick up a government vehicle. He did not speak to any of us four Investigators. I don't know if it was through choice or with instructions. He was gone from the District Office a few hours. Of course, we don't know who he talked to during that time. We can only assume. A few hours after, he returned to the office. Evidently his investigation was completed. We managed to overhear his conversation when he reported to the Southern Regional Commissioner, and his report was, "Yes, Sir, boss. They did it." That was a brief report, but it was enough for the Southern Regional Commissioner to make up his mind that we were guilty and would get no assistance through the Service. Legal assistance can be very expensive, and none of us was in any position to be hiring civilian lawyers for our personal defense, but as far as the Justice Department was concerned, we were on our own.

It didn't take long for our former FBI friend who was now eager to get four Investigator scalps to come back with word from his superiors that any contract we had with the AFGE didn't mean anything to the FBI, and he was going to take statements. Once again, he got no statements, as we were unwilling to make them, and he went scurrying back to his office when we told him we had not been given sufficient time to obtain counsel. While he was checking with his superiors to see what sufficient time was, Joe Frangi, our shop steward, had contacted the AFGE. Fortunately, there was another organization that many Immigration Officers belonged to. It was the FCIA; that is, the Federal Criminal Investigators Association. Those of us who were not members immediately joined. We then acquainted them with our problem and the need for legal assistance.

There was a lawyer in Long Island, New York, who had assisted Immigration Officers in New York and was on retention by the FCIA. We contacted him, Jack Solerwitz, and he indicated his willingness to come to Puerto Rico and represent us on a specific date and be with us during the FBI interview. When our eager FIB agent again came back insisting that we be interviewed and give statements, we gave him a time which would be agreeable when our attorney would arrive from New York.

In the meantime, Jamall's lawyer and the Independence Party were having a field day in the newspapers. They were using this incident as an example of why all North Americans should be removed from Puerto Rico. They believed that Puerto Rico should be for Puerto Ricans. They objected to the U.S. Courts being conducted in the English language. They claimed responsibility for several acts of violence. One of those acts had been a bomb placed alongside the telephone conduit cables form the Hato Rey section to the city of Old San Juan. The bomb had severed the telephone cables, disrupting service for many weeks. We also suspected they were responsible for the numerous bomb threats we were receiving at the Pan American Building.

There were at least two or three each month. They were a source of harassment more than anything else. We had to take each threat seriously. There were so many that we had it down to a routine as to how we would evacuate the building. Each person was responsible for searching the area immediately around his desk, in the desk, and the trash can. Then they would evacuate the building while a selected team searched the hallways, restrooms, and other areas of the building not directly under someone's watchful eye. We would then return to work. This happened several times without incident until there was a fire of mysterious origin that got into the electrical wiring of the building. The insulation around the wiring burned with such an acrid smoke which was circulated throughout the building that we had to evacuate and remain away from the building for two days while the smoke was blown out.

We Investigators tried to carry on our work as normal, but there was no such thing as normal with a Civil Rights Investigation hanging over our heads. Our District Officers, Mr. Savage and Mr. Longo, never wavered in their support of us Investigators. Although the Regional Office had abandoned us, our District Officers never did. This case was doing nothing to help relations between the Puerto Ricans, including our office secretarial staff, and some of the Anglo Investigators. The feelings bordered on enmity, and there was constant bickering. One of the Investigators, who for personal reasons disliked the Puerto Ricans most, was Dan McKaskill. Dan was a marathon runner and ran about seven miles every morning before breakfast just to keep in shape. He usually ran the same course, and as he would run along the road, Puerto Ricans would pass in their automobiles and throw beer cans at him. He, in turn, never missed a chance to denigrate the Puerto Ricans, and he tried to show that they were stupid people. He called them "polly-glots" to their face.

I had to go to the dictionary to find the definition of a "polly-glot." They disagreed with him about everything, including the Spanish language. The Puerto Ricans would not concede that anything we had learned in a book was correct; the only correct Spanish was their version of the Spanish, even though we thought they were funny when they called orange juice "china." They also called buses "Gua Guas," that sounds like it should be spelled wawa or waawaa, but it's really guagua. They had other expressions which we had not learned in our Border Patrol Spanish.

When the secretary started making fun of how the Americanos spoke Spanish, Dan would ask one of his fellow Investigators if he had ever told them the story about the Puerto Rico fisherman. Someone would say, "No, Dan, I don't remember that story," and he would tell it again for the umpteenth time, always loud enough for the secretaries to hear. He told how there were three Puerto Rican brothers who went out in a small boat every day into the Bay, near San Juan, to catch some fish to eat and enough to sell. This had been going on for a long time when the oldest brother complained to his younger brothers that he was really feeling bad and was afraid he was going to die. The younger brothers assured him that, oh, surely there was nothing wrong, but he insisted that he really believed he was doing to die, and he wanted them to promise that in case he did die they would bury him at sea. Of course, the younger brothers promised, and the older brother died. In trying to keep their promise, the two younger brothers drowned trying to dig his grave. The other

Investigator would then tell McKaskill that that sounded like the brothers who had found the good spot to fish and decided they better line up that position and mark the boat with an X. One of the other brothers said, "No, that won't do any good, dumby. Tomorrow we might not have the same boat."

McKaskill just laughed when an alien attempted to get away by running. He would occasionally give one the chance to think that he could escape, and after the alien ran until he was exhausted, McKaskill would trot up beside him and say, "Run, come on, run, you're not really running." Tony also had a personal reason to dislike Puerto Ricans; someone had stolen his motorcycle. One day I was with him in the heavy traffic in the Hato Rey Section near the office when someone on a motorcycle passed us. Tony says, "That's my motorcycle. I would recognize it anywhere." He then attempted to keep up with the motorcycle in heavy traffic. The man in the motorcycle realized we were following him and attempting to catch him. He then started taking evasive action by cutting corners at a service station. We followed him right through the service station on to the next street, but when we came to a traffic stop for another red light, he drove on the sidewalk, passing cars that we could not get around. He was soon gone, and we never saw him again.

The Jamall case was slowly being moved to the back burner. As soon as the FBI entered the investigation, the case was taken away from the Immigration Investigations. I believe that a thorough investigation would establish the truth of the admission that he had made, but Mr. Longo ordered me to cease any efforts in that investigation. He said the case now belonged to the FBI. I knew the FBI was not interested in establishing whether he was a citizen or alien; they were only interested in successfully making a Civil Rights violation case.

A few weeks after the incident, a man and a woman arrived at the office asking to see me. They turned out to be the uncle and aunt, who claimed they had raised Jamall. They said they wanted to show me that he was really a citizen of the United States and brought with them a copy of his birth certificate. The copy of the birth certificate only reinforced what he had told us. It was a delayed registration for a child four years old. It was issued based on affidavits of the relatives, who claimed the child had been born in Puerto Rico. They also claimed the child's mother had died when he was about six years old, as Jamall had claimed. I told the uncle it should be an easy matter to interview Jamall's father and get the real truth. He said no, that would not be possible, because the father had gone insane and was in an institution and could not be interviewed. That ended our investigation of Jamall as far as the Immigration Service was concerned.

The date which we had agreed to be interviewed by the FBI came. Attorney Solerwitz had arrived from New York. He reviewed the facts of the case of each of the Investigators to make sure there were no discrepancies in our story. We then met with the FBI Officer. I was to be interviewed first. We entered the room in which he was waiting. We were seated, and he asked if I was represented by an attorney. I told him yes, the man accompanying me was Mr. Solerwitz, my attorney. He then asked the other three Investigators if they were represented by an attorney. Each in turn replied that yes, he was represented by an attorney, and Mr. Solerwitz was his attorney. I don't know what effect this had on the FBI Officer, the fact that we were all four using the same attorney and had obtained the services of an attorney. It would have been his responsibility to advise us of our rights, which is called a Miranda Warning. I am sure he knew that Mr. Solerwitz would not let any one of us say anything that could be used against us. The FBI Officer then decided that a sworn statement would not be necessary, and his investigation would be an unsworn interview only. That would be our last contact with the FBI. Months would drag by, and we would hear nothing on the progress of the Justice Department's Civil Rights Investigation.

Mr. Savage had given me a full caseload. A few of the cases involved marriage frauds between Iranians and Puerto Ricans. He also gave me four cases involving neighborhood investigations of families who were petitioning to adopt Vietnamese orphans. In these cases, I found that the adoptive parents who had been selected by the Catholic Welfare Services, who were caring for the orphans, had really wanted to adopt a child and had prepared a nursery and were financially able to support another child. I recommended in favor of the adoptions, even though I suspected that in some cases, the children were not truly orphans, but were unwanted children that had been given up for adoption by their mothers. I hoped those babies truly found a better life.

I was getting quite a few prosecution cases from the airport. These cases usually were detected by the Immigrant Inspectors who encountered people bearing altered passports. The passport usually contained a valid Visitors Visa, which had been issued by the American Consulate, but after the visa stamp was placed in the passport, an imposter would remove the original owner's picture and substitute their own picture, relaminate the photo page of the passport, and attempt to enter the United States using another person's passport.

Another type of fraud was counterfeit alien registration cards. These had several ways of identifying counterfeit cards by special printing processes and codes entered on the card. The Assistant U.S. attorneys like to get these cases, as they were usually open and shut cases since we had the document itself as evidence. We had the testimony of the Immigrant Inspector, and in cases of a counterfeit card, I would track down the file relating to the actual alien registration number that was on the counterfeit card. Then I could attest that that card did not relate to that individual. A six-month sentence was usual in these convictions. My participation included going to the airport, taking custody of the alien and the documents, preparing a written Report of Investigation, and preparing a Prosecution Report for the Assistant U.S. Attorney. These convictions looked good on his record, but they were not always open and shut.

One of the better cases I remembered involved a beautiful woman from Colombia and six aliens who were accompanying her. The Immigrant Inspectors were suspicious of this group who were traveling together. It seemed obvious that she was their guide and was trying to herd them through inspections at the airport. They detected that the passports this group were carrying had been altered. The group had not come directly from Colombia, as normal tourists would do. Evidently this woman was experienced and knew that Colombians were checked very closely at the airport, as they were suspected of carrying narcotics. She had guided them across the border into Bolivia, and they then had boarded the plane in Bolivia en route to Puerto Rico, with the final destination of New York City. The bearers of the passport had been matched up fairly well with the physical description and ages of the persons to whom the passport had originally been issued. They had been told to memorize all of the personal data on the passport. They had not been able to do that, and that was an initial point of suspicion with the Immigrant Inspector. Then his closer examination disclosed the alteration in the passport.

I was called to the airport to take custody of the woman and the smuggled aliens. I prepared the Prosecution Report and took her before the Magistrate who found probable cause for her detention and trial and set a bond for her. Two of the men refused to cooperate, and they were immediately deported back to Colombia. That left four witnesses against the woman; that seemed to be enough. It looked like another open and shut case. The trial date came, and the U.S. Attorney presented a good case, in my opinion. I was there beside him to offer any information and assistance that I could. The lady showed up for her trial impeccably dressed, her hair combed, her makeup on, and she was really a beautiful sight. The witnesses against her consisted of a middle-aged man, a young man, and a young woman and man who were sweethearts. It was up to me to make sure the witnesses were present for the trial. I had found them a boarding house with reasonable rates where they could stay together and I could keep an eye on them. They could also find work, even though it was menial work, pending the trial. A few days before the trial, I went by the boarding house to check on them. There were only three present. The young man had disappeared. The other three said he was there the night before, but he was not there that morning; he simply had disappeared. I don't know if he just went into hiding or if he had found a way of continuing on to New York. Anyway, I was left with three witnesses, which seemed to be enough.

The trial proceeded; the Assistant U.S. Attorney presented the documents, so we had the documents themselves as evidence. We had the word of the three witnesses. The older man was a little bit indecisive in his testimony about where the documents were delivered to hi m and he was not a very good witness for the prosecution, but he testified that she was the person whom he had paid for the documents and who had guided him across the border into Bolivia, then made the travel arrangements for them, and accompanied them to Puerto Rico. The young man was real precise and more definite in his testimony; so was the young lady. We had presented our evidence, and it was the defense attorney's turn to impress the jury. He was an eloquent speaker. He pointed out the faulty memory of the elderly man, classified him as being almost senile. He gave his story, which the defendant brought out in her testimony to the jury, in which she declared her innocence.

She claimed the old man was surely getting something from the Immigration Service for telling such lies against her. She further claimed that the young man was the former sweetheart of her sister, and he blamed her for the break up of his romance with her sister. She claimed he was lying out of revenge. She claimed that the girl accompanying him was his new sweetheart, and she was lying, that she was saying what her sweetheart told her to say. The defense attorney then gave his eloquent closing argument. He pointed out the honesty of the young woman; he asked for the jury's sympathy, stating how she was young and had her whole life ahead of her, and could not possibly look like a criminal, much less be a criminal. He asked how would they feel to be in her shoes and have their life destroyed by three dishonest witnesses. It was obvious they were dishonest because they were carrying fraudulent documents and lying about his client. He pointed out the instability and inconsistency of the testimony of the elderly man. He reiterated what the defendant had said about the young man and young woman's testimony being lies and based on his dislike for her. She shed a tear or two at the appropriate time, and the jury was obviously impressed. They were not out very long when they reconvened to announce: defendant was not guilty.

Her application to enter the United States as a visitor was denied, and the airline that brought her had to return her to Colombia. The other three were then deported back to Colombia, and the young man was never seen nor heard from again. He is probably still living in New York City.

I was having some success with my marriage fraud investigations. A few of the cases involved aliens who had already been issued a resident alien's card. The investigation was based on a complaint form the U.S. citizen that they believed the alien had just used their marriage as a means of gaining residence, and they had not intended to remain married. In some cases, the citizen had learned that the spouse had hidden previous marriages in their native country, or, in fact, were still married to someone in their native country. The other cases were applications for permanent residence still pending, and the Immigrant Inspector suspected that the marriage was fraudulent. In these cases, it was essential to get the cooperation of the American citizen who would sometimes admit that they had entered into the marriage for a certain amount of money. The petitions, I noticed, were often submitted through an attorney's office. It appeared that the same attorney was a third party arranger in many of these marriages and had found someone willing to go through with a sham ceremony.

It seems like I remember the cases in which I was not successful more than the ones in which I was. One of the ones in which I was not successful concerned an Iranian. My investigation disclosed that he was not living with his citizen wife. I located him on the western end of Puerto Rico in a town called Mayaguez. He was employed as a merchant selling rugs and used clothing. I then went to his wife, who was living in a small village on the eastern end of the island. She lived alone with no source of income other than welfare assistance. She admitted that he was not supporting her. My interview with her was recorded on a cassette tape. I understood her to say that she would be willing to be a witness at a hearing after I explained that her husband would probably be ordered to leave Puerto Rico. She further stated that she was going to ask for a divorce, which in Spanish is "pedir."

The day of the hearing came, and she appeared as she had promised she would do, but she was in the company of an attorney and was holding hands with the husband. I knew something had not gone as I had anticipated. I asked our secretary, who was also the court stenographer, what had happened, and she told me the woman had not said she would ask for a divorce, she had said she would impede the divorce. I dug out the cassette tape and listened to it, and sure enough, the word I had understood to be "pedir," meaning to ask for a divorce, was "impedir," which meant she would impede the divorce. He had obviously made some kind of financial arrangements with her, and true love had once again conquered all.

Something unique about the San Juan District was called "home leave." Anyone who was willing to extend their two-year tour in Puerto Rico would receive a bonus for extending called "home leave." The government would pay their round trip airfare and give them an extra thirty days' leave besides their regular annual leave in order to get them to stay in Puerto Rico another year. A few of the Investigators were interested in extending their tour another year, and Joe Frangi, who owned a nice home in Puerto Rico, continued to maintain that his permanent home was in New York City. To him it was just an additional paid vacation every year to go back to New York. I would not be interested in extending my stay, and my leave would be my regular annual leave. I would fly back to New Orleans with Jerry for our Christmas vacation at my own expense.

    I first learned about home leave when Mr. Savage called me into his office and explained that the Trial Attorney who represented the Service before the Immigration Judge was going on home leave and that every year someone took his place as the acting Trial Attorney while he was away. He asked me if I would be willing to be the Trial Attorney during his absence. I thought that was a good opportunity and was glad to be the Trial Attorney. I didn't have very many days to look over the cases which the Immigration Judge would be hearing during the Trial Attorney's absence. We didn't have a full-time judge at San Juan. Periodically, a judge would fly down from the New York District to be our Immigration Judge. The judge arrived, and I had selected ten cases for him to hear. The full-time Trial Attorney seemed to me like he was too lenient with the aliens at their hearings. He would present the case and get a finding of deportability from the Immigration Judge, then the alien's attorney had the opportunity to ask for voluntary departure in lieu of deportation. The full-time Trial Attorney had been permitting these requests to go unchallenged, and most of the decisions resulted in the Deportation Order and then an opportunity for an alien to abscond before his time for departure.

    In my first case, I presented the Service's position and evidence that the person was a deportable alien. The Judge rendered his decision that he did, indeed, find deportability. Then the attorney for the alien made his request for voluntary departure in lieu of deportation. My inexperience cost me in that case. The alien's attorney told how long he had been residing in Puerto Rico, how he had money in the bank, how he had a job which he was unwilling to leave, but would leave within the time prescribed by the Immigration

Judge. I was not prepared to debate these facts, and the Judge granted the alien sixty days in which to depart from the United States. This was just sixty more days the alien could hold a job, and for each amount of time he remained in the United States, his lawyer would be paid that much more money, so it was the lawyer's aim to keep the person in Puerto Rico just as long as he possibly could.

In the next case, after the question of deportability was settled, the attorney for the alien asked for the opportunity to depart voluntarily rather than be deported. The Immigration Judge asked what is the Service's position. This time I was prepared. I used as my justification that the person had been in the United States a long time, that he had accumulated enough money to buy a ticket to New York or to any other place that he wanted to go, and that he had no reason to leave his job in Puerto Rico until just now, when he had been ordered deported, and if given a chance he would surely abscond. The judge ruled in my favor, and the alien was ordered detained until he could be deported.

I went through the same procedure for the next five cases. On the fifth case, when the time came to answer the question, "What is the Service's position?" I told the Immigration Judge, "Your Honor, the Service must once again oppose voluntary departure." The judge was getting tired of my opposing voluntary departure. This was something unusual; it didn't happen with the regular Trial Attorney, and I could see he was becoming perplexed when he said, "Bruce, you don't have to oppose anything," but he did rule in my favor and ordered deportation rather than voluntary departure. Out of the ten cases, I was successful in opposing voluntary departure in six of them. The Detention and Deportation Section was truly amazed at my success, as this was unusual.

The aliens receiving voluntary departure and absconding from Puerto Rico to New York were just a drop in the bucket of the total number, using Puerto Rico as a stepping-stone to the mainland United States. There were Dominicans and Haitians who were admitted to Puerto Rico only who had decided to go farther. There were British West Indians from all of the British Islands who wanted to use Puerto Rico as a means of getting to New York or other American cities. Some of them were admitted to the Virgin Islands only and continued on. In an attempt to prevent this from happening, a program called

"Pre-inspection" was instituted at the airport. This meant that everyone boarding the plane would have their immigration documents checked before they were allowed to board. This was only as effective as the Immigrant Inspector doing the inspecting. Most of them took this seriously, but some who didn't like the work would just make a token appearance and not check every passenger before they boarded.

I was about to fall into disfavor with Supervisory Investigator Vyse. There was another of our many bomb threats, and the building was evacuated. Our security check disclosed an inner officer door had been left unlocked between the files room and another one of our Immigration offices. Technically, the door should have been locked, and the files room supervisor was responsible for seeing that her employees had evacuated and secured the doors when they left. One of our Investigators with the responsibility of double-checking found the unlocked door. Mr. Vyse assigned me to do an internal type investigation, with the object of placing blame on the files room supervisor, who happened to be Puerto Rican. My investigation disclosed that there had not been a violation or compromising of any classified material, as the classified files were kept in a separate locked room, and as far as I could determine, no one had disturbed any of the other files or compromised them in any other way. Mr. Vyse was not satisfied with my investigation.

I had not been critical enough of the files room supervisor. He advised me that if I was not with him, I was against him. I told him I was neither for anyone nor against anyone, that I had simply written my report based on the situation I found. After that, we would not be very close friends. That was all right with me, as I was wanting to distance myself from him. He was having a problem waiting until after duty hours to have a drink. He would also cause havoc and friction between the Anglo Investigators and the Puerto Ricans. One day I came to work, and he was already in his office almost having an apoplectic fit. I asked him what was wrong, and he was saying, "It's witchcraft. This is a case of witchcraft." It took me a few minutes to find out what he was talking about. There was something on his desk. It looked to me like someone had emptied a pencil sharpener contents on his desk. He was scraping the contents into a glassine envelope and told me he was sending the contents to the FBI for analysis because someone was obviously trying to use witchcraft to put a hex on him. It would be a couple of weeks before the report came back from the FBI laboratory. When it did come back, it showed that there was pencil lead mixed with bird droppings; so who knows, maybe someone really was practicing witchcraft. Anyway, Mr. Vyse would soon be rotating back to the States.

    I found myself working with Jewel Gross again. We were working one of his cases, and when we finally found the address we were looking for, it turned out to be a bar, high on the side of one of the mountains. There were living quarters in the basement of the bar, and a couple of women were mopping and cleaning the bar in preparation of a new day's activity. While Jewel checked the identity of one of the women who lived downstairs under the bar, the other one told me she lived across the street, and I accompanied her up a few steps to a long, low building which was divided into three bedrooms. I began to suspect that we had found another house of prostitution, as a man was getting dressed, I noted, as we walked by an open door. I checked the woman's alien registration card and asked the man who was just leaving to identify himself. He was a citizen of Puerto Rico. I asked him who was the woman, and she was just a friend with whom he had just spent the night. I checked her identification, and she turned out to be a Dominican woman who had been admitted to the United States as a permanent resident. I took her alien registration card and gave her one of my business cards with an appointment time for her to come to the Immigration Office.

    Although we had not had any previous success in deporting prostitutes, I thought I might have better success with this one. She arrived at the time I had given her for her appointment. I used one of our secretaries to take her sworn statement in shorthand. She would also be my witness, since I was interviewing a woman. I managed to get the woman to confess that she had been working as a prostitute. I reminded her that I had the man as a witness, if I needed him, to get the truth. He might have been willing to cooperate and he might not, I really didn't know, but that was my leverage in getting her confessions. I got sufficient information about how long she had been practicing prostitution, how much she charged, and all of the details. I then issued her an Order to Show Cause, and she was eventually deported back to the Dominican Republic.

That was the ultimate result, but in the morning Jewel and I first encountered her, I noticed a large German Shepherd dog lying beside the sidewalk in front of the house. I walked right beside the dog, and he never moved a muscle other than to roll his eyes, as to let me know that he saw me. However, when Jewel walked across the street to join me, I heard this awful racket, like the dog was attacking; then I heard whimpers. I rushed outside to see what had happened, and evidently the dog didn't like Jewel's looks. For some reason, he had become vicious, and Jewel had sprayed him with his ever-present fountain pen container of mace. I had an example of the mace before and knew that it didn't work on people, but it certainly had worked on the dog. The dog was pawing at his eyes with his front paws, and whining and whining, but he couldn't wipe the mace out of his eyes. I felt sympathy for the dog.

I was not involved in every escapade, but Tony was such a hard charger, it seemed he was involved with everything. He and Jewel were working together when they spotted a figure that was familiar to both of them. The man was a British West Indian who was a resident alien. He was known to all of the Investigators because he had the contract to maintain our vehicles. The contract had been taken away from him and awarded to someone else when we suspected that the Service was being charged for repair and parts and work that was never done. Later, we received information that this man was somehow managing to assist or smuggle other BWIs through the airport. Jewel and Tony spotted the man's car. There were two passengers in the car with him. They decided to check the identity of the passengers. When his car finally stopped, the male passenger quickly admitted that he was in Puerto Rico illegally, without any documentation. They then asked for the identification of the woman. The driver proceeded to interfere. He told them it was none of their business who the woman was, that she was his wife. They didn't care whose wife she was, if she was an illegal alien. They proceeded to tell him the woman was under arrest and would have to accompany them. He said that they could not take her, and the fight was on. They eventually overpowered the man and did arrest the woman. They then proceeded to charge him with assaulting Federal Officers because he fought with them.

The Assistant U.S. Attorney took this case. I sat in with the Assistant U.S. Attorney to assist him any way I could. The trial came; the jury selection was interesting to me. Speaking English was a sore spot. The Puerto Ricans would refuse to speak English. One of the Assistant Attorney's questions was, do you speak English well enough to be a juror? Never once did anyone say they did not speak English well enough to be a juror. Another question was, "Are you employed?" Unemployment was the highest in Puerto Rico of any place in the United States. However, not once did a prospective juror say that he was unemployed. The English speaking self-employed jury was selected, and the testimony was presented.

I believe the testimony of the two Immigration Officers was sufficient to get a conviction. However, I could tell the sympathy of the jury was not with the officers, but was with the BWI. Our Supervisors and Investigators at the office were interested in the case, and when I went back to the office at noon, they wanted to know how it was going. I told them I was afraid the jury was not sympathetic. The defendant was a large man with huge hands. His lawyer's defense was that he only defended himself when the two officers attacked him, and he had not really injured the officers. The strategy of the defense attorney was to show that there were no marks on either of the Immigration Officers. Tony testified that the man had struck him in the face with his fist. The defense attorney asked for permission for the defendant to walk in front of the jurors with his hand folded into a fist and show them what a huge hand this man had. His defense testimony was that he had previously been a professional boxer, and if he had struck the Officer in the face with that huge fist, there certainly would have been some kind of mark. In the end, the testimony of the Immigration Officers was disregarded, and the verdict was not guilty. Now that the BWI had been declared innocent of assaulting the officers, there was nothing to prevent him from turning right around and bringing suit against the officers whom he claimed had used excessive force when they kicked him in the groin. Now the Immigration Service and Tony and Jewel were on the defense.

Supervisory Investigator Vyse's vacancy was announced, as he would be rotating back to the States. I thought about the job. It would not be a promotion for me, or involve a pay raise, as I was already a Field Grade 12, but I thought that it would give me a wider choice of assignments when my rotation date arrived if I had experience as both a Field Investigator and a Supervisory Investigator. So I applied for the position and was selected.

There would be several vacancies to fill, first of all, the position I had just vacated. There was another vacancy when Investigator Leo Neit rotated back to the States, and one of our Investigators died. He was called Ace because of respect for his ability, not for a derogatory reason. I knew Ace was a hard worker even when he was in the Border Patrol at Brownsville, Texas, and in Puerto Rico he had become the office expert on false documents. He knew how many stitches should be in the binding of a passport. He would examine passports to see if the bindings had been resewed when pages of another passport had been placed inside a passport that contained a legal visa stamp. He knew the color combinations, and how many lines should appear in the under printing of the visa page. He also was the best at detecting counterfeit alien registration cards and had deserved the nickname, "Ace." I was surprised that Ace had not been promoted instead of me when I first came to Puerto Rico.

I suspected that it was a personal matter because he was in a constant battle with the bureaucracy and red tape of the Immigration Service. When he transferred to Puerto Rico, he had been transported by ship. He was afraid to fly and would not return to the United States by air. He insisted on being returned in the manner that he had been brought to Puerto Rico. In the meantime, the Service had quit using sea passage for transportation. They would not approve his travel by sea and insisted that he and his family use air transportation. He had written memos and contacted almost every official in the Service to seek help in solving his problem. We could tell he was a nervous wreck. The end result was that on his way to work one morning, he had a tremendous heart attack and subsequent attacks until it proved fatal. That was a tragic ending for an Investigator and a problem that really should not have been a problem.

It was time for Mr. Savage to rotate back to the States before I completed my first year in Puerto Rico. His vacancy was announced, and a few days later he came to me and asked, "Aren't you going to apply for my vacancy?" I told him I had not yet completed a year in Puerto Rico, and most vacancy announcements had the requirement that an applicant must have one year in grade. He told me to reread the announcement and then put in my application. When I read the announcement the second time, I noticed that there was no one-year in grade requirement. So I did apply for his vacancy. Sometime later I received an answer to my application. It stated that someone with an identical score but with more time in the Service had been certified, and I was not on the certification list. We learned that the person with an identical score who had been certified was Ed Sullivan. Since Sullivan was already at San Juan, we felt sure he would be selected. This was reinforced by the Deputy District Director who also believed Ed would be selected. After a couple of weeks went by without Ed receiving his confirmation telegram, it looked like he would not be selected. We didn't know the reason why, and every day someone would ask him if he had received his telegram. When it was obvious that he had not been selected, he would shortly rotate back to the States himself. The person selected was an Investigator from Chicago. Investigators were arriving to fill each of our vacancies. They included Blackwell, Rosemond, and Limon. Since each of these names related to a color, the secretaries nicknamed them the "Rainbow Boys."

Income tax time came, and I was due for another lesson in the operation of the government of the Commonwealth of Puerto Rico. First of all, income tax stays with the Commonwealth. I filed my return, along with a few thousand Puerto Ricans. The Governor, after the deadline for filing had passed, published a little article in the newspaper thanking the few thousand who had filed their returns for again doing their duty and filing their tax returns. I learned that most Puerto Ricans didn't bother to file a return. If they waited long enough, there would be a new Governor elected who would give them an amnesty, and they could pay a percentage of what they owed and be forgiven. My return was audited, and I was called in for an interview. The lady at the tax office informed me that I had claimed deductions for moving expenses. The moving expenses the government had given me was taxable in Puerto Rico, and I was required to come up with five hundred dollars cash. Ouch!

All was not work and no play in Puerto Rico. Jerry and I were taking advantage of the Caribbean beach hotel's swimming pool just across the street from where we lived. We both had enviable tans. In fact, the secretaries at the office would come by my desk, place their arms alongside mine and say, "Gee, Mr. Sims, you're one of us now," because my arm was darker than theirs. We had done all the things tourists do in Puerto Rico. We visited the casinos. We also drove all over the island. One of the most scenic places is the eastern end of the island where a mountain is covered by a rainforest. It is called El Yunque. The mountain is so tall that it blocks off the clouds which deliver the rain to the eastern end, forming a jungle, but caused the western end of the island to be desert-like. That part is covered with cactus and mesquite, and what crops they have at the western end of the island must be irrigated. The major crop is sugar cane, which is turned into very popular Puerto Rican rum. The Bacardi Rum factory is a tourist attraction, and Jerry and I took many trips across the bay on the Catano Ferry boat. There was a contortionist who made the ferry boat his stage and entertained the passengers, and he always collected a handful of quarters. The rum distillery would furnish samples, and a person could drink too much if he was so inclined.

We also had visited a unique place called Florescent Bay because of the phosphorus in the water in that particular area. It was just west of Ponce, on the south side of the island. It was visible in the darkness; so on the day we visited, we had a nice seafood supper waiting for darkness. We then boarded a ferryboat type boat to go the few miles from the dock around the coast to the bay. On the way to the bay, a young boy and his father were sitting in the back of the boat near Jerry and me, and the boy asked his father, "Dad, what is that?" He pointed to the sky, and everybody looked in the direction he was pointing. It took us a few seconds to see what he was talking about, but way high in the heavens, higher than any plane could possibly fly, was a light steadily tracking from the western horizon towards the east. The boy wanted to know what it was, and no one could be sure, but we agreed with his father who told him it was probably a satellite. The phosphorus in the water in that particular place was a mystery, but it was impressive to see the shimmering wake of our boat and see silver streaks flashing through the water as fish scurried out of our way. We anchored in the bay, and the deckhand hoisted several buckets of seawater and poured it on the deck. Each bucket was a bucketful of stars as each drop sparkled as it ran off the deck.

Dear Chief

Parking was scarce in Old San Juan, so Jerry and I would more often take the bus to the plaza where we would enjoy a cup of coconut-flavored ice cream and join the shiploads of tourists walking the streets, visiting the souvenir shops. We usually waited until after sundown when it was a few degrees cooler than in the middle of the day. It never really cooled down in San Juan. The night temperature was only a few degrees lower than the daytime temperature.

On one of these visits, we were walking behind two women who were headed back to their ship, which was only three or four blocks away, when I saw movement in the shadows as the women walked by, and a man darted out. I heard the women scream as he wrenched away one of the purses the woman was carrying. Instinctively, I took off after him as he ran down the street toward the waterfront. He was a tall, lanky Puerto Rican, and I wasn't gaining on him very much, but it was downhill, and I stayed behind him. When we reached the bottom of the hill, he turned east along the street that parallels the waterfront. He was around the corner and out of sight from me for a minute or so. He must have been rummaging through the lady's purse as he ran. When I rounded the corner, I could not see the purse in his hand any longer, but I continued to chase him. Another block away, there was a group of people in front of a cantina, and I yelled to them as he ran toward them, "Stop him, stop him." They all turned to look to see what the commotion was, but showed very little interest. One man detached himself from the group, and as the purse-snatcher ran by, he got in his car and overtook him. He passed him and then turned in the street, squarely in front of the running purse-snatcher and let him run right into the side of the car. He got out of the car and grabbed the purse-snatcher, and I came running up and grabbed him by his other arm.

The man who assisted me was an undercover police officer. I told him what had happened, and he asked our suspect, "Where is it?" The suspect answered, "I don't know." The police officer asked him again, "Where is it?" and this time gave him a sharp blow to the solar plexus. The guy doubled over, and the third time he was asked, where is it, he answered, "It's there, it's there," and the cop had him retrace his path until we found the lady's purse where he had dropped it in some weeds beside the sidewalk. I don't know what he did with her money but he had somehow disposed of it, whether he also hid it in the weeds or whether there was a companion whom he had run by during the chase and handed the money. The lady's purse and her passport were returned to her, but her money was lost. I asked the policeman what he would do with the thief. He said he would lock him up and keep him detained overnight, but in the morning the ship would leave, and the lady would no longer be available as a witness against the thief, and his case would be dismissed for lack of evidence. In Puerto Rico crime does pay.

As soon as Jerry and I were eligible to use our vacation plan, we decided to spend a week in St. Thomas, Virgin Islands. We had already visited St. Croix. It is a very small island, and the Investigator who met us took us all over the island in just a little while. St. Thomas is a little bigger, and the island of St. John is just a short ferry ride, and the British Virgin Island, Tortola, is just on the skyline from St. John. St. John has beautiful beaches, and after looking around the mainland, we decided we would visit both St. John one day and Tortola another day. We were waiting for the bus that would take us to the village of Red Hook where we would catch the ferryboat to St. John, when a car pulled up to the bus stop and a black man called, "Mr. Sims, Mr. Sims." I looked around to see who knew my name, as I didn't expect anyone to know me in St. Thomas. The man saw that I did not recognize him and said, "You don't know me, do you?" I replied that I didn't, and he said, "You caught me in Puerto Rico and sent me home. That was the best thing that you could have done because it caused me to get my resident card," and he took an alien registration card from his wallet and held it up for me to see that he was now a legal resident. He offered me a ride, but Jerry and I wanted to see things the way the tourists see them, and we declined.

The ferryboat ride was pleasant. On the way over, we both noticed one person that stood out from the group of passengers. He sat in the back of the boat by himself, and I commented to Jerry, "I wonder what that Mexican is doing in the Virgin Islands." We thought no more about him and enjoyed our day swimming in the warm water with the whitest, sandiest beach we had ever seen. The stay in St. Thomas was pleasant, and we did a little shopping. The day came when we had decided to go to Tortola. The ferryboat ride was a little longer. We didn't know what to expect, and we were surprised at how poor the people are in Tortola. What I remember most is a Black lady holding out her infant who could not have been more than a few weeks old and asking us if we wanted to buy the baby. We didn't feel like spending much time in Tortola and got the next ferry back to St. Thomas.

It was back to work for me. Now that I was a Supervisor, I was determined that I would not be a "sit in the office" Supervisor like my boss had been in San Francisco. I would get out with my Investigators as much as I could. I would work with Jewel Gross, who took over my caseload. Naturally, I would go with Tony whenever time permitted, and I also worked with Ferrer, and Foy on Area Control. One of the little techniques I had come up with to detect the BWIs and Dominicans from the Puerto Ricans was to ask them about the United States flag. One day, we were checking a small construction site. I noticed one person who didn't seem to have anything to do and was apart from the rest of the workers. I approached him and gave him my usual questions, "How many starts on the United States flag?" Without hesitation, he responded, "24, sir." I thought, oh, I better put him in the car. As I led him toward the car, a young man detached himself from the other workers and came running after me, saying, "Wait, wait, you have my brother." He explained by making a motion toward his head with his finger, saying, "He is a little slow." He said there was no one at home to leave his brother with, so he had to bring him with him to work every day. You never know what you will run into.

One day, Tony told me he was going to apprehend a maid and wanted someone to go with him. Since I was free at the moment, I agreed to go. We arrived at the home in the richest residential area of San Juan. We rang the door and the maid opened the door for us. As soon as she realized we were Immigration Officers, she tried to slam the door, but Tony had his foot in it. She whirled and ran through the house with Tony in hot pursuit. I was several steps behind. I saw them both go out the door in the back of the house, and the maid put her arms on a wall in the back yard and pulled herself over before Tony could get there. Instead of rolling over the wall like the woman had done, Tony jumped the wall and soared out into space. The woman must have known there was a big ditch behind the wall, and she was able to ease over the wall and slide down the bank of the ditch. Tony landed in the ditch so hard that he was badly injured; I could tell when I looked over the wall. I clambered down the bank to where he was laying, and he told me that he was afraid his leg was broken, but he thought he could make it back to the car if I could help him. It turned out he was right, but the severity of his injury was worse than we both had feared. Tony feared that the doctors in Puerto Rico would be unable to mend his leg because they were talking about the possibility of amputating it. Tony knew he could get better treatment back in the States and asked to go home to Texas. There was some hassle about letting him go back to the States, but in the end he came back to Texas for treatment. That was my last day of duty with one of the hardest-working Investigators I ever worked with.

I was getting along very well with the Puerto Ricans who worked in our office, but I was about to sample a bit of the animosity that McKaskill had experienced. I thought the bay near the airport would be a good place to fish, but it was hard to get to, except for the main entrance from the marina where powerboats and sailboats were berthed. The main channel was used by water skiers. I decided a rubber raft would be just the thing for me to scoot around among the trees and the shallow water. I had gone fishing and had tied my little raft to a tree branch beside the main channel and was not paying any attention to the boats going up and down behind me as I fished back toward the bank. When I heard a ski boat come zooming by, I turned just in time to see a skier come directly at me. But just in the nick of time, the ski rope pulled him away from me, and he turned a sharp turn which sprayed a wall of water from his ski. I heard him laughing as they towed him away. They were gone a few minutes, and had changed skiers. Two people were in the boat, and one on his single water ski. I was a little more alert this time and was looking at the skier as he approached; he made his turn a little too soon to spray any water on me.

While they were gone this time, I noticed some large pods growing on the tree that I was tied to; some were within reach. They reminded me of the large pods of seeds that grow on American locust trees. I reached up and broke off one of the pods, which was more than six inches long and resembled a hunting knife in its shape. I figured the third skier would take his turn at spraying me when they came back, but I continued my fishing as if I were paying no attention to them as I heard them approaching for the third time. The third skier was determined that he was going to get close enough to spray me, but when he was almost within distance, I turned to face him with the seed pod in my hand, drawn back ready to throw like a throwing knife. I flipped it just as he was approaching the critical point. It upset him so that he lost his concentration, and by the time he veered away from me, the towline jerked him forward again, and he went tumbling head over heels. He was floating around in the channel waiting for the boat to make a turn and come back for him, and I called him everything that I could think of, including stupid son-of-a-bitch, and asked him if he thought he was a water skier. The boat came back to lift him aboard, and I heard them asking him, "What happened; what did he say; what did he say?" The guy was too embarrassed to tell them and said, "Nothing, nothing; let's go." I obviously had spoiled their fun.

Maybe I needed to go to charm school; that is what they called the course the Immigration Service offered us Supervisors. The Border Patrol Academy had been moved from Port Isabel, Texas to Glenn County, near Brunswick, Georgia. There was an old Naval base there that was now known as FLETC (Federal Law Enforcement Training Center), Glenco, Georgia. All of the Immigration training, as well as several other government agencies, was being conducted there. It was my first trip, and I was looking forward to seeing old friends from all over the United States. It was also an interesting flight up the coast of Florida to Jacksonville. We flew almost directly over Cape Kennedy and could see rockets standing on their launch pad, or at least a rocket. A bus would meet us at the Jacksonville airport and transport us the additional forty miles to Brunswick. Sure enough, there were acquaintances from every part of the United States.

The first couple of days we got together and said, "What an opportunity this was to get away from home, and get some exercise." We really planned to shed a few pounds by jogging. The first day, three or four of us got together and did jog a mile or so. The next day we didn't jog hardly as far, and about the third day was, well, let's just jog over to the mess hall. The food was delicious, the best I've ever seen at any government facility. Instead of losing a few pounds, I ended up gaining a few. I was seated in the mess hall one day when someone slapped me on the back so hard I spilled my coffee. I turned around to look over my shoulder at a bearded face I didn't recognize. The person who had slapped me saw that I didn't recognize him and said, "You don't recognize me, do you?" I said, "No, I'm afraid not." He said, "I'm Taylor. We were stationed together at Stockton." I had not recognized him with the beard. I wondered why, and he told me that he was working for the ATF agency and that he was responsible for the explosions we had been hearing. He was teaching a new class of trainees how to blow up whiskey distilleries.

There wasn't much to remember about the training except the three-minute speech that each of us was required to present before the other members of the class. It was up to us to determine the three minutes without looking at a watch, so we conspired with a buddy to start drumming his fingers on the table within a few seconds of the time our three minutes were up, so we could start concluding our speech without going too much overtime. I don't know why the flight back to Puerto Rico seemed longer than the one coming to Glenco. It's usually the other way around. A person in anticipation of arriving at his destination seems to take longer than the trip back.

I have mentioned that vacancies were constantly occurring in San Juan. Usually the District Director selected the person to fill each vacancy without consulting anyone else. I had never had any input into a selection until Sullivan's vacancy was filled. It looked as if the DD was going to select some one from another office, but the DD went on vacation before the selection was made. I talked with the Deputy District Director, Mr. Bobeck, and convinced him that it was bad for morale for most of our vacancies to be filled with someone from outside our own district when we had qualified people sitting there waiting for an opportunity. We decided that Jim Heishman was qualified for the Grade 12 position, and we notified the Regional Office that he had been selected, and he got his telegram confirming his promotion before the DD returned from his leave.

Our new Assistant District Director for Investigations, Robert Karol, arrived from Chicago. He let it be known that he had heard about what a trouble spot he was coming to and had been told to take charge with a firm hand and not to trust anyone. That would work out fine, and Puerto Rico would become just the home Robert was looking for.

Transfers to and from San Juan continued at a rapid pace. Another Investigator Joined the Rainbow Boys. Al Redman came to San Juan from a position as Immigrant Inspector on the Northern Border. Everyone who came to San Juan was not suited to work as an Investigator. It was my opinion that Al was one of those. He had worked in the Northern Border where I am sure he did a good job as an Immigrant Inspector for so many years that his fluency in Spanish had left him. I couldn't assign him to work casework alone, so I assigned him to work Area Control with one of my best and most aggressive Area Control Investigators. The Investigator came to me after a couple of weeks working with Al and requested that I either reassign him or assign Al to work with someone else because he didn't want to work with him any longer. I asked why. He told me how they had gone to a house looking for a suspect. Al was to guard the back door while the other Investigator tried to get someone to open the front door. The house was like so many in Puerto Rico with a hallway down the center, and one could see from the front door to the back door. When someone finally came to the front door to let the Investigator in, he saw his suspect going out the back. He rushed to the back door expecting Al to have the alien in custody. Instead, he found Al standing with his arms folded. When asked, "Where is the alien?" Al just pointed in the direction the alien had gone and said, "He went that way." Al had made no attempt to stop or pursue the alien as he fled. I made no apologies for the rating I gave Al at the appraisal period, which was not a high rating.

Supervisory Investigator Cochran was transferred back to the States with a promotion. His replacement was Gene Smithberg who had been an instructor at the Border Patrol Academy. His Spanish was great, and he was a very knowledgeable Supervisor. Shortly after his arrival, he and I were both told to attend a Supervisor's Training Course sponsored by the GSA. The class consisted of more women than men. The emphasis of the training would be on personnel problems and how to get employees to work together as a team. At the end of our course, our lady instructor gave us a ball of yarn, which she called a warm fuzzy, and we would give her a going-away lunch at one of the nice restaurants. The meal was fairly expensive, and since each of us would order individually, I ordered a chicken dinner, which was the cheapest thing on the menu. I noticed some of the men and women were having lobster or combination seafood plates, which were very expensive.

As we finished the meal, I noticed that some of the men were drifting away to the bar. Some of the women were headed for the ladies' room, and many of them were not returning. As a result, the GSA Representative, who was hosting the training session, was attempting to collect money to pay for the bill, but she was way short. Even though Smithberg and I contributed much more than our fair share, she was still short more cash than she had and had to put a large charge on her credit card. I felt sorry for her. I don't know if the people who failed to pay thought the meal was at government expense or why they had no responsibility for at least paying for their own, but maybe the GSA Representative needed to take her own class in how to work as a team.

Jerry and I have always liked dogs. When we moved to Puerto Rico, we only had one that we took with us. She was an AKC registered miniature greyhound named Lady Genevive, with a pedigree as long as your arm, but to us, she was just a gentle pet that we called Ginny. We had been in Puerto Rico only a short time when our paper boy became interested in this strange-looking dog which was too small to be a greyhound and too large to be a Chihuahua. On his delivery route one day, while I was home, he approached the gate at the carport with two smaller boys who were about eight years old from their appearance and could have been friends or his younger brothers, but he had brought them along to see the dog. He asked me in Spanish if she was a Chihuahua. I told him she was a greyhound, and he asked me again, since he didn't have knowledge of greyhounds, if she is not a Chihuahua. I told him, "No, she is not a Chihuahua; she is a greyhound." He turned with his two companions shaking his head in disbelief, and I heard him tell them as they left the driveway, "Yes, she is a Chihuahua."

It wasn't intentional, but it just worked out that Ginny was about to have company. In Puerto Rico, there is an ambivalent attitude toward dogs, and all things, for that matter. If God put them there, then it shouldn't be any person's intent to change things, so all kinds of stray dogs from mangy, dying, hairless mutts to helpless young dogs are permitted to roam the streets unmolested. I don't believe they even have a dog pound or dogcatcher. I had seen the ugliest dog I ever saw in my life scrounging food across the street at the hotel garbage dumpster. She almost defies description. She was a brown, mixed with black. I have seen the same color in cows, and they are called brindle. Her ears didn't stand up nor did they hang down like a beagle. They were just something on the side of her head, and she was obviously very pregnant.

One night, I heard howling, and I got up to see where it was coming from. I took my flashlight, and followed the sounds to the garbage dumpster. I shined the light inside, and there was this ugly-looking dog. In the States we would call her a "Heinz 57," but Americans sarcastically referred to those mutts in Puerto Rico as "Borinquin Terriers." She was so big that she could no longer climb out of the dumpster. I arranged some cardboard boxes so she could climb out, and she managed to get out and run away. I realized she could no longer scrounge for food in that manner, so I began taking some canned dog food on a paper plate across the street and setting it on the ground near the dumpster. She was curious about it, but would not approach and eat the food while I was standing there. I returned to the house but kept an eye on her, and after I left she did eat the food. I also had to put out some fresh water because water is scarce in Puerto Rico. There is an abundance of seawater, but very little fresh water.

Over the days, she came to look forward to my putting out the food and would get closer and closer while I stood nearby. Eventually, she would come and eat the food while I stood there. She was getting so big I told Jerry that she was going to have more puppies than our beagle had in Texas when she had eight puppies. The time for her delivery was drawing near, I could tell. One day I came home and went to check on her and give her some food, and she wasn't there. I looked around and finally heard some squeaking from under the steps leading up to the walkway of the hotel. She had dug a hole in the sand in which to have her babies. I couldn't tell how many she had, but there were so many she couldn't tend to them. I could see a couple of others that had been mashed and were all covered with sand. As I neared the hole she was in, she bared her teeth and growled, but I kept talking to her and told her she needed some help, and that I wasn't afraid of her. I knew she was not going to bite me, that I knew she was just protecting her puppies. I was able to reach the dead ones, and throw them in the dumpster, but I still couldn't tell how many there were. Each day, when I came home from work, I went over to see about her, and each day there were more dead puppies.

Finally, I could tell that she had a total of twelve, but there was only one left alive. I don't believe they were getting any milk. When there was only one left, I said, What a shame for a dog to have twelve puppies and none of them survive," so I got a cardboard box and told her to come along. She trotted along beside me with her nose against the box. We went through the house to the patio. I put down the box and more food and water for her and realized that the dog was not able to nurse, and if it was going to survive, I would have to feed it with a medicine dropper. I tried giving it some warm milk, and it lived until the following day, but when I came home the following evening, it was also dead. I told Jerry that we might as well let the dog stay. She seemed content in the cardboard box. Obviously she had never had anything, and now she had a home.

If we were going to keep her we had to give her a name. She had been so alone and looked so pitiful we decided to call her Lonesome. Ginny, our greyhound, had grown up with other dogs, and she accepted Lonesome as a sister without showing any jealousy whatsoever. Lonesome was not going to be a favorite with my wife. She was not as neat as Ginny. She always ran around with her tongue hanging out, dripping saliva, and she had longer hair than the greyhound, and it would shed and blow around the carport and the patio. Jerry said we didn't need another dog, but if we were going to keep her, we had to get her distemper and rabies shots, which we did. Jerry complained about the dog, and one day I came home from work and she was missing.

I wondered if she had decided to run away, but I doubted that. She had become so domesticated, and she would not leave a place where she had food and water and a bed. Finally, Jerry admitted that she had taken the dog several miles down the beach where there were other stray dogs and had put her out. It took me about three days to make Jerry feel so guilty about what she had done that she told me where she had taken the dog and agreed that if I liked the dog so much that we would go back where she had left her and look for her. We went to the place Jerry said she had put the dog out, and she had been around there because there were several dog tracks in the sand. I began calling her name, and several hundred yards down the beach I saw this animal coming running toward me getting larger and larger as she approached. I could tell it was Lonesome. When she was about ten feet from me she sprang through the air, right into my arms, and began licking my face like we had been separated forever. With devotion like that, we could never get rid of her, at least I couldn't, and spent the several dollars it would take to get her ready to travel and bring her back to the States with us when I eventually rotated back home.

As my rotation date neared, I submitted my "Dear Chief" memo, informing the personnel office that I did not intend to extend my tour in Puerto Rico and listing three locations that I would like to be assigned to when I rotated. Jerry was concerned about where we would be going. The three locations I asked for were in the Southern Region. The Regional Commissioner was Mr. Salturelli, the same Commissioner who had stated we would get no assistance when we were accused of violating Jamall's civil rights. I also received some communications from the personnel office indicating that my name should have been on the list for the ADDI's job that I had applied for and had been informed that another person with the same score, but more time was certified. That entitled me to priority consideration for another GS-13 job. I also finally received word from the Department of Justice that there would be no further investigation of the civil rights complaint because of insufficient evidence. So, as far as I was concerned, everything was in good order, and I was ready to leave Puerto Rico.

A month before my rotation date, one of my friends from the FBI came by to visit. He had visit4ed me one month after I arrived in Puerto Rico. He said he had heard I was there and came by to visit since we had been in the Border Patrol in the same class together. He was under the same two-year.Tour that I was, and I was surprised that he already knew his assignment, and I had not heard anything from my request. He let me know that he was leaving exactly at the end of his two-year tour. Jerry kept saying no one was interested whether we rotated back on time or not. I kept telling her the Immigration Service would take care of its own; just give them a chance.

I began to believe Jerry when I saw vacancies posted at one of the places I had asked to go. I began calling everyone who would listen at the Central Office Personnel Office and at the Regional Office Personnel Office. No one seemed concerned that my time had come and gone. I finally reached Mr. Salturelli on the phone and told him that my rotation date had passed, that I had seen vacancies posted for one of the places that I had asked to go to and would like to be rotated to that position. Mr. Salturelli was as sarcastic as anyone I had talked to. He told me he kept the list of vacancies on his desk in front of him, and he decided who would fill them, and that it might be a long time before I got one of those vacancies. His last comment was, "What is your hurry anyhow?"

That evening when I went home I told Jerry what had transpired. She had been saying all along that the only way we would get out of Puerto Rico was to contact our Senator. I told her that we would contact her Senator from Mississippi and that I would help her compose a letter. I thought everyone has a boss, even Regional Commissioners. At that time her Senator was Senator Stennis. We composed our letter to him, in which we requested that he contact the Commissioner of Immigration in Washington in the Central Office and request that he expedite my transfer back to the States, as my rotation date had already passed without anyone making any attempt to transfer me, and that vacancies had been posted in locations where I had asked to be rotated to.

It took a little over a week for us to receive an answer from Senator Stennis. His short note just stated that he hoped that he had been of assistance to us. He will never know how much assistance he really was. Even before we received his answer, I began getting phone calls from the Southern Region. I no longer had to make the calls; now they were calling me and telling me where there were vacancies and asking if I would like one of them. When he mentioned San Antonio, Texas, I stated that was the one I wanted. They told me that a GS-12 Investigator would be retiring on the last day of August. They also told me I could not report for duty in San Antonio before he was officially retired. I told them that was fine with me, that I would report for duty on the first day of September. The wind down to rotation was anticlimactic, but not uneventful.

Dear Chief

    The Rainbow Boys were a mild-mannered group compared to the excitement that Investigators like Vyse, MacKaskill, and Hobert had stirred up. Blackwell was about to solve one of the mysteries regarding our telephones. He and I were working late one evening; everyone else had left the office and secured the doors to the hallway, but we could still go from office to office through the inner doors. Blackwell was going to do the security check, which consisted of making sure the outer doors were locked, that no files or classified material had been left on the desktops. He would then secure the doors behind him as he came back to the Investigation Section. He was in the file room when I heard him yell, "Sims, Sims!" I rushed to see what he was excited about, and he pointed to the Supervisor's desk which no longer had the telephone sitting on it, but the cord was under her desk. I got to a position where I could see what Blackwell was pointing at, and I could see a man curled up under the desk with the telephone. We got him out, asked him for his identification, and he was at first reluctant to give his true name. Then we went through his billfold and found out his true name and identification as an employee of the GSA who had responsibility for cleaning the building. He was one of their janitors.

    For months, strange telephone numbers, mostly to New York City, had been appearing on our long distance phone bill. There was a system of telephone service called the FTS, and our Investigators knew that they could call New York through the FTS operator, who would then ring the number in New York City, and it wouldn't be charged as a long distance phone call. But every month, anywhere from eight to a dozen calls were appearing on our long distance bill. When our secretary checked the log of phone records on the form, G-40, these would be unaccounted for. Mr. Karol would then divide them between Smithberg and me and we would have to concoct some story of why that number was called without using the FTS system. After we fabricated a reason for the call, Mr. Karol would then certify that the call had been a necessary call, and a G-40 matching the long distance call would be filed away. I hated doing this every month. It was not truthful, and I didn't want to sign a form certifying I had made a call that I had actually no knowledge about, but the mystery was solved with the apprehension of the GSA employee.

It turned out that he had girlfriends in New York whom he was calling on our phone. As a janitor, he had access to all of the building and could get into the Immigration offices. We asked him why he didn't use the phones in his own section, and he said his supervisors would not let him make calls from the GSA office. We told Mr. Karol what we had found, and he contacted the GSA Supervisor to have some disciplinary action taken against the man who was running up our phone bill, but to my knowledge, nothing was ever done about it. At least the calls stopped.

My sister-in-law has two sons, my nephews, who I fondly refer to as my number one nephew and my number two nephew. Number one nephew has a close friend about his age. They are together so much that I began calling Ricky my number three nephew. Number one had mentioned he would like to come to Puerto Rico for a visit before we left. We reminded him that time was running out, and he better come if he wanted to visit while we were still there. On the appointed date, we met the plane, and off of the plane stepped number three nephew, but number one, who was employed at the bank, could not get away, and at the last minute had to cancel his plans for the trip. We tried to show number three nephew a good time. Jerry was so glad to see him that she kept him up until three o'clock in the morning asking questions about everyone she could remember in Greenville.

I let Ricky wear one of my jackets so he could visit the casino, which required a jacket. Before that, we had visited the old fort in old San Juan. We'd also taken the boat ride across the bay to the Bacardi Rum Distillery. The fact that my jacket was three or four sizes too large didn't bother Rick. The sleeves hung down over his thumb, almost to the tips of his fingers, but he didn't care. It seemed like the streetwalkers didn't care, either. They would walk along beside Ricky, who was walking with Jerry and me, and ask him if he wanted to have sex with them. He must have looked like a real tourist. He was amazed at how brazen they were. There was certainly nothing like that in Greenville, Mississippi.

The next day, cockfights were scheduled at the arena near the El San Juan hotel. I had been once before, so I knew what to expect, but it was something new and different for Ricky. It's an exciting place. The arena is circular with a small circle at the floor level.

Dear Chief

Everyone gets a good view of the roosters as they fight, but the real money is not in the prizes awarded to the best or winning rooster. The money is in the side bets. Number three nephew was so amazed to see so many people with a handful of money, wanting to bet with their neighbors. They would bet before the fight started, then when it looked like one of the cocks was getting the best of the other, there would be more offers to bet with everyone shouting their bets to each other, some accepting and some declining.

The cocks are fitted with steel spurs that fit over the spur on the leg of each rooster. The spurs are razor sharp. The owners let each cock pick at the other a little bit to get them agitated, then when they turn them loose, they are ready to fight. The roosters jump into the air and slice at each other, and sometimes there's a lot of blood flying around if one gets sliced across the neck. The vulnerable part of the rooster is the back, and a good rooster will jump high in the air and sink a steel spur into the back of his opponent. When this happens, you can see the other one shudder, and it takes the fight right out of them. Many of them are killed. If one is not putting up a good fight, its owner may let the other one kill his rooster. If he has put up a good fight, and even though he is losing, the owner can surrender and save his rooster to fight again another day. Ricky seemed to have a good time, and I was glad he could visit with us.

Our next-door neighbor was visiting in the opposite direction. He had gone to Florida to look for a house to live in, in anticipation of moving to Florida. When he left, he told me that his avocado tree in his back yard had fruit almost ready to pick and if I wanted them, to help myself. He left the key to the gate between the yards with me. I picked a couple, and they were still a little bit green. I thought I would wait a few days before picking any more of them. The weekend came, and I opened the gate, went into the yard, and was amazed that there was not an avocado left on the tree. Someone had scaled the wall and picked every avocado. The lots behind the house I lived in and a couple of my neighbors' houses had a cinder block fence about seven feet high. This fence separated the houses on one street from the houses facing the street behind.

One night, just after sundown, Ginny and Lonesome began barking and raising a fuss. I knew there had to be someone there, or they wouldn't bark that way. About that time I heard two shots, Spat,

Spat, from a small caliber pistol. They sounded like they were coming from my back door, it was so close. I grabbed my own pistol and ran out the side door to the carport so I could see the back yard. On top of the fence was a young man that I recognized as our neighbor from two houses down the street. When the shots were fired, the dogs were as silent as a mouse, and I figured that he had shot my dogs, but they were just a bit gun shy. When he fired his pistol, they had run around to the other side of the house to the patio.

He explained that he and his mother and father were sitting on the front porch trying to get a little bit of the ocean breeze that you can feel at sundown. He had heard a noise inside the house and knew that all three of them were out front, so he suspected a burglar was inside. Then he went inside, sure enough, he surprised a man who was trying to steal their television set. The man ran out the back, and my neighbor grabbed his pistol and ran out behind him. The man was very agile and had climbed the seven-foot cinder block wall and was running on top of it toward my house. The neighbor had climbed up on the fence and pursued him and fired two shots as he jumped off the fence into the yard facing the other street behind us. That just proved that nothing was safe in Puerto Rico, from fruit to bicycles to televisions.

Coconuts were also considered public property, no matter whose yard the palm tree was in. Teenage boys would climb the tree and knock off the green coconuts. They could be sold by roadside vendors who usually had an old cold drink box with some ice in it and would chill the green coconuts and advertise them as coco frio. The coconut milk wasn't bad if it was cold. Another thing that Jerry and I like was coconut flavored ice cream.

Time was running out in Puerto Rico. I took the car to the port to be shipped back to New Orleans in plenty of time for it to be waiting for us when we arrived. Jerry was counting the days. In fact, she had never liked living in Puerto Rico. It was too hot; the temperature at night was only a few degrees cooler than it was in the daytime. During our second winter in Puerto Rico, it had cooled down to 69 degrees during a cold spell. All the neighbors were breaking out heavy coats and sweaters and complaining about the cold. Jerry got along good with the neighbors, and they would converse in their limited English and she in her limited Spanish.

Dear Chief

However, she understood a lot more Spanish than she was willing to speak. She had made a few friends; one worked at the bank where we did business; another was a wife of a jewelry storeowner in Old San Juan. Mostly, our friends were other government employees. They were there on two-year tours like us, and we knew they would be leaving, but it was kind of depressing every time when one of them left.

The last two Investigators to come to Puerto Rico did not come with promotions. They came as Investigator Trainees with permanent assignments to Puerto Rico and would not be entitled to the two year rotation.

I could understand some of Jerry's displeasure with Puerto Rico; not only was there the language, but there was discrimination against Americans. The Puerto Ricans wanted Puerto Rico for Puerto Rico and resented people being transferred to their Commonwealth to be their bosses. I had been with Jerry to the grocery store when she would be ready to check out and put her groceries on the checkout counter; the Puerto Rican woman operating the register would attempt to reach around Jerry's items to get items for the woman behind her and check her out ahead of Jerry. Jerry never hesitated to put a stop to that and tell them, "Hey, I'm next." She also got discourteous remarks when she walked our dogs. There was a vacant lot on the street behind our street, and if she took them there she walked by a building under construction several weeks. The employees would yell and whistle and gesture and make rude remarks to the blonde-haired Americana. There were perverts on the public beaches who were exposing themselves to the tourists. I just called them "weeny wagers" and laughed at them, but it was better for her to swim in the hotel swimming pool. Jerry also didn't like to fly. She was nervous about the trips we made to the Virgin Islands on the little Prinair Airlines, even though they were probably the safest in the world. They were small planes, but had four engines. She said that if the good Lord would just let her get safely back to the good old United States of America, she would fly one more time, but that would be the last time.

I must have gotten along well with the Puerto Rican employees at the Immigration Office. They gave me a nice going-away party. Everything was in readiness. The movers took the furniture. We had travel cages and medical certificates for the dogs so they would not have any problem with quarantine once we returned to New Orleans. Jerry and I could sleep late at the hotel the last night. We could take a midday flight and still arrive at New Orleans in the early afternoon. Investigator Blackwell took us, with the dogs, to the airport. The dogs were slightly sedated so they would have no problem with the trip. I took Jerry to the lounge and made sure she drank a couple of double shots of vodka before boarding the plane so she would also be slightly sedated. As I said before, she had counted the days. After two years and two months and twenty-two days, we waved goodbye to Blackwell and boarded our freedom bird.

CHAPTER SEVEN: SAN ANTONIO

With no more inconvenience than a taxi trip from the airport in New Orleans to the port to pick up our car, we were on our way to San Antonio. Jerry and I had crossed the United States several times, and there was not much new for us to see as we traveled down the interstate, watching one green sign after another. It was repetitious, seeing the name of a road or town and next exit, and I began to wonder about America's attention for brevity.

I really believed we should adopt the women's equal right belief that the abbreviation for a lady should be Ms. It was only logical that if the abbreviation for mister should be Mr., then the abbreviation for a lady should be Ms., and one would not have to wonder if he was using the correct designation, as he might make a mistake if he used Miss for a married lady or Mrs. For a single lady. In that line of reasoning, I wondered why someone had not taken the words "next exit" and shortened them by taking the "tex" out of next exit and leaving the "nexit," shortening the word to "nexit." There could be no mistake for what nexit meant. Just think of all the reflectors this would save if used on all the next exit signs throughout the United States.

It had been five years since I was last in San Antonio for two weeks Air Force Reserve duty. At that time, Jerry and I had stayed at a motel near the entrance to Lackland Air Force Base. The motel there was reasonable, and the restaurant had good food, so we decided to stay there temporarily while I once again let Jerry look for a house that she would be content to live in.

I didn't know just what to expect at San Antonio. It is one of those places that Investigators want to go to, but never have the opportunity. The office was small considering the geographical area we had to cover. I felt a little better when the first person I met in the Investigation Section was Hoyle Thompson, whom I had met years ago at the Journeyman Investigators class. He told me that the Assistant District Director for Investigations' positions was vacant. He told me it would be filled by an old buddy of mine from San Francisco, Ed Molina, who would be arriving in a couple of weeks. In the meantime, he told me I was the senior, because I had been a

Supervisor Investigator for a year at Puerto Rico, and he had just become a Supervisor Investigator, so I was to be the acting ADDI until Mr. Molina arrived. The first thing I had to do was prepare the monthly activity report to be submitted to the Regional Office. Fortunately, the secretary who had been typing the report knew what was required, and the other people who contributed portions of the report submitted their reports, and we consolidated all into a passable monthly activity report.

It had been so long since I had been in Texas that I had forgotten how everything either sticks you, stings, or bites you, that I was surprised when, in my second week, I was bitten by a spider on the top of my foot. There is something about a spider bite that deteriorates the skin, and in a couple of days, the pimple had grown to a hole in the top of my foot the size of a dime. My foot was swollen, and I could hardly walk, so I went on sick leave. I was on sick leave when Mr. Molina reported for duty, and I was not there to welcome him. I had looked forward to working with Molina again. I respected him for the work he did in San Francisco, and I believed he would be a good person to work for in San Antonio. Maybe we weren't as good friends as Thompson had believed, because when I reported back for duty, it was as if I was a total stranger, and he had never known me at all.

The manning of the San Antonio office was similar to other small offices. The ADDI was a grade GS-13. There were two supervisory grade GS-12's and two non-supervisory GS-12's I expected the office to have several very old Investigators, as there were never vacancy announcements for San Antonio, and I had never had another opportunity to go there. There were a few old timers ready for retirement, but I was surprised at the number of young Investigators. When I asked them how they got to be at San Antonio, I learned that most of them had taken a reduction from their grade as Border Patrolmen and came to San Antonio as Investigator Trainees. However, in a couple of years, they were at a higher grade as Investigators than they had been as Border Patrolmen.

I learned that we had an annex located on South Main Street, about five blocks from the District Office. The annex housed the Detention Facility and the Area Control Squad, which I would supervise. I would also supervise the General Squad, which was located in the District Office, and I would stay in the District Office the first few weeks of my assignment at San Antonio. During that few weeks the Regional Commissioner would visit the District Office. I knew the Regional Commissioner had not chosen my assignment to San Antonio, and it had been politically forced on him. I was not surprised when I overheard him talking to the District Director outside my office door asking the District Director, "How is he doing, anyhow?" I don't know what kind of person he thought I was or what I would be doing. But regardless of his feelings, I was glad to be at San Antonio.

Investigators tend to find little niches for themselves that they feel comfortable in, and San Antonio was no different. They had assigned an Investigator as a processing officer who took care of some walk-ins and prepared Orders to Show Cause. Another investigator was assigned to check the local jail and prepare cases for prosecution. I always like to get out of the office as much as possible. Moving to the annex would mean I could spend more of my time with the Area Control Unit and less time devoted to the casework of my General Investigations.

There were only four Investigators at that time assigned to Area Control work. They had teamed up as a matter of convenience, in more or less permanent partnerships. I noticed that my oldest Investigator, Ralph Marsh, and his partner would come into the office about nine-thirty or ten o'clock in the morning with four or five aliens they had apprehended and would have cardboard boxes of personal effects with them. My other team would come in about the same time with three, four or five aliens who were traveling light with no baggage. These two investigators would have dusty shoes where they had been running or walking through construction areas. I wondered why the difference, and someone finally told me that Ralph and his partner were going by the bus station every morning and apprehending the aliens who were sitting around in the bus station with their baggage. The other team was getting out into the outer areas of San Antonio, where the construction was going on, and were getting apprehensions of aliens employed in construction work. They would then have a coffee break, sit around awhile, maybe process the aliens they had brought in, or they might even wait until the afternoon to process the aliens in custody and not get back out into the field at all in the afternoon. Or, if they processed the ones they had in custody, they might go back into the field in the afternoon and make a couple more apprehensions. I noticed there were no females in the group.

I suggested that the two teams work as a unit instead of working separately; that way, they would have four people to cover a construction site and apprehend some of the aliens who were running and escaping. They would also know where each unit was working and not come around covering the same places one after another. They didn't seem amenable to my suggestions. Old habits are hard to break. I also learned that the Detention Section had more panel trucks than they were using, and it would be possible for us to borrow a panel truck, which would seat about thirteen to nineteen passengers depending on how the benches or seats were arranged in the panel truck. They all informed me that they did not drive a panel truck, and I replied that that was okay, that I would drive the panel truck myself. Apprehensions had been about two hundred or two hundred and fifty per month. I knew we could greatly expand that number by working together as a team.

I gradually eased into the team concept by leading my team to some small factories and shops in the local San Antonio area that I had chosen from looking at the apprehension records which our "Girl Friday" maintained in our records. She was named Guadalupe Gonzales. Lupe was our combination receptionist, secretary and file clerk at the annex. Investigator Marsh was not in favor of the idea of checking tortilla factories. He told me that most of the employees at the tortilla factories were women, and they did not apprehend women. This was strange to me, and my reply was that, "Women were just as illegal as the men, and from now on we would apprehend anyone who was illegal, women included."

The increase in the number of apprehensions and having women among them would work a slight hardship on the Deportation Section. If there were women in the group to be transported back to the border, a female employee of the Deportation Section would be sent along as a matron on overtime, to escort the women back to the bridge. Many days the apprehensions would not exceed one load in a panel truck, but with my assistance and using more vehicles to transport the apprehensions back to the office, we would soon be

Dear Chief

apprehending too many to send back on one panel truck. Fortunately the Deportation Section had a bus similar to civilian-type Greyhound buses with which to transport larger numbers.

I knew I was upsetting my oldest investigator, Ralph. He had enough years service and was old enough to retire, but he was just coasting along and enjoying his work in Area Control until we started working as a team. Then Area Control became more like a job. We stopped coming into the office at nine-thirty and continued to work in the field until we apprehended as many as our vehicles would haul, and then we came back to the office to do the processing. As we apprehended more and more women, it wasn't long before I heard from the Deputy District Director. He informed me that he had been advised that I was not following the guidelines. I knew what he was referring to, but I also knew there were no written guidelines on apprehending females. No one would put in writing that a segment of the illegal population was to be ignored, so I felt free to make apprehensions on any and every nationality of illegal aliens, whether they be male or female. Most of the apprehensions would be Mexican Nationals. There would be some other South American countries represented. The aliens from other countries were referred to as OTM's. That meant other than Mexico. We would be apprehending many Iranians who had entered the Untied States as students, but were no longer in status. But the great majority would be Mexicans whom we could put on the bus and transport back to the border on the same day they were apprehended. These aliens were not formally deported, but were granted voluntary departure.

We Investigators also had some unwritten guidelines of our own. If we found an alien who had been apprehended many times, we would issue a WA and OSC and have the alien formally deported. Also, those we took out of jail for minor violations of civilian law for which they had been apprehended by civilian authorities were usually deported. If an alien was carrying a weapon or fought with us and resisted apprehension, we might have him deported or prosecuted. Investigator Rocamontes had very good liaison with the Assistant U.S. Attorney, and if we told an alien he was going to spend six months in jail, then he was going to spend six months in jail. He actually spent one day less than six months, a total of 179 days, then he had to serve every day of his sentence.

A prosecution case just before I came to San Antonio had received wide publicity in the San Antonio press. The owner of Mario's Restaurant had been prosecuted and convicted of aiding and abetting aliens illegally in the United States. As a result, when I visited employment places in San Antonio, I found very few owners or managers who would deny me the opportunity to question their employees. I knew they really didn't want to lose their illegal alien employees, but they would tell me, "You aren't going to get me like you did Mario," and I had very little problems questioning the employees.

We often received comments from the employers, such as, "Why don't you leave these people alone? They aren't bothering anybody. They aren't criminals. They only do work that nobody else would have anyway." I found this was not the case. One place in particular, I remember, was a brick factory on the outskirts of San Antonio. When my team and I first went there, we apprehended eleven illegal aliens and left only one. He was the foreman and was an immigrated alien who was carrying the Alien Registration Card. The owner was very upset that we had apprehended his employees and told me that I was putting him out of business. I had heard that before, but really didn't believe it. We waited a few weeks and went back to the same location. This time, we only caught about half a dozen illegal aliens, and he had some black employees. He had no black employees previously, so I knew we at least provided an opportunity for some local people to accept employment. We waited a few weeks and went back to the same place again. This time, nearly all his employees were black, and the others were legal aliens. He had cleaned up his act and had not gone out of business.

Before I had been at San Antonio for three months, Ralph decided he would join the District Director, the Deputy DD, and a couple of other Investigators in retirement at the end of the year. We would receive two Investigator Trainees to replace Ralph, and life would go on in the Area Control Unit.

I couldn't spend all of my time with my Area Control Unit. I had to devote some of my time to the General Investigators. Without seeing them work, I would not know how they organized their work and how well they did it for appraisal purposes, so I tried to go with each of them an occasional day in the field to observe their work.

Dear Chief

We checked a lot of employment records, just as I had done when I was assigned to Investigations in New York and San Francisco; not much had changed. One of the questions or statements that I could dispute through my experience was the claim that illegal aliens weren't hurting the employment situation in the United States and that they were paying taxes and were paying their way. This is not true. Many of them are using completely fraudulent Social Security numbers or a number that someone had given to them and told them they could use, and we were getting reports of as many as four or five people paying into one Social Security account. They might be located in Los Angeles, with another one in Dallas, and another one in San Antonio, and someone else somewhere within the Untied States. Each time one of these people was located, they claimed to be the real person whom that account number pertained to, and only occasionally was a false claim case successfully made against one of them. Also, people who do not speak English are not dumb. They are just as smart as anyone else. They know that if they claim to be married with five or six or seven dependents, even though they may be single, no income tax is taken from their wages. Then at the end of the year, for tax purposes they have paid no taxes; they do not file a return, and they have not "paid their way."

I found through my work around San Antonio in the construction industry, one of the largest employers of illegal aliens was the Zachry Construction Company. He employed more simply because he was the largest employer. The claim that aliens were not taking jobs from Americans is disputed by the fact that his company and many others have a standard pay scale. Regardless if the person is legal or illegal, he will earn the same wages. By far the most employees are doing concrete work, but some are working in metal work and as equipment operators, which certainly are jobs that Americans would like to have.

Another type of case my General Investigators were assigned were locate cases on Iranian students. I always thought we were spinning our wheels looking for these Iranians who should not have been admitted to the United States in the first place. We would occasionally find one, and we would institute deportation proceedings by issuing a Warrant of Arrest and an Order to Show Cause which had to be approved by Mr. Molina, the ADDI. He was a little bit reluctant to be as harsh with these out of status students as we would like for him to be. We would ask for a bond, and if he would approved a bond at all, it would be a minimum bond. Then the alien would not show up for his hearing, and we would have to go looking for him again.

1978 came and would prove to be an eventful year for the Immigration and Naturalization Service. That was the year the Social Security Administration decided that the Freedom of Information Act pertained to their records, and that they should no longer furnish information on aliens' places of employment to the Immigration Service. After that, if we needed information, we would have to obtain it through the U.S. Attorney's Office, then only to assist in a criminal prosecution.

The Internal Revenue Service also decided that their records were covered by the Freedom of Information and Privacy Act and would no longer disclose information at our request. There were very few cases that merited criminal prosecution. For all practical purposes, we had lost two of our best sources of detecting the workplace of illegal aliens in the United States.

Before I get too far ahead in the story, let me tell you that Jerry had not been idle. She was diligently looking for a house for us to live in where she would be satisfied. I've said that if it pleased her, it would certainly please me. She was not in as big a hurry this time to find a place. We would use more of our temporary quarters allowance. When the rates were cut, she looked around for another motel with a kitchenette that might have cheaper rates than the one we were living in.

She had checked with the Belvedere Motel on the Austin Highway. She returned that evening to tell me that the motel was run by people from India, whom she believed to be illegal aliens. At the first opportunity, I went by the motel and checked their identity, and sure enough, they were a family of tourists who had decided to stay in the United States. They were in an illegal status. Jerry was correct once again. Jerry had always had a pretty good eye for spotting illegal aliens.

Other people were also constantly reporting the location of illegal aliens. We received anywhere from 100 to 200 reports per month. It seemed like our secretaries were constantly on the phone taking reports. This was a good source for making apprehensions. Often when we would apprehend a relative of a United States citizen or legal resident alien, they would ask me, "Why do you do this work?" I usually answered them the same way. I would say that, "If I wasn't doing the job, someone else would be." It was a pretty good job that I enjoyed, and I was paid to do it to the best of my ability. Then I would usually ask them a question, "Why do you want to keep illegal aliens in the United States?" and I usually got the same answer from them. It was, "Son mi sangre, they are my blood."

My Area Control crew was telling me they had not been on a detail to Austin, Texas in a long time. They said they sued to go on overnight detail. The DD told me that we did have enough money for the detail. The DD was Mr. Staley. Even though he had retired at the first of the year, he agreed to stay on until someone was named as his replacement. There were a few awkward moments after his retirement when our secretary, who was preparing Warrants of Arrest and Orders to Show Cause for the DD signature asked Mr. Staley what his title would be during his temporary duty until his replacement came on board. She asked him if he would be the Acting District Director or Temporary District Directory, and he told her that his signature would still be District Director.

Since this was my first trip to Austin, I let the more experienced Area Control Investigators lead the way. I tagged along in the panel truck ready to transport the aliens they apprehended. They knew which construction sites and what businesses they wanted to check. True to their word, Austin was running over with illegal aliens. We began apprehending them before we even got into town. There were housing construction sites on the outskirts of Austin as we approached where we found several aliens working. There were also restaurants on the outskirts of town that my men wanted to check, and they made apprehensions there. We found a large number working at a salvage yard. In fact, by the time we finished checking the salvage yard, we had so many in custody we had no more room for them in the vehicles. We then transported them to the city jail where they would hold them temporarily in the drunk tank until transportation could be arranged to send them back to the border. We wrote booking slips, then went out in the afternoon to continue our Area Control work. There was a poultry processing plant my men wanted to check. Once again, we apprehended all we could transport at the poultry plant. Before the end of the shift, I called San Antonio to report to Mr. Molina the progress we were making and the number of apprehensions that would need transportation back to the border. We had already apprehended over sixty illegal aliens at that time, and Mr. Molina's comment was that he believed we had exceeded our capacity.

We had more in custody than the Deportation Section could transport in one load, even using the bus. The problem was solved by chartering a civilian bus. Nearly all these illegal aliens requested immediate voluntary departure back to Mexico. Very few of them claimed to have any property or personal effects to take back with them. Some of them, I know, didn't want to disclose their living quarters as there were other aliens there that would be apprehended, and others thought they would return so quickly that they could have their same jobs back and return to the same place they were living to recover their personal property.

At that time, there was no penalty for employing an illegal alien, and many of them would be successful in returning to their same employment. We had heard for years that the employers would be penalized for hiring illegal aliens if the pending legislation, called the "Rodino Bill," could be passed. Each year it was introduced in Congress, but each year it was not passed.

While we were making out the booking slips at the jail, a policeman wanted to talk to me. He wanted to discreetly tell me about an apartment that we should check. He told me we would find 22 illegal aliens in the one apartment. This sounded like a high number to me to be occupying one apartment, but I told him that we would check the building. Early the next morning, to start our day, we went by the apartment before they had a chance to get up and go to work, and we located 21 illegal aliens living in a one-bedroom apartment. Four or five of them were sleeping on the one bed. Two or three were sharing a couch, and the rest were sleeping on the floor. The only reason we didn't get 22 instead of 21 was because one of them had found a girlfriend with whom he could spend the night and wasn't home that morning. I thought we had had a very successful detail, and this was verified by the Austin paper the following morning, whose bold headlines read, "INS Blitz Austin."

Dear Chief

Later on, it would not be possible to apprehend 21 aliens at an apartment because of Service Policy. Service Policy is set by the Commissioner of the Immigration and Naturalization Service and is his way of choosing how he wants the Immigration laws enforced. These are not written laws, but are his directives. At that time, the Commissioner was Leonel Castillo, an Hispanic from Houston, Texas. I'm sure Mr. Castillo did some fine things for the Immigration Service during his short time as the Commissioner, but he did not live up to the expectations I and others at the San Antonio office had for him. When I first arrived in San Antonio, I attended a reception party in his honor at one of the local country clubs. We thought since he was coming back to Houston, that he would be coming on over to the San Antonio District Office, but we were disappointed. We had to hold a reception without the guest of honor, and he got no closer than Houston. It turned out that his priorities would be modernizing the Service, computerizing the INS records, and speeding up the applications process for those who had petitions and other applications pending and were unsympathetic to the sometimes long delays they were having in getting their applications approved. His emphasis would not be on apprehending illegal aliens who were already here. In fact, we began to hear rumblings of an amnesty. It would be his directive that Investigators would no longer go to residences to apprehend illegal aliens. We could still apprehend them at their workplace or at entry. I remember sending back dozens of form G-330's that were sent to the San Antonio office reporting illegal aliens residing at various addresses. Since his directive was that we would not go to addresses, I had to return the forms to the sender with no action taken on them. Some even contained a picture of the subject. I would check our immigration records, and if I could find where the alien had been previously apprehended or had a service file number, I would assign those to a General Investigator, but most of them were returned with a notation that we were prohibited from going to residences. So much for Service Policy.

I would be making a few other changes in the Area Control operation. First of all, I relaxed the dress code. My Investigators would no longer have to wear a sports coat; they could wear sports clothes, even blue jeans and sneakers. I would also change the way of processing walk-ins. When I arrived, it wasn't unusual for the Radio

Operator to call a team of Investigators who were working in the field and direct them to come into the office because someone was there waiting to be processed. This just destroyed our Area Control operation. I decided that it would be more convenient for the Immigration lawyers, who were bringing their clients to the office, if there was a certain time set aside for them. I designated one Investigator to stay in the office on Tuesdays, and it worked out very well. There would be enough walk-ins on that one day to keep the Investigator busy and justify his staying in the office, and it didn't disrupt what we were doing in the field.

By using the panel trucks and working as a team, our apprehensions had gone up dramatically. Now it was not unusual to apprehend six hundred aliens per moth, and that number would go up even higher as we used the detention bus to accompany us on our Area Control operations. Just as there were policy changes, there were also personnel changes. Investigators would be rotating their duty assignments. Gary Osburn would go from the Area Control Squad back to the District Office where he would become one of our most proficient computer operators. Part of the modernization and computerization of our service records would be done by an Administrative Assistant to the District Director. A lot of money would be spent earlier under the Castillo regime than at any other time in my career. We would run out of money as early as June, and the annual appropriations would not be available until October. There would be a period to time when our Administrative Assistant would predict how much money we would have to spend, and we would be limited to four tanks of gas per month. This meant that our Area Control operations would come to a screeching halt. I would have the gas guzzling large engine sedans use up their gasoline and then remain parked. We would use the smaller sedans, but would be limit3d to trips to the jail and the local train yards.

We had two yards in San Antonio, one on the south side and one on the east side. The Railroad Detectives would often call us when they found a boxcar concealing several aliens, and we were able to keep up our apprehensions through their assistance. We also had two bus stations in San Antonio, and checking the northbound buses became one of my favorite activities as long as I was at San Antonio. I tried to get others interested in bus check, but found a general lack

Dear Chief

of interest. In fact, someone resented the fact that I was checking buses and reported to the Regional Office that I was stopping buses. A Regional Investigator contacted me and asked me where and how I was stopping the buses. I had to assure him that I was not stopping buses, but was checking buses while they were in the station. What I usually did was take an Investigator with me to lunch. There were three restaurants where one could buy Mexican food or Chinese or American food near the bus station. We would finish lunch in time to check the northbound bus which traveled through Dallas to Chicago. Since I had done transportation check as part of my Border Patrol assignment in Harlingen, I had no hesitation or reluctance to step to the front of a bus and announce to the loaded passengers that this was an immigration check and to please tell me their citizenship as I came to them. I would repeat the instructions in Spanish, then proceed to check every passenger on the bus so no one could claim that only the Mexicans were being checked while the Anglos were not questioned. I let everyone tell me they were a United States citizen or produce their immigration documents.

We also occasionally checked an eastbound bus. On one of the eastbound buses I found a young man who was a citizen of Japan, who was destined to Florida, but had left his passport and immigration documents in San Francisco. I took him off the bus and asked Investigator Rocamontes to prepare a prosecution report for the Magistrate, who found the young man guilty of failing to carry his immigration documents and gave him a small fine and then we let him proceed on his way to Florida. This would prove to be a good decision later on as one of the local attorneys filed suit, or attempted to file suit, against me in Federal Court for discriminatory enforcement of the Immigration laws when I also prosecuted one of his clients for failure to carry proof of alien registration. Rocamontes dug through the files and found where we had prosecuted other nationalities, including the Japanese boy and some Iranians, and the case was thrown out of court.

One morning I was sitting at my desk engrossed in paperwork, and one of the Investigators wanted me to meet a newly assigned Investigator. I looked up to see before me Tino Garcia. He was returning from an overseas assignment in the Virgin Islands. It took me a few moments to realize where I had seen Tino before. Then I remembered he was the person my wife and I had seen on a ferry boat when we were visiting Saint John's in the Virgin Islands. We had wondered who the Mexican was; I had the answer. He was an Investigator assigned to Saint Thomas, who was going to Saint John's to do Immigrant Inspection work. Tino would take his turn in assignments to the General Investigations and Area Control Sections and would turn out to be a pleasure to work with.

On an Area Control operation checking construction sites, the word would go out that Immigration was present, and aliens would be running all over the place. When Tino trotted up beside one who was unsuspecting and told him Immigration is here, the alien would say, "Where, where," and Tino would say, "Here, it's me."

An Anti-Smuggling Section was formed at San Antonio. This seemed to be the latest phase that Immigration was going through. They saw smuggling as a priority problem. Two of our Grade 12 Field Investigators would be assigned to the Anti-Smuggling Unit. There would also be a chance for some of our Grade 11 Investigators who were assigned to the unit to be upgraded, and there would be a couple of promotions from other offices and a later transfer of an Investigator who was already a GS-12. There were several Investigators who would have qualified as a Supervisor of the Anti-Smuggling Unit, but no one was selected.

Shortly after the formation of the Anti-Smuggling Unit, I was outside the ADDI's office when I heard his secretary discussing his plans for the unit. Since the ADDI was a GS-13, he desired to be upgraded to a 14 to put him on a par with other officers, and his plan for doing that was to name the other Supervisor at San Antonio as the Anti-Smuggling Section Supervisor. He would be supervising other grade12 Investigators and would be entitled to an upgrade to a 13. Once that was accomplished, the ADDI could then make his own appeal for upgrading to the GS-14 grade. This plan did not include me and seemed a bit devious. I let it be known to Mr. Molina and to the Regional Office that if anyone was going to be named as the temporary supervisor to the Anti-Smuggling Section, it should be me. That put me in disfavor with Mr. Molina. I was already on the verge of disfavor. The Regional Office, in turn, notified him that no other GS-12 Supervisor would be supervising the Anti-Smuggling Section, that he would be their supervisor. It would be years before anyone was promoted to the supervisory position. Since the Anti-Smuggling Section needed room at the District Office, I moved my section of General Investigators to the annex with me. Our Steno/Secretary was also in disfavor of Mr. Molina. In fact, he wasn't getting along well with any of the Spanish surnamed employees, and Mamie was pleased to move her desk from the District Office to the annex to be with the Investigators whose work she was doing.

Mamie was one of the most efficient secretaries I have ever seen. She could type the reports that were submitted to her and do her office work so quickly that it looked like she had a lot of free time, and one of the Border Patrol officers who came by our office to process some aliens he had in custody asked me, "Doesn't Mamie ever work?" I told him she was so efficient that she did her work so quickly that it looked like she had lots of free time. She decided to use some of that free time to be the representative of women who were seeking equal opportunity in the Service. Mamie deserved an incentive award. When I recommended her for her proficiency and quality of her work, a recommendation was returned with the comment that "Wasn't that what she was supposed to do?" Mamie was going to college at night, and after obtaining her degree, eventually she left the Immigration Service to work for another government agency.

Since neither Thompson nor I would be the temporary supervisor of the Anti-Smuggling Unit, Thompson decided to apply for a vacancy as an Assistant Chief in the Border Patrol. He was selected for the position. I would concentrate on running the annex and apprehending as many illegal aliens as possible. Things were working out very well for the Area Control Section. We were using the detention bus on our details to Austin, and apprehensions were at a record high. We were apprehending over 800 per month. I had not set a goal, but my men themselves had decided that it would be possible to apprehend 1,000 illegal aliens. When we reached 900, someone wrote in our apprehension book, at the end of the month, "Close but no cigar." They knew we wanted to reach that magic 1,000 number.

Not everyone was interested in working Area Control; some GS-11 Investigators thought that was beneath their grade level, and someone complained to our Central Office that they were being required to do lower grade work. The Central Office published operational instructions indicating that an Investigator could do 40% Area Control work without jeopardizing his higher grade. This was interpreted to mean that Investigators MUST do 40% Area Control work. Subsequently, I had plenty of Investigators to assist me. What I was asking them to do was assist in processing the aliens we brought in near the end of the shift. Everyone at the office, at that time, pitched in and helped do the processing and claimed that as their 40% time spent on Area Control. Finally, we did reach that sought-after number. By going on several details where we could apprehend large numbers of aliens at poultry processing plants and working some areas we had not worked before, we did reach one thousand aliens apprehended in one month.

    San Antonio is a large city. It is now the tenth largest city in the United States, but removing one thousand aliens in one month's time from the San Antonio District area sure put a dent in the alien population. They began to be scarce. I believed that I was proving that an aggressive enforcement policy was the best method of dealing with the illegal alien problem in the United States. I was very proud of the accomplishments of my Area Control Unit. It had taken an extraordinary effort on the part of every man assigned. At the Incentive Award rating period, I could not single out one individual. The accomplishments had been a unit accomplishment, and I asked Mr. Molina to submit a recommendation for a unit award rather than an individual award. Such a recommendation was submitted to the Incentive Awards Committee, but I was not shown a copy of the recommendation until after it had been submitted. I was immediately disappointed in how weakly our case had been stated. We would be further disappointed when the Incentive Awards Committee turned down the recommendation. All we would have was the personal knowledge that we had done one hell of a job.

    Tom Forest would replace Thompson as Supervisor. I like Tom, and we would get along well together. Things were not getting better with Mr. Molina. I withdrew more and more to the annex and found less and less reasons to visit the District Office. In fact, things were so bad that I could not get a bond set on aliens we apprehended and instituted formal deportation proceedings against. The first thing he would say to me when I called him on the phone requesting that a bond be set was, "No, I can't go along with that," and whatever I was asking for would be reduced, or the alien might be released without a bond. There was a much better chance of getting a bond set if one of my men called him instead of me. There was still a good chance if I could somehow bypass the ADDI and reach the District Director that I would get the bond that I was requesting. The ADDI unexpectedly announced his retirement, and I breathed a sigh of relief.

It would be about six months before his position was filled. In the meantime, Tom Forest and I would take turns as the Acting ADDI. We would each serve as the Acting ADDI for a 30-day period. That way, neither of us had enough time to appeal for upgrading to that position or to appeal for the Anti-Smuggling Supervisor's position. When the ADDI vacancy was finally announced, we would both apply for the job and would be on the promotion list. In fact, that was the only promotion that I would apply for. There had been one grade GS-13 vacancy announced at San Francisco that I was interested in, but when I mentioned it to Jerry she said we had lived in California three times already and that was enough. She was not going back there ever again, so I never applied for that vacancy. Two vacancies had been filled prior to the ADDI's retirement. One was in the Anti-Smuggling Unit where Sam May was transferred from Atlanta to San Antonio, and the other was an Investigative Trainee position in the Area Control Section which was filled by John Tellis.

John came to San Antonio from Kansas City where he had been a Detention Officer. There was some skepticism expressed about John's becoming an Investigator. Some of the Investigators were willing to bet that he would never succeed because he was black. I took a special interest in John. Here was an opportunity for me to influence a trainee and instill in him some of the desire to apprehend illegal aliens that I had always had. The skeptics said he would never pass his Spanish test. John did study hard and did pass his test, and I would work more with him than any other Investigator. If John was available at noon, I would invite him to go to lunch with me. We both liked Church's Chicken. John called chicken wings his flight food and claimed it helped him to apprehend illegal aliens that ran from him. After having our chicken, we would then proceed to the bus station, and almost always apprehend some illegal aliens. I showed him how I checked the buses. If we weren't successful in locating any northbound aliens, we would go on to a couple of food processing plants in the downtown area, and occasionally we would just find some on the streets.

One day we spent a couple of hours at what they call "sharp shooting," which was just spotting suspects on the streets of San Antonio. It was fairly easy to tell by the way they were dressed and their demeanor. Some of the people from the country had not been to large cities and were awe-struck. You could see them standing on the corner undecided as to which way to go or gawking at the tall buildings. On this particular day, we were seeing how many we could spot without questioning a citizen. On that particular day, we apprehended nine illegal aliens off of the streets. We only questioned ten people. Only one of the ten turned out to be a citizen and was offended that we had asked him about his citizenship. He wanted to know, "What are you talking to me for? Do I look like a wetback?" In those situations, about the only reply one can make is, "Yes, you certainly do," and then get into the car and drive away while he is still thinking of something else to say.

In processing the apprehended aliens it was usual to ask the question, "Why did you come to the United States?" Then we would hear a long story about how many brothers and sisters there were in the family that he had to support; how his father was sick or injured and couldn't work and why he had the economic need to come to the United States. One of those we took off the streets had a different answer. When asked that question, his answer was, "Para ver las vistas, senor," which is in order to see the sights, sir.

John and I were together on another occasion checking a small restaurant on the south side of town where we could almost always apprehend two or three illegal aliens. We would usually get the dishwasher and the busboy and maybe a waitress or two. On this particular day, it was nearly noon, and the diners were beginning to fill the restaurant. We immediately apprehended the dishwasher, and I began talking to one of the waitresses that I had not seen there before. She had no documents to show that she was an immigrated alien, and, in fact, claimed that her place of birth was Houston, Texas. She did not speak a word of English, and I suspected that she was an undocumented false claim. Sometimes those without documents are harder to get to confess than those who have documents, and you can detect information from the document that they do not know.

The young woman was getting more nervous and perspiring and was getting less forceful in her claim to being a United States citizen. She had no explanation for not having a Social Security card. It was obvious that she wanted to walk away from us, but couldn't. Her boss was glowering at her. Having an illegal alien apprehended at his restaurant was nothing new to him. He obviously wanted her to tell us the truth and get out of there. We were seated at one of his back tables, and although I spoke to the woman in a low voice, we still attracted a lot of curiosity. Now the woman was really nervous and perspiring. She was saying, "I have work to do," and I was telling her that "I also had work to do, and I cannot leave knowing you have not told the truth." I wanted her to feel that her false claim was hopeless. Finally, she gave a sign of resignation and said, "Well, I will tell you the truth. I am a citizen of Mexico, and I have no papers." That was good enough for me. I wanted Tellis to know that it was possible to obtain a confession from an illegal alien claiming to be a citizen of the United States, even though they had noting to show. We could get the rest of her story back at the office. She then appealed to our generosity and wanted us to send her back to Mexico immediately. I was determined that she would not get off that easily, so I had a Warrant of Arrest and Order to Show Cause prepared for her.

The waiting period for a deportation hearing after the issuance of an OSC is normally one week. That meant she would be sitting in the Bexar County Jail for a week. On the second day, she left word that she wanted to see an Immigration Officer. The Investigator doing the jail check told me that she wanted to tell the truth a second time. The second truth was that she was not a citizen of Mexico, but was a citizen of El Salvador. There is no way of knowing how many illegal aliens from countries other than Mexico have claimed to be Mexicans when apprehended in order to get immediate voluntary departure back to Mexico.

It was during one of my stints at the District Office that Sam May and his partner returned to the office without the car they had left in. He had an interesting story to explain what had happened to the car. He told me that they had found a load of illegal aliens at the roadside park east of San Antonio. They suspected that the driver was the smuggler, so they handcuffed him and put him in the back of their sedan while they talked to the load of illegal aliens to try to get the truth from them about the arrangements of their smuggling case. They were surprised to look up and see that although the driver had been securely handcuffed in the back of their car, he was driving away in their car. Sam had fired a shot at the car as it went by him, but the driver was on his way back to the border. When Sam told me about the incident, I told him that firing a weapon was a serious thing, and that he should prepare his own "Dear Chief" memo and set forth the facts in a manner satisfactory to the Regional Office, that his life was in danger when he fired his weapon trying to protect himself from the alien who was about to run over him. His memo must have been satisfactory because I heard no more about the incident, but I always teased Sam after that. I told him that he was the only person in the INS that I had ever known that shot his own vehicle.

In due time the ADDI's position was filled. Tom Forest was selected. It would have been nice to get the promotion, but I never had any animosity against the District Director, Mr. Casillas, for selecting Tom. Tom was probably the best choice. He would be content to stay in the office and do the paperwork. I would have been chomping at the bit to get out of the office every day. Now I could go back to what I liked to do best, leading the Area Control Team in our constant search to detect illegal aliens.

One of the things each officer had to do was respond to inquiries from the surrounding law enforcement agencies. They would encounter illegal aliens for traffic violations or other minor incidences such as fights at bars and would call an Investigator to determine the alien's legal or illegal status. We would ask that they put the alien on the phone, and we would ask him how he entered the United States. Usually, there was no problem. The alien was already in custody and preferred to be in the Immigration custody rather than the local law enforcement custody and would readily admit that he had entered the United States illegally. We would then advise the local law enforcement agency to detain the alien until we could come and get him the next duty day. I had received such a call from the city of Gonzales, Texas. They told me they had two aliens in custody, and I talked to them and ascertained that they were, indeed, illegal aliens and advised that someone would come to pick them up the next duty day.

The detention officers were the ones who usually made their rounds and would visit several city or county facilities, but that particular day they were shorthanded, and I told them that I would go to Gonzales to pick up the two that I had asked to be detained. When I arrived in Gonzales, I noticed a person just leaving the county jail. I thought to myself, "There goes an illegal alien right now." But I went on inside, and a lady jailer said that she would get the alien right out for me. I noticed that she had said "alien" rather than "aliens," and I reminded her that I had asked that two illegal aliens be detained, not one. She told me that there was only one now because the other's owner had just come by and posted a bond for him. I asked her how long ago, and she said, "Just a few minutes ago." I took the one she had brought for release as quickly as I could, rushed him out to the car, and started circling the blocks in downtown Gonzales, looking for the one I had seen leaving just as I arrived. A couple of blocks from the jail I spotted him using a telephone. There was another young man with him at the public phone. I stopped the car beside them and grabbed the one that I knew was an illegal alien that I had seen leaving the jail. When the other boy who had been too surprised to run away and was still standing there answered my questions, he also turned out to be an illegal alien. Before I put him in the car, I took the precaution of giving him a quick frisk search and found a butcher knife in his belt, sticking down his pants leg. It was a regular kitchen butcher knife, and I don't see how he kept from injuring himself. I confiscated the butcher knife, and it is one of my souvenirs that I am still using today. I thought: "Only in Texas can an owner post bond for his illegal alien."

When money was available, I would again take my Area Control team on a detail to Austin. We would be accompanied by a detention officer driving the Immigration bus. We would go with the particular purpose of checking a large furniture factory. I had my men surround the factory while I went inside to talk to the owner, who turned out to be a lady. She knew she had some illegal alien employees and gave me permission for my men to enter the factory and check them. Immediately, people were running everywhere and trying to hide. Some were running outside, but were caught by my men waiting for them outside. Some of my men came inside to help me question the ones who remained and who were hiding. Once again, several women went inside the ladies room thinking they would be safe there, but we eventually managed to catch a busload of aliens from that one factory. The owner was so surprised at the number we had apprehended that she was upset and said if she had known we would take so many, she would never had given me permission for my men to come inside.

I would not be able to go on every detail. My men went to Ft. Hood a couple of times by themselves and each time managed to apprehend a large number of illegal aliens employed in construction on Ft. Hood. Since the office was two supervisors shorthanded, I had more responsibility than I would normally have had. In fact, there was another vacancy which remained unfilled for about five months. That was the Deputy Director's spot.

I ended up attending an Intelligence Officers' Conference, conducted by the Southern Region Intelligence Office at Bandera, Texas. Bandera is in the Texas Hill Country and is a nice place to visit. I enjoyed seeing old friends from all over the Southern Region, even some who had been in my Border Patrol class and others I had met at the Journeyman Investigator's School and at other stations. The conference was informative. It was interesting to find out the types of problems other offices were having. After the duty hours, we had some time to enjoy Bandera. I remember the canoe trip they had planned for us on the Medina River. It turned out to be enjoyable, but could have been dangerous. My canoeing partner was an Immigrant Inspector from El Paso. We were attempting to be the first canoe down the river and stay in the lead. We were ahead by a short distance when we unexpectedly hit swift water just before a low water bridge. I could see we would have a hard time going underneath the bridge because of the low headroom. At the last moment, we tried to swerve over to the edge so we could portage the canoe around the bridge, but the swift water hit us, and the canoe capsized. My partner was pinned between the canoe and the bridge. I was also behind the canoe, but in a little bit shallower water. We were both trying to keep the canoe from going under the bridge and becoming wedged, and we were tiring quickly. Fortunately, the canoers behind us arrived and were able to beach their canoe before reaching the swift water and

Dear Chief

came to our rescue. They pulled the canoe to the shore, and we were then able to get out of the river. One of the ladies who was rafting on an inner tube came to the bridge and was able to scoot right on through the bridge. Her husband, who was a short distance behind her, didn't see her go through the bridge and was alarmed thinking something had happened to her, but he called her name, and she answered from the other side of the bridge.

I would also attend an Anti-Smuggling seminar at El Paso. The emphasis of this seminar was ways to make it more unprofitable to the smuggler. We would implement a program of vehicle seizures. I brought the information back from the seminar, and we appointed Sam May as our Vehicle Seizure Officer. It was not long before we had several vehicles stored on government property on Ft. Sam Houston. Our storage area was not very secure, and vehicles we were storing there were soon vandalized. We needed a vehicle for surveillance work, and soon thereafter the El Paso office notified us that they had seized a panel truck which they believed would be ideal for our purpose. An Anti-Smuggling Officer was detailed to El Paso to bring the panel truck back to San Antonio where it would be modified and radios installed.

Breaking up a ring of smugglers and getting successful prosecution was certainly specialized work. It might require weeks of surveillance and all the resources of the Anti-Smuggling Squad, but individual loads of smuggled aliens might be encountered at any time by any Investigator. John Tellis and I were working the east side of San Antonio when we discovered a pickup load of aliens parked on a side street whose driver had abandoned them. There were about twelve aliens seated crisscrossed in the back of the truck just sitting there waiting when we drove up to them. Their driver must have been inside a building close enough to see that we had discovered them because he never reappeared, and after looking around a bit and waiting, we finally had to take them to the office without discovering the driver.

On another occasion, I had accompanied Robert Lowery on his casework to the very eastern limits of our district area. We were on our way back to San Antonio on Interstate 10 when we neared a roadside park. I was always alert to the possibility of discovering aliens who were resting at the park and had told Robert to slow down where we could see the vehicles parked at that roadside park. It was in the afternoon, and the sun was in such a position that we could see into the cars. Although we were headed back towards San Antonio, and the roadside park was on a slight rise on the eastbound side of the road, I still noticed two passengers in a pickup truck near the entrance to the highway. I told Robert to make a U-turn and we would check that truck. With a nifty piece of driving, Robert managed to stay right beside the truck until his merge lane ended, and he was on the shoulder of the road with nowhere to go. Since there were some roadside metal signs ahead of the truck, he would be forced to either run over the signs or stop. I had my window down with my badge in my hand telling the driver to stop, and as soon as vehicle stopped moving, I rushed to the passenger's side of the pickup truck.

As soon as I could see inside, I saw a young man crouched down in the passenger's floorboard. I asked him if he was a citizen or alien, and he admitted that he was an alien who had no immigration papers. By this time, Robert was at the driver's side of the pickup truck. While he watched the driver, I lifted the canvas which was covering the bed of the truck just enough to see that the whole truck was loaded with illegal aliens. I didn't want to disturb them too much, so I put the canvas back like I had found it. Robert took the pickup driver and the passenger from the front seat into custody and secured them in the back of his sedan. The driver would be kept apart from the passengers and interrogated separately. I would drive the pickup. We made detours back on the westbound lane of Interstate 10 and headed for San Antonio. When we arrived at the District Office, the load of smuggled aliens and I were both surprised. They were surprised that they were not in Houston, their planned destination. I was surprised that there were fourteen passengers crammed into the back of the pickup truck. I didn't know how many we had until the canvas cover was removed.

After a long vacancy, the Deputy District Director's job was filled by a new man from the Dallas District Office. I might have liked him under other circumstances, but he didn't get off to a good start with me and some of the other investigators. He was very young to be a Deputy District Director and had short, curly hair. He wanted to get into the things and be one of the regular guys, I suppose. He wanted to play softball with our softball team, but we saw that as an attempt to take over. His youth was against him, and some of the Investigators immediately nicknamed him "Lt. Fuzz," after the character in the comic strip. I probably had some resentment against him, especially when I learned that he was the son-in-law of the Regional Commissioner. He may have gotten his promotions on merit, but there is also the suspicion there had been favoritism. I also resented his being my second line supervisor and trying to run the Area Control Squad. He staged a couple of raids of local factories and invited the television media to accompany him. I saw this as just looking for individual publicity, and we had been doing our job for all these years because it was our job, and we were supposed to, rather than staging a show for the media.

I began to think about retirement. I would complete my 20 years' service in April, but would have to wait until my birthday on the 29th of June to be age 50 and eligible to retire. I knew that my ten years' Air Force duty and work as a civilian guard would be added to give me a total of 31 years' Federal service. If my mind was not already made up, there were a few things that would help me.

I wanted to take my Area Control Section on another detail. I learned that the Service was, once again, short of money, and there was only enough for two people to go on detail. I decided that Investigator Reininger and I would go to Waco. We worked our way to Waco and checked into a motel. We then proceeded on up to the little town of West, Texas. West is right on the county line that separates the San Antonio District from the Dallas District. I had never been there before. The town is very small, and someone must have noticed the green Immigration panel truck and spread the word. We wanted to check a chicken ranch on the edge of town, and by the time we got there, the word had already gone ahead of us. As we approached the chicken houses, we could see at least a half dozen people walking across a plowed field so far ahead of us that we would have never been able to catch them, and as we didn't know the farm roads enough to go ahead and cut them off, they were home free. There are always a few that do not run. Reininger and I started checking the ones who remained and sorting out the illegals from the legals. We neared the rear of one of the chicken houses and heard voices coming from behind the house. Obviously, there were some hiding behind the house who weren't sure where we were. We exited the chicken house, and as we went around the corner, they saw us and began running. Reininger was in hot pursuit when he tripped over a barbed wire fence and went sprawling in the manure which always surrounds a chicken house. It was damp, and he got it all over his chest. I never smelled anything so bad. I told Reininger we had better get back to the motel as quickly as we could so he could shower and change clothes. So much for West, Texas.

After getting cleaned up, we went by a poultry processing plant in Waco. We got there at the evening shift change. There were carloads of aliens arriving to go to work, and all we had to do was check them as they attempted to enter the gate until we had our panel truck loaded. We took them to the county jail for processing and to be detained until the Deportation Officers could bring the bus the next morning. We asked those we had in custody when the shift would change again, and we went back the next morning to intercept those who were coming off of the midnight shift and those going to work on the day shift, and we once again loaded the panel truck. We left a busload of aliens in jail in Waco and then worked our way back to San Antonio. We had had a very successful detail.

I was to the point that I must decide whether or not I was going to retire, and if so, when. I would be required to submit a "Dear Chief" to the Regional Personnel Office notifying them. I found myself working on the southwest side of the city with John Tellis. We were driving by one of the seedier motels that was known to us for its drug transactions and as a stopover for loading illegal aliens. We noticed two men standing in the parking lot of the motel that we thought should be identified. As John was driving, I was prepared when he pulled to a stop beside them. I had my identification in one hand, and when I opened the car door, the men turned to face me. I had time to say one word, "Immigration." That was all it took for the younger of the two to whirl around and head for an open door to one of the motel rooms. I was only a few steps behind him. When he reached the room, he didn't bother to close the door, and I went in right behind him. He went on through the room to the bathroom, and when I reached the bathroom door, he was standing there waiting for me with a pistol in his hand. I don't know if he had the pistol in his belt or if he knew it was in the bathroom of the motel room, but he was prepared for me. I was in shock to find myself looking down the barrel of the largest nickel revolver that I have ever seen. I remembered that it was not shiny chrome or blue, but was nickel. It seemed to be growing every second. It was a cannon compared to my little snub nose .38, which was still in my holster, and that's where it would stay, at least for the moment.

I realized that I was just a twitch of the finger away from having my career ending prematurely. The person holding the pistol obviously, from the way it turned out, didn't want to shoot me. He just wanted to get away, and when he motioned for me to step aside, I certainly stepped aside, and he kept the pistol pointed at me as he backed toward the door. He then whirled around and ran out the door. I didn't know where my partner was or what he would do, but when I reached the doorway, I saw that he had stayed beside the car to question the other person, and it turned out that he was a Cuban who had immigrated to the United States and had his alien registration card.

The person I was after had fled around the corner of the motel. I cautiously peeked around the corner with my gun in hand, but he had already reached the street behind the motel and was out of sight. I cautiously approached the street to see whether he had gone north or south or east on the street that ran beside the end of the motel. He was not in sight on the street, either. A boy on his bicycle was only a few yards away. Evidently the commotion had caught his attention. He told me the man got away in a Trans Am. I returned to the motel parking lot to interrogate the man who had stayed behind. He was a resident of the motel, and it was his room the other person had run into. He claimed that he did not know who the person was. He claimed that he had only stopped to ask for directions. He was a funny-looking individual with curly black hair and a swarthy complexion. I suppose he was another Cuban because he was speaking Spanish like a Cuban, but he could have been some other nationality. I will never know.

If my mind had not been made up before, it was now. Retirement was so near and looked so desirable. I came back to the office and told Tom Forest what had happened and that I had decided to retire. He told me to submit my memo, then move back to the District Office and they would announce my vacancy. That way, maybe my position wouldn't be vacant as long as he and I had taken turns awaiting a new ADDI. This would give my older GS-11 Investigators a chance to be the Acting Supervisor of the Area Control Squad and gain a little experience. I would spend the last couple of months at the District Office doing appraisals and shuffling paper. The countdown to retirement would be anti-climatic after chasing aliens every day. I would still check the northbound bus every day. In fact, Tom Forest would accompany me to lunch and also check the bus with me several times. This was more than Ed Molina had ever done. In fact, I don't believe we ever had lunch together, much less check a bus together. Tom was turning out to be a very good ADDI. He was enforcement minded, and I had had no problem getting Warrants of Arrests and bonds. In fact, he had gradually raised the minimum bond and even put a few "no work" conditions when we knew an immigration attorney was just trying to prolong an alien's stay in the United States so he could work longer.

Sam May stirred up a little excitement one day. He and I had had lunch together and checked the northbound bus. We found three Mexicans sitting together near the rear of the bus. They presented alien registration cards, and I immediately detected that one of the cards was a counterfeit card. I was lucky to have Sam with me that day because he had experience as an Immigrant Inspector and was more familiar with documents than I was. He decided that one of the other two cards had been altered by a picture substitution and that the third card looked to be valid. We both looked at it and could not find any evidence of tamper or being fraudulent. I really couldn't find a violation to bring the third subject to the office. Sam had a different logic. His logic was that if something was wrong with the two of them and all three were traveling together, then there must be something wrong with all three of them. He convinced me to bring the third subject with us back to the District Office. I did take a precaution of recovering his ticket from the bus driver so if we had to turn him loose later, we could send him on his way.

Sam's intuition turned out to be right. Fortunately, the file number for that person was located at the San Antonio District Records Room. When we obtained the file, Sam determined that the person we had taken off the bus was not the person to whom that file related. He was an imposter who had grown a mustache and combed his hair so he would look like the person whose picture was on the alien registration card and in the service file. I was proud of Sam when he got the admission from the alien that he was an imposter. Apprehending three aliens with alien registration cards was a good day's work.

As my days grew shorter, I endured all of the short time jokes. They would ask me, "How short are you?" and I would tell them I was to short to engage in a long conversation, or I was too short for a long drink of water, etc. There was still time, however to ruffle the Deputy District Director's feathers. As the Service grew shorter and shorter of money, we went through another scare as we had done several times before. The employees were assembled and advised that we might run out of money, and unless we were advised differently by Friday afternoon, we would be placed on leave without pay, and only the essential employees would remain on duty. The list of essential employees was prepared by the Deputy District Director. Although the Deputy District Director's job had been vacant for about five months prior to the arrival of Lt. Fuzz, he placed himself at the head of the list of the essential employees. By now, I had no reluctance to express myself freely. I told him I didn't see how he could be an essential person when his job had been vacant for so long. He got red in the face, but didn't say anything until later, when he followed me to my office to tell me that I had embarrassed him in front of the employees. We were notified before quitting time on Friday that we could come back to work the following Monday, and no one would be placed on unpaid leave. Those last few days gave me plenty of time to remember some of the little things about my career in the Immigration and Naturalization Service.

I remembered some of the unusual Spanish names, such as a family named *Borrego*, which means "sheep." I also remembered processing an illegal alien with the unusual name of *Seis Dedos*, which means "six fingers." I wondered why an alien would be called Six Fingers until we checked his hands, and sure enough, there must have been a gene passed along the family line to cause the family to bear the name Six Fingers. This young man had an extra thumb beside his regular thumb, and he actually had six fingers.

I had plenty of time to become melancholy about leaving my work family. I thought about all of the Border Patrolmen that I had spent long hours on line watch with in the Border Patrol and whom I would never see again. There would always be a place in my mind for the haunting music drifting across the river from the cantinas. There was something unforgettable about the sound of an accordion or the plaintive sound of the trumpet. It has always amazed me how much sadness Mexicans can put into their music. Now I would only chase the elusive wetback in my dreams.

There was no reason to work a day longer than I had to. I had notified the Region that I would be retiring on my birthday, the 29th of June, which was on a Tuesday. I declined the offer of a retirement party, but I knew there would be a little office ceremony at the end of the day where I would be presented my Retired Investigator's Badge mounted on a plaque. My office family surprised me that morning at coffee break by presenting a birthday cake. Since it was a Tuesday, the timekeeper wanted to know if I was willing to finish out the pay period. I told her, "No." She then asked if I wasn't going to finish out the week. I told her, "No. I was going to finish the day." I decided this day should not be much different than any other, so I kept working. I went by the bus station and checked the northbound bus and found two undocumented aliens sitting unobtrusively in the back of the bus. For me, it was a moment to remember, apprehending the last two aliens of my career. How well I remembered the first two I had apprehended working with Arnold Cope almost twenty years ago.

The end of the shift meant time for me to say *Adios* to my work family. It also meant time for a bus ride back to the border for the two apprehended aliens. They had failed this time in their attempt to find work in *El Norte*, but for the illegal alien looking for a better life, the attitude is *Siempre Manana*, "There is always tomorrow."

The End

ABOUT THE AUTHOR

Bruce R. Sims is a retired Air Force Lieutenant Colonel who combined an Air Force and civil service career. His writings are based on true experiences. His assignments have taken him to the Far East, Africa, Europe and Puerto Rico. His travels and interest in people influenced him to get a BS Degree in Geography from Florida State University.

He now resides with his wife Dorothy Jeroline (Jerry) who shared moving experiences with him. They now reside in his hometown of Hiawassee, GA.

Printed in the United States
79674LV00004B/229-234